Come and Get It!

Published by:
The Junior Welfare League of Talladega, Alabama
Post Office Box 331
Talladega, Alabama 35160
1990

Cover art by Janie Cravens

The purpose of The Junior Welfare League of Talladega is to engage exclusively in work calculated to improve the social, charitable, benevolent, and cultural betterment of humankind and to provide relief for the poor, distressed, and underprivileged.

Proceeds from the sale of **"Come and Get It"** will be used to support community projects sponsored by The Junior Welfare League of Talladega, Alabama.

For additional copies, use the order forms at the back of the book or write directly to:

COME AND GET IT
Post Office Box 331
Talladega, Alabama 35160

Please enclose your return shipping address with check payable to "The Junior Welfare League of Talladega" in the amount of $14.95 plus $2.50 postage and handling per book.

Library of Congress Catalog Card Number: 90-060367

ISBN 0-9626929-0-5

Copyright © 1990
The Junior Welfare League of Talladega, Alabama 1990

FIRST EDITION
First Printing: 5,000 copies — 1990
Second Printing: 5,000 copies — 1992

Printed in the USA by
WIMMER BROTHERS
A Wimmer Company
Memphis • Dallas

Come and Get It

Cookbook Committee
1989-1990

Tracey Barber
Donna Edmiston
Brenda Hollingsworth
Teresa Lawson
Linda McCardle
Jody Parker
Pam Riley
Heidi Yates

Janie Cravens
Winser Hayes
Donna King
Amy Mathison
Frieda Meacham
Pam Phillips
Kaye Spears

Active Members of The Junior Welfare League of
Talladega, Alabama
1989-1990

Tracey Barber
Janie Cravens
Donna Edmiston
Jenni Griffin
Nancy Hare
Susannah Herring
Nancy Hopewell
Donna King
Amy Locklin
Frieda Meacham
Linda McCardle
Jody Parker
Pam Phillips
Pam Riley
Alicia Rogers
Debbie Smith
Mary Taylor
Charlene Walker
Mary Alice Wood

Jeannette Bice
Cay Davis
Laura Gaines
Leigh Hardy
Winser Hayes
Brenda Hollingsworth
Emily Jacobs
Teresa Lawson
Amy Mathison
Genie Medders
Barbara McCormack
Kaye Patterson
Beth Ralston
Cary Robbs
Sylvia Sims
Kaye Spears
Judy Vinyard
Margaret West
Heidi Yates

We sincerely appreciate every recipe of the hundreds submitted. Regrettably, we were unable to incorporate all the wonderful recipes and ideas due to space.

The Junior Welfare League of Talladega, Alabama

The Junior Welfare League of Talladega, Alabama was organized by 14 dedicated ladies in 1932. It is one of the oldest charity leagues in the state of Alabama. The charter members gave to the League its purpose: "to foster interest among its members in the social, economic, cultural, and civic conditions of their community, and to make efficient their volunteer services..." Each year every League member contributes 60 or more charity hours and as a group raises thousands of dollars to support worthy charitable projects in the community. Among these projects are: Christmas baskets for the needy, Dial-a-Story, children's books for the Talladega Public Library, hospital volunteer work, Meals-on-Wheels for the elderly, support programs for abused children, and the purchase of playground equipment for our local park.

FROM THE EDITORS

The Junior Welfare League of Talladega proudly presents **"Come and Get It,"** a sequel to **"When Dinnerbells Ring,"** first published in 1978. The cookbook committee would like to express our warmest thanks to those of you who shared your ideas and your favorite recipes. Many thanks also to all the dedicated League members who tested recipes. A special thanks goes to Janie Cravens for sharing with us her talents by creating the art for our cookbook and to Phillip Rogers whose poem in our preface depicts our title so well. We are grateful to Sharon Goldsworthy and Richard Anderson of Wimmer Brothers for being patient and generous with their professional advice. Special appreciation goes to our families who have been so understanding and supportive during the past two years.

Our goal had been reached after endless hours of work by members of our organization, their families, and friends in the community. We have set the pace for your festivities, so let's set the table and call *"Come and get it."*

Linda McCardle, Publishing Chairman 1989
Donna Edmiston, Publishing Chairman 1990

TABLE OF CONTENTS

PREFACE
By Frieda Meacham

When Dinnerbells Ring, our first cookbook, has been an exemplary and often used illustration of the culinary arts so a part of our heritage. In **Come and Get It,** the Junior Welfare League of Talladega continues the tradition of Southern cooking at its finest. Sections are included which we hope will be resources in today's transitional world. As lifestyles are transformed, the desire has been to meet current needs while retaining the spirit of graciousness and hospitality so typically Southern. Perhaps the personification of what we want to hold in our hearts is reflected in the poem below:

Lazy afternoons. Sunday clothes.
Gracious fun. Forgotten woes.

An elegant silver haired grandmother
we can never forget...

Ringing the family dinnerbell
and calling, "Come and get it."

Phillip J. Rogers
July 1989

Appetizers and Beverages

Come and get it, honey
Come and get it while it's hot —
The hoecakes' in the oven
And the coffee's in the pot.

HOT CRAB SANDWICH

16 slices white bread, crusts removed
8 slices pasteurized process cheese
2 6½ ounce cans crabmeat
6 eggs
3⅓ cups milk

1 teaspoon Worcestershire sauce
Dash red pepper
1½ teaspoons salt
1½ cups corn flakes
½ cup butter, melted

Arrange 8 slices bread in 9x13 inch pan. Top bread with cheese, sprinkle crabmeat and top with other bread. Beat eggs, milk, and seasonings. Pour over sandwiches. Cover with plastic wrap and refrigerate overnight. When ready to bake, sprinkle with corn flakes and drizzle butter over top. Cook at 350 degrees for an hour or until puffy and lightly brown.
Yield: 8.

Doris Munroe

HAM AND SWISS ANGEL BISCUITS

½ cup butter
¼ cup prepared mustard
1 tablespoon poppy seeds
¼ cup onions, finely chopped

1 package angel biscuits (24 count aluminum pan, in bread section)
Swiss cheese, thinly sliced
Ham, thinly sliced

Melt butter, add next 3 ingredients and stir until smooth. Split entire package of biscuits and spread with butter mixture. Layer cheese and ham and replace top half of biscuits. Seal with foil and bake 20 minutes at 350 degrees or until cheese melts. Separate by cutting through with sharp knife.
Yield: 24 appetizers.

Denise Murray
Montgomery, Alabama

MOLDED SALMON

2   envelopes unflavored gelatin
½   cup lemon juice
1   15½ ounce can salmon
5   hard boiled eggs, grated
¾   cup celery, finely chopped
2   tablespoons chives, chopped
1   cup mayonnaise

¼   cup horseradish
2   tablespoons capers
Salt, pepper, hot sauce, and
    Worcestershire sauce to taste
1   cup mayonnaise
2   tablespoons horseradish

Dissolve gelatin in lemon juice, then set in pan of hot water to heat thoroughly. Mix gelatin mixture with drained and flaked salmon, eggs, celery, chives, mayonnaise, horseradish, and seasonings. Pour into ring mold (4 to 6 cup) that has been rinsed with cold water. Refrigerate for several hours before unmolding. Garnish with parsley, olives, and capers. Serve with 1 cup mayonnaise and 2 tablespoons horseradish mixed together.
Note: This recipe can be made in a fish mold; decorate with sliced olives, chives, and paprika. Serve with crackers for hors d'oeuvres.

Mrs. W.A. Davis (Mona)

TUNA DIP

1   12 ounce can white tuna,
    packed in water
¼   cup Parmesan cheese, grated
1   cup sour cream
1   egg, hard-boiled and chopped

1   tablespoon lemon juice
1   7 ounce package Italian
    dressing mix

Flake tuna. Combine all ingredients and serve with chips or crackers or use as sandwich spread.
Yield: 2 cups

Mrs. J.B. Boykin (Evelyn)

SALMON SPREAD

2   8 ounce packages cream
    cheese, softened
1   7½ ounce can smoked
    salmon, drained

2   teaspoons lemon juice
1   teaspoon prepared mustard
½   teaspoon seasoned salt
1   dash hot pepper sauce

Combine all ingredients. Blend well. Cover and chill.
Yield: 1½ cups
Note: Will keep in refrigerator for up to 4 weeks.

Mrs. Billy Mills (Faye)

CHEESE TOASTIES

1 cup Cheddar cheese, shredded	¼ teaspoon dry mustard Dash of paprika
1 tablespoon mayonnaise	Garlic powder to taste
1 tablespoon onion, chopped	2 English muffins (4 halves), split and toasted
1 teaspoon milk	
½ teaspoon Worcestershire sauce	4 slices bacon, cooked and crumbled

Mix cheese, mayonnaise, onion, milk, Worcestershire sauce, mustard, paprika, and garlic powder. Spread 2 tablespoons on each muffin half. Sprinkle ¼ bacon on each. Place on cookie sheet and bake at 350 degrees until cheese melts. Cut each muffin half into 4 wedges. Serve warm. Yield: 4 meal servings or 16 appetizers.
Note: Good as an appetizer or at a meal with salad.

Mrs. Dewayne Clark (Marion)

CHEESE PUFFS
"Make these ahead to have on hand"

1 8 ounce package cream cheese	5 egg whites
1 cup margarine	2 loaves French bread
8 ounces sharp Cheddar cheese, shredded	

Melt cream cheese, margarine and cheese together in a microwave or top of range until hot. Beat egg whites until stiff. Fold into cheese mixture. Remove crusts from 2 loaves of French bread. Cut bread into 1 inch squares. Dip each cube into mixture and put on ungreased cookie sheet. Chill for 4 hours. Bake at 400 degrees for 5 to 10 minutes. May freeze cubes after chilling time. Can be placed in a bag, then can take out amount needed. Yield: 50 to 60 servings.

Mrs. Robert W Weaver (Janette)

PECAN CHEESE PUFFS
"A great party favorite"

½ pound mellow cheese, shredded	½ teaspoon salt
1 cup margarine	1 teaspoon sugar
2 cups all-purpose flour	¼ teaspoon red pepper
	Pecan halves

Cream cheese and margarine. Sift flour, salt, sugar, and red pepper. Mix with cheese. Drop by teaspoon on greased cookie sheet. Press pecan half on top. Bake at 325 degrees for 7 to 10 minutes.
Yield: 60 to 70 cheese puffs.
Note: May increase red pepper to ½ teaspoon if you like cheese puffs more spicy.

Mrs. Raymond Shepherd (Margie)
Starkville, Mississippi

CHEESE PINEAPPLE MOLD
"Very festive."

1½ pounds sharp Cheddar cheese, shredded	½ cup butter, softened
½ pound Swiss cheese, shredded	½ cup apple juice
1 8 ounce package cream cheese, softened	2 tablespoons lemon juice
¼ pound bleu cheese, crumbled	1 tablespoon Worcestershire sauce
	Sliced green olives
	Paprika

Combine cheeses with butter. Slowly add juices and Worcestershire sauce. Blend well. Shape into a pineapple. Cover and chill. Before serving score the cheese with wooden toothpick to make pineapple diamonds. Decorate with green olives and sprinkle with paprika. Olives can be used to make the pineapple crown or a crown can be used from a fresh pineapple. Good served with wheat crackers.
Yield: 3 cups.
Note: For a holiday party, cheese can be shaped into a holiday wreath.

Valerie B. McWilliams

CHEESE BALL
"Put this together for a party pleaser."

1 pound sharp Cheddar cheese, shredded
1 8 ounce package cream cheese, softened
1 tablespoon Worcestershire sauce
1 tablespoon onion, chopped
1 tablespoon green pepper, chopped
1 teaspoon lemon juice
1 2 ounce jar pimento, chopped
Dash of salt
Pecans, chopped

Mix all ingredients together (can be done in food processor.) Shape ball and roll in chopped pecans. Serve with fancy crackers.

Mrs. Marty Phillips (Pam)
Similar recipe submitted by *Mildred Goodpasture*
Variation: Omit green pepper and pimento.
Mrs. Bailey Dixon (Gail),
Clinton, South Carolina

PARTY CHEESE BALL

1 8 ounce package cream cheese, softened
3 ounces bleu cheese
¼ cup margarine
⅔ cup well drained ripe olives, chopped
⅓ cup walnuts, chopped

Blend cream cheese, bleu cheese, and margarine. Stir in olives. Chill slightly, form into ball. Roll in chopped walnuts. Refrigerate until serving time.

Linda B. Miller
Kenner, Louisiana

CREAMY HAM AND CHEESE BALL

½ pound medium Cheddar cheese, shredded
1 3 ounce package cream cheese
1 7 ounce jar sharp pasteurized process cheese
1½ teaspoon garlic salt
1 dash red pepper
1 teaspoon mustard
½ cup smoked ham, finely chopped
Pecans, finely chopped

Mix all ingredients, except pecans. Form a ball or log. Roll in chopped nuts. Chill and serve with crackers. Variation: Use regular ham. May be rolled in chili powder.

Angela H. Dempsey

CRABMEAT PARTY SPREAD

1 envelope unflavored gelatin
1 tablespoon water
1 10¾ ounce can cream of
   mushroom soup, undiluted
8 ounces crabmeat, chopped
1 8 ounce package cream
   cheese, softened

1 cup celery, finely chopped
1 cup green onions, finely
   chopped
1 cup mayonnaise
1 dash hot sauce

Dissolve gelatin in water. Heat soup, add gelatin, and mix until smooth. Add remaining ingredients and mix well. Press into a mold and chill for 6 hours. Unmold. Serve with crackers.

Mrs. Stuart McConnell (Pat)
Riverside, Alabama

Similar recipe submitted by *Alicia Rogers*

CHEESE AND BEEF LOG
"Make this ahead—It freezes well."

2 8 ounce packages cream
   cheese, softened
½ cup butter, softened
2 tablespoons mayonnaise
1 teaspoon lemon juice
2 tablespoons horseradish
   sauce
1 tablespoon Worcestershire
   sauce

1 5 ounce can potted ham or
   corned beef spread
4 dashes hot pepper sauce
1 5 ounce jar dried beef,
   shredded
Round buttery crackers

In a large bowl, mix all ingredients except dried beef. Working on waxed paper, form mixture into 1 or 2 logs. Roll in shredded dried beef. Refrigerate. Serve with crackers. Reshape when needed as log is being served.
Yield: 20 to 24 servings.
Note: Better when served 24 hours after preparation.

Cay Davis

BEEFY CHEESE DIP

1 pound sausage
1 pound ground beef
2 pounds pasteurized process cheese spread

1 10¾ ounce can cream of mushroom soup
Nachos or other chips

Brown sausage and ground beef. Drain well; melt cheese. Mix sausage, ground beef, cheese, and soup. Pour into a crock pot on low or medium heat. Serve warm.

Jerry Woodard
Similar recipes submitted by *Marion Molliston* and *Jeannie Hill.*

HOT BEEF DIP

1 8 ounce package cream cheese
2 tablespoons milk
1 2½ ounce jar dried beef, chopped
2 tablespoons dry minced onion

¼ cup bell pepper, finely chopped
½ cup sour cream
¼ cup nuts, chopped
2 tablespoons butter or margarine

Mix cream cheese and milk in mixing bowl. Add beef, onion, bell pepper, and sour cream and blend well. Sauté nuts in butter. Pour cream cheese mixture into a glass pie plate. Put nuts on top. Bake at 350 degrees for 20 minutes. Serve warm from oven with melba toast rounds.

Mrs. Mike Riley (Pam)
Similar recipe submitted by *Mrs. Jackie F. Stephens (Elaine)*

CREAMY CHICKEN DIP

2 10 ounce cans cooked white chicken
1 8 ounce package cream cheese, melted
1 10¾ ounce can cream of mushroom soup

½ teaspoon Worcestershire sauce
⅛ teaspoon garlic salt
2 ½ ounce packages sliced almonds
Assorted crackers

Drain chicken and mix together with all other ingredients. Pour into medium size boiler and heat on stove. Serve hot with crackers.
Yield: 4 to 6 servings.

Jenni Griffin

TEX-MEX DIP

1   16 ounce can refried beans
1   6 ounce can tomato paste
1   4 ounce can chopped green chili peppers, drained
3   tomatoes, chopped
2   teaspoons lemon juice
¼   cup sour cream
½   cup mayonnaise
1   package taco seasoning mix

1   bell pepper, chopped
1   bunch green onions, chopped
1   2 ounce jar pimentos, chopped and drained
1   4½ ounce can black olives, chopped and drained
2-3 cups Cheddar cheese, shredded

Mix together the refried beans, tomato paste, and chili peppers. Spread in the bottom of a 9x13 inch casserole dish. Next mix together the chopped tomatoes and lemon juice. Spread on top of the bean mixture. Mix sour cream, mayonnaise, and taco seasoning. Spread on top of tomato mixture. Mix chopped bell pepper, green onions, pimentos, and black olives. Spread on top of sour cream mixture. Cover with cheese. Garnish with tomato slices and more green onion. Serve with nacho or corn chips.

Mrs. James Barnett (Lynn)

MEXICAN DIP

2   cans bean dip
2   avocados, mashed
2   teaspoons lemon juice
1   cup mayonnaise
½   cup sour cream
1   1¼ ounce package taco seasoning

2   tomatoes, chopped
6   green onions, chopped
1   4½ ounce can black olives, sliced
1   cup sharp cheese, shredded

Arrange layers in order as follows in a 9x13 inch dish or casserole. First layer—bean dip. Second layer—mix avocados with lemon juice; add salt and pepper to taste. Third layer—mix mayonnaise, sour cream, and taco seasoning. Fourth layer—mix tomatoes, onions, olives, and cheese. Serve with tortilla chips or nachos.

Gloria Hughes
Birmingham, Alabama
Similar recipes submitted by *Faye P. Cooley* and
Mrs. Samuel Earle Yates (Heidi)

TACO SAUCE DIP

1 10 ounce can tomatoes with
   green chiles
2 fresh tomatoes, preboiled
   5 minutes and chopped
1 large onion, chopped

1 6 ounce can tomato sauce
1 teaspoon hot pepper sauce
Dash garlic salt
Dash Worcestershire sauce
Salt and pepper to taste

Mix all ingredients together and refrigerate for 2 hours or overnight. Serve
with tortilla chips.

Alicia W. Rogers

GARDEN SALAD SANDWICH

1 8 ounce package cream
   cheese, softened
1 tablespoon lemon juice
¾ cup carrots, grated
¼ cup bell pepper, finely
   chopped

¼ cup celery, finely chopped
¼ cup onions, finely chopped
¼ cup cucumbers, finely
   chopped
¼ to ½ cup mayonnaise

Mix cream cheese and lemon juice. Add other ingredients until mixed well
and can be easily spread. Makes about a loaf and a half. Good on whole
wheat or oat bran bread.

Judy B. Vinyard

CURRY DIP FOR VEGETABLES

1 cup mayonnaise
1 teaspoon curry powder
1 teaspoon tarragon vinegar

1 teaspoon garlic salt
1 teaspoon prepared
   horseradish

Combine all ingredients, mix well and chill.
Note: This is pretty served in a small hollowed-out purple cabbage and sur-
rounded with fresh vegetables, such as broccoli, cauliflower, carrots,
zucchini, celery, cucumber, bell pepper, radishes, etc.

Mrs. Tom Barber (Betty)

HOT ARTICHOKE DIP

"Even non-artichoke lovers love this."

½ cup mayonnaise
½ cup sour cream
1 14 ounce can artichoke
   hearts, chopped and drained

⅓ cup Parmesan cheese, grated
⅛ teaspoon hot sauce (optional)

Stir all ingredients until well mixed. Spoon into small ovenproof dish. Bake for 30 minutes at 350 degrees or until bubbly. Serve warm.
Yield: 2 cups.
Note: Delicious served on crackers as an appetizer. May be heated in the microwave.

Mrs. Tommy Spears (Kaye)

Variation: Add ½ cup shredded Cheddar cheese.
Melanie Hughes, Birmingham, Alabama

CAJUN ARTICHOKES

4 large, fresh artichokes
1 small onion, chopped
¼ cup lemon juice
3 cups white or cooking wine
1 teaspoon Worcestershire
   sauce

2 to 3 drops hot pepper sauce
1 teaspoon salt per artichoke
Enough water to cover
Melted butter with lemon juice
   according to taste

Use a serrated knife to cut off stem and tops of artichokes. Use scissors to snip off tips of leaves. Be careful—they stick. Place stem down in large pot. Add other ingredients except melted butter. Bring to a boil and keep rolling 30 minutes or until leaves pull off easily. Turn off heat, leave covered and in liquid for another 30 minutes. Drain upside down quickly so they don't cool. Serve with melted butter and lemon juice.

Mrs. John T. Robbs (Cary)

ARTICHOKE HEART APPETIZERS

2   8 ounce cans crescent rolls
¾   cup mozzarella cheese, shredded
1   3 ounce can Parmesan cheese, grated

½   cup salad dressing
1   14 ounce can artichoke hearts, drained, chopped
1   4 ounce can green chiles, drained, chopped

Unroll dough and press flat down in 15x10x1 inch jelly roll pan to form crust. Bake at 375 degrees for 10 minutes or until dough is brown. Combine next four ingredients, mix well. Spread over crust. Bake at 375 degrees for 15 minutes or until cheese is melted. Garnish with green chiles. Cut into squares to serve.

Mrs. Larry Edmiston (Donna)

ZUCCHINI HORS D'OEUVRES

1   cup biscuit mix
½   cup onion, finely chopped
½   cup Parmesan cheese, grated
2   tablespoons fresh parsley, chopped
½   teaspoon salt

½   teaspoon ground oregano
⅛   teaspoon pepper
1   clove garlic, minced
¼   cup vegetable oil
4   eggs, beaten
3   cups zucchini, thinly sliced

Combine all ingredients except zucchini, mixing well. Stir in zucchini. Spread evenly in a lightly greased 13x9x2 inch baking pan. Bake at 350 degrees for 30 minutes. Cut in 1½ inch squares. Serve warm.

Mrs. Frankie Newman

PEPPY JELLY TARTS

1   7 ounce jar sharp pasteurized process cheese
½   cup butter or margarine
1   cup all-purpose flour

2   tablespoons water
1   jar (4 or 8 ounce) green or red pepper jelly

Cut cheese and butter into flour. Quickly stir in water and roll into a ball as for pie crust. Roll out dough ⅛ inch and cut into 2 inch circles. Put ½ teaspoon pepper jelly in center, fold edges over. Flour index finger and thumb. Pinch edges together, then flour fork and crimp edges with fork. Bake at 375 degrees for 10 minutes.
Yield: 4 dozen.
Note: May be frozen before or after cooking.

Betty Lou Camp

MUSHROOM PASTRIES

1 17¼ ounce package frozen
   puff pastry
½ cup margarine
1 3 ounce package cream
   cheese

Garlic salt to taste
1 8 ounce can mushrooms,
   sliced

Thaw pastry in refrigerator overnight or at room temperature until pliable. Mix margarine, cream cheese, and garlic salt with mixer. Stir in mushrooms. Cut pastry into 2 to 2 ½ inch rounds. Place a teaspoon of filling in center of round, fold over and seal edges carefully. Bake at 350 degrees for 10 to 12 minutes or until brown.
Yield: 24 servings.

Mrs. Allen Gray McMillan, Jr. (Jean)

MUSHROOM LOGS

1 8 ounce package cream
   cheese, softened
1 4 ounce jar mushroom stems
   and pieces, drained and
   chopped
1 teaspoon seasoned salt (garlic
   salt is best)

1 tablespoon onion flakes
2 8 ounce cans refrigerated
   crescent rolls
1 egg, beaten
1 to 2 tablespoons poppy seeds

Room soften cream cheese. Combine cream cheese, mushrooms, salt, and onion flakes. Mix well. (If needed, a small amount of mayonnaise may be added.) Separate rolls into 8 rectangles—press seams to seal. Spread filling in equal portions over the dough. Starting at long side, roll up like a jelly roll. Pinch seams to seal. Slice into 1 inch pieces and place on lightly greased cookie sheet, seam side down. Brush each piece with egg and top with poppy seeds. Bake at 375 degrees for 10 to 12 minutes or until lightly browned.
Note: May be frozen before baking. To bake, thaw for 1 hour.

Dorothy R. Parker

STUFFED MUSHROOMS

36 fresh mushrooms
½ cup butter, softened
1 clove garlic, finely chopped
  (or ¼ teaspoon garlic powder)
⅔ cup Monterey Jack cheese,
  shredded
⅓ cup corn chips, finely crushed

2 tablespoons wine or cooking
  sherry
2 tablespoons soy sauce
1 1.2 ounce package dry onion
  soup mix

Wash mushrooms and remove stems. Mix other ingredients and fill mushroom caps. Broil until light brown. Can be prepared ahead of time and refrigerated before cooking, then broiled when ready to serve. Serve hot. Yield: 12 servings.

Mrs. Jack R. Wood (Jackie Smith)
Heflin, Alabama

BACON AND DATE WRAPS

1 pound sliced bacon
1 package pitted dates

Toothpicks

Cut slices of bacon in half. Wrap bacon around pitted date and secure with a toothpick. Bake at 350 degrees. They may also be broiled. Check while baking and/or broiling until bacon is crisp. Serve warm.

Hattie Wallace Coker

HUNGARIAN ROUNDS

1 pound sausage (mild or hot)
1 pound lean ground beef
1 pound Velveeta cheese
½ teaspoon garlic powder
2 tablespoons green onion,
  chopped

1½ teaspoon Worcestershire
  sauce
1 teaspoon oregano
Party rye or pumpernickle bread
Paprika

Brown meats together, drain and add cheese. Add other ingredients, except bread and paprika, mix well and cook until heated. Spread on party rye or pumpernickle bread. Freeze slices on cookie sheet. When solid, stack in plastic bags in freezer. Take out as needed and bake 15 to 20 minutes at 350 degrees. Sprinkle with paprika.
Yield: 50 slices.

Becky Heacock (Mrs. James W.)

SAUSAGE BALLS

1   pound mild sausage
2   cups biscuit mix
1   cup sharp Cheddar cheese,
    shredded

1   cup water

Scramble sausage in pan and brown slightly. Pour off all grease. Put in bowl and add remaining ingredients. Form into small balls using your hand to roll them. Freeze. Take directly from freezer and bake at 400 to 450 degrees for about 15 minutes.

Mrs. Robert Kline (Marilyn)
Childersburg, Alabama

MINI-PARTY PIZZAS

2   pounds hot sausage
2   pounds sharp pasteurized
    process cheese spread
1   2 ounce can mushrooms,
    chopped

2 or 3 dashes Worcestershire
    sauce
2 or 3 dashes hot pepper sauce
Brown party rye bread, lightly
    toasted

In skillet brown sausage and drain well. Cube cheese. Return sausage to heat and add cheese. Stir until cheese melts. Add remaining ingredients except bread. Spoon mixture on warm lightly toasted bread slices and serve while hot.

To freeze: Lay mixture-topped bread slices on cookie sheet and place in freezer. When pizzas are frozen transfer to plastic bag. Remove as needed and heat in medium oven until hot. When freezing, do not toast the bread before hand.

Yield: 30 to 40 slices.

Note: May use 1 pound hot and 1 pound mild sausage if desired. Recipe may be halved.

Judy B. Vinyard

PIZZA CUPS

1   6 ounce pizza crust mix
1   pound ground beef or
    sausage
¼   cup onion, diced

1   15 ounce jar pizza sauce
1   cup mozzarella cheese,
    shredded

Mix pizza crust according to package directions. Grease 36 miniature muffin cups. With greased fingers work dough into muffin cups. Brown meat and onion. Drain excess fat. Mix pizza sauce with meat and onion. Spoon into pastry cups. Bake 5 minutes at 400 degrees. Take out of oven and sprinkle with cheese. Return to oven and bake 5 minutes or until brown on edges. *Note:* May be frozen before cheese is sprinkled.

Mrs. Carl Reaves (Joyce)

TANGY BITS

½   cup oil
1   teaspoon lemon pepper
1   teaspoon dillweed
1   teaspoon garlic salt

½   1 ounce package dry ranch
    style dressing mix
1   10 ounce box miniature
    round buttery crackers

In a measuring cup combine and stir first five ingredients. Pour the mixture over crackers and lightly toss. Cook at 250 degrees on a cookie sheet for 15 minutes.
Note: The longer they sit, the stronger they get!

Dot Wallis Moosmann
Sun City Center, Florida

GOLDEN NUT CRUNCH

1   12 ounce can mixed nuts
¼   cup margarine, melted
¼   cup Parmesan cheese, grated
¼   teaspoon garlic powder

¼   teaspoon ground oregano
¼   teaspoon celery salt
4   cups graham cracker
    breakfast cereal

Mix nuts and margarine in bowl until well coated. Add next 4 ingredients, toss until well coated. Spread in ungreased jelly roll pan. Bake, stir occasionally. Remove from heat and stir in cereal, cool. Store in airtight container. Yield: 6 cups.

Cecil Avery (Mrs. Arnold)
Tuscaloosa, Alabama

PARTY PUNCH

1 46 ounce can pineapple juice
1 46 ounce can apple juice
Juice from 2 lemons (optional)

2 small packages of lemon-lime
flavored unsweetened soft
drink mix

Mix all ingredients. Add enough water to make one gallon. Serve with cracked ice.
Yield: 20 servings.

Mrs. Robert M. Wikle (Berniece)

CHERRY SLUSH PUNCH

2 small packages cherry
flavored unsweetened soft
drink mix

1 46 ounce can pineapple juice
1 2-liter lemon-lime carbonated
drink

Mix soft drink mix as directed on package in a gallon container. Add pineapple juice. Stir. Transfer to 2 half gallon containers and place in freezer. Stir several times during the day to keep it slushy. When ready to serve, add lemon-lime carbonated drink.
Yield: 20 to 25 servings.

Mrs. Britt Parker (Jody)

BRUNCH PUNCH

1 fifth blended bourbon
½ cup rum
1 cup unsweetened pineapple
juice
1 cup unsweetened grapefruit
juice

½ cup lemon juice
2 quarts champagne or ginger
ale
Fresh strawberries or orange
slices for garnish

Mix together first five ingredients and refrigerate. When ready to serve, add champagne or ginger ale. Garnish with strawberries or orange slices.
Yield: 24 servings.

Renita C. Holman

STRAWBERRY LEMONADE PUNCH
"Such a pretty punch."

2 cups boiling water
½ cup sugar
2 teaspoons peppermint flavoring
2 10 ounce packages frozen strawberries

5 cups water
2 6 ounce cans frozen pink lemonade concentrate, thawed and undiluted
½ gallon strawberry ice cream

Combine first 3 ingredients. Stir to dissolve sugar and let stand five minutes. Add strawberries, stirring until dissolved. Press strawberry mixture through a strainer and discard pulp. Add water and lemonade, stirring well. Chill thoroughly. Spoon ice cream into punch just before serving.
Yield: 4½ quarts.
Note: Fresh strawberries make a pretty garnish.

Mrs. Jenni Griffin

HOT BUTTERED RUM MIX
"An excellent wintertime warm-up"

1 pound butter, softened (no substitutes)
1 16 ounce package confectioners sugar
1 16 ounce package light brown sugar
2 teaspoons ground nutmeg

2 teaspoons ground cinnamon
1 quart vanilla ice cream, softened
Light rum
Whipped cream
Cinnamon sticks, optional

Combine butter, sugars, and spices, and beat until light and fluffy. Add ice cream and stir until well blended. Place mixture into a freezer container and freeze. To serve, thaw slightly. Place 3 tablespoons of mixture and 1 jigger of rum into a large mug and fill with boiling water. Stir well. Top with whipped cream and serve with cinnamon stick. Any unused portion of mixture can be refrozen.
Yield: 20 to 25 cups.

Susan M. McCrary

HOT MULLED PUNCH

1   1½ quart bottle cranberry juice
2   1 quart bottles apple juice
½   cup brown sugar
½   teaspoon salt
4   cinnamon sticks
1½ teaspoons whole cloves

Pour fruit juices into 30 cup coffee maker. Place remaining ingredients in basket and perk. Upon completion of perking cycle, remove basket. Serve hot.
Yield: 3½ to 4 quarts.

Mrs. Don Medders (Genie)

WASSAIL BOWL

1   gallon apple cider or juice
1   cup packed brown sugar
1   6 ounce can frozen lemonade
1   6 ounce can frozen orange juice
1   tablespoon whole cloves
1   tablespoon whole allspice
Cinnamon sticks, optional

Mix cider, sugar, undiluted lemonade, and orange juice together in a large pot. Tie cloves, allspice, and cinnamon sticks in cheesecloth, add to cider mixture. Simmer, covered, for about 20 minutes. Remove spice bag. Serve hot.
Yield: 24 small servings.

Valerie B. McWilliams

RUSSIAN TEA

6   cups water
3   large tea bags or 6 small
1   cup sugar or 8 packets low calorie sugar substitute
1   teaspoon whole cloves
1   stick cinnamon

Mix all ingredients and boil for 5 minutes. Add:
3   tablespoons lemon juice
1   12 ounce can frozen orange juice
3   12 ounce cans water
1   18 ounce can pineapple juice
5   packets low calorie sugar substitute
2   cups apple juice

Heat, strain, and serve.
Yield: 1 gallon or 21-6 ounce servings.

Mrs. Moody Scroggins (Joan)

MOCHA PUNCH

SYRUP

2 cups sugar
2 cups boiling water

1 ounce instant coffee

Mix together until sugar is dissolved, then cool. Makes 2 cups.

PUNCH

1 gallon chocolate ice cream
1 gallon vanilla ice cream

1 gallon milk
2 cups syrup

Mix ice creams and milk in a punch bowl. Add 2 cups of syrup to 2 gallons of ice cream.
Yield: 48 servings.
Note: May be doubled.

Faye Cooley

TROPICAL MIMOSAS

1 6 ounce can frozen orange juice concentrate
1 12 ounce can pineapple juice
1 12 ounce can apricot nectar

¾ cup water
1 25.4 ounce bottle champagne, chilled

Combine first four ingredients, stir well, and chill. Stir in champagne immediately before serving.
Yield: 8 one cup servings.

Amy M. Mathison

EGGNOG

6 eggs, separated
6 tablespoons sugar
1 cup bourbon
1 cup milk

2 cups heavy cream, lightly whipped
Freshly ground nutmeg

Beat egg yolks and sugar thoroughly. Slowly add bourbon and milk. Fold in stiffly beaten egg whites and whipping cream. Sprinkle nutmeg on top.
Yield: 8 servings.

Mrs. Edward T. Hyde (Dorothy Brunson)

Breads

CHEESE CROISSANTS

1 8 ounce cream cheese with
   chives and onions
4 ounces mozzarella cheese,
   shredded

8 large croissants

Mix cream cheese with mozzarella cheese until smooth. Slice croissants and spread cheese mixture in the center. Wrap in foil and bake at 400 degrees until cheese is melted. (Approximately 15 minutes.) Serve immediately while warm.
Yield: 8 servings.

Mrs. Mike Baker (Joni)

FRENCH TOAST WITH ORANGE BUTTER

12 1 inch thick slices French
   bread
6 eggs
4 cups milk
½ teaspoon salt

½ teaspoon ground nutmeg
½ teaspoon vanilla extract
2 tablespoons butter or
   margarine, divided

Place bread in a 13x9x2 inch pan. Combine eggs, milk, salt, nutmeg and vanilla; beat well. Pour mixture over bread, cover and refrigerate overnight. Melt one tablespoon butter in an electric skillet at 300 degrees; remove 6 slices of bread from dish and cook in butter 10 to 12 minutes on each side or until cooked thoroughly. Repeat procedure with remaining butter and bread. Serve hot with orange butter.

Orange Butter
1 cup butter, softened
½ cup orange juice

½ cup confectioners sugar

Cream butter until light and fluffy. Add orange juice and confectioners sugar; beat until thoroughly blended.

Mrs. Florence Kaylor

Rub a slice of raw potato over the griddle before cooking pancakes to keep them from sticking.

MRS. NELLIE'S WAFFLES

3 eggs
2 cups all-purpose flour
1¾ cups milk
4 teaspoons baking powder

1 teaspoon salt
1 tablespoon sugar
¾ cup corn or peanut oil

Separate eggs and beat whites until stiff and set aside. Beat yolks in separate bowl until fluffy. Add other ingredients, except egg whites, to yolks and beat well. Fold in egg whites. Heat waffle iron to medium heat. Spray with non-stick vegetable spray when iron reaches medium heat. Add ½ cup waffle mix. Cook until lightly tanned.

Mrs. Dorothy R. Parker

OATMEAL MUFFINS

1 egg
1 cup buttermilk
½ cup brown sugar, packed
⅓ cup shortening
1 cup quick cooking oats
1 cup all-purpose flour (if using self-rising flour omit baking powder and salt)

1 teaspoon baking powder
1 teaspoon salt
½ teaspoon soda

Preheat oven to 400 degrees. Grease bottom of 12 medium muffin cups. Beat eggs, stir in buttermilk, brown sugar, and shortening. Mix in remaining ingredients just until flour is moistened. Batter should be lumpy. Fill cups ⅔ full. Bake 20 to 25 minutes or until light brown.

Mrs. Nancy Hare
Montgomery, Alabama

ORANGE POPPY SEED BREAD

1 box butter pecan cake mix
1 3⅛ ounce package coconut cream pudding
4 eggs, slighlty beaten

½ cup oil
3 tablespoons poppy seeds
1 tablespoon orange peel
1 cup hot water

Combine all ingredients well. Pour into 2 (8x3¾x2½) greased loaf pans. Bake at 325 degrees for 40 minutes. Let cool in pans.
Yield: 2 loaves.

Mrs. Nauburn Jones, Sr. (Margaret)

29

SWEET POTATO MUFFINS

½ cup margarine
1½ cups sugar
2   eggs, beaten slightly
1¼ cups canned sweet potatoes,
     mashed
1½ cups all-purpose flour
2   teaspoons baking powder

¼ teaspoon salt
1   teaspoon cinnamon
1   cup milk
¼ cup pecans, chopped
½ cup raisins

Cream margarine and sugar. Add eggs and potatoes. Sift together flour, baking powder, salt, and cinnamon. Add these dry ingredients alternately with milk. Fold in pecans and raisins. Fill greased miniature muffin tins ⅔ full. Bake 25 minutes at 400 degrees.
Yield: 3½ to 4 dozen mini-muffins.
Note: May be frozen.

Elaine Stephens

BANANA/PINEAPPLE NUT BREAD

1½ cups vegetable oil
2   cups sugar
3   eggs, beaten
2   cups ripe bananas, mashed
1   8 ounce can crushed
     pineapple, undrained

2   teaspoons vanilla
1   teaspoon cinnamon
1   teaspoon salt
1   teaspoon soda
3   cups all-purpose flour
1   cup nuts, chopped

Mix all ingredients in order listed. When adding flour, stir only until moistened. Pour batter into two greased and floured loaf pans. Bake at 350 degrees for 1 hour. Cool 10 minutes before removing from pans.
Yield: 2 loaves.

Mrs. Dalton (Imogene) Morgan
Similar recipe submitted by *Mrs. Tom West (Margaret)*
Variation: Omit pineapple and add 1 6 ounce jar red cherries, chopped.

Mrs. Harvey Hendrix (Laura)

ORANGE WALNUT BREAD

2½ cups all-purpose flour,
    unsifted
1¼ cups sugar
2   teaspoons baking powder
½   teaspoon baking soda
½   teaspoon salt
2   eggs, beaten

¼   cup butter, melted
2   tablespoons cold water
2   tablespoons orange peel,
    grated
½   cup fresh orange juice
1   cup walnuts, chopped

Sift first five ingredients together. Set aside. Combine eggs, butter, water, orange peel, and juice. Add (by hand) and stir quickly to dry mixture until just moistened. Stir in walnuts. Turn into a greased and floured loaf pan. Bake 1 hour at 350 degrees.
Note: This may be made and frozen or served immediately with butter. May be doubled but not halved.

Mrs. Ernest A. Hammett, Jr. (Gladys)

STRAWBERRY BREAD

2   10 ounce packages frozen
    strawberries, thawed
4   eggs
1¼ cups vegetable oil
3   cups all-purpose flour

1   teaspoon baking soda
1   teaspoon salt
3   teaspoons cinnamon
2   cups sugar
1   cup nuts, chopped

Stir together strawberries, eggs, and oil. Mix together flour, baking soda, salt, cinnamon, sugar, and nuts. Add to strawberry mixture and stir until blended. Pour into 2 greased and floured loaf pans. Bake at 350 degrees for 1 hour or until done.

Nancy Hare
Montgomery, Alabama

PEAR BREAD

½   cup vegetable oil
1   cup sugar
2   eggs
¼   cup sour cream
1   teaspoon vanilla
2   cups all-purpose flour

½   teaspoon soda
¼   teaspoon nutmeg
¼   teaspoon cinnamon
1   cup fresh pears, grated
½   cup pecans, chopped

Mix oil and sugar. Add eggs, sour cream, and vanilla. Sift, then add dry ingredients. Fold in grated pears and pecans. Bake in loaf pan for 1 hour at 350 degrees.

Ruby Richardson
Tuscaloosa, Alabama

PINWHEEL PUMPKIN BREAD

Bread

3 eggs
1 cup sugar
⅔ cup canned pumpkin
1 teaspoon lemon extract
1 teaspoon ginger

¾ cup all-purpose flour
1 teaspoon baking powder
2 teaspoons cinnamon
½ teaspoon nutmeg
Dash of salt

Beat eggs and sugar, blend in remaining ingredients for bread. Spread on cookie sheet lined with wax paper and coated in oil. Bake 375 degrees for 15 minutes. Turn out on linen towel coated with confectioners sugar. Roll up in a towel (like a jelly roll) until cold.

Filling

1 8 ounce package cream cheese
3 teaspoons milk
1 teaspoon vanilla

2 tablespoons butter
1 cup confectioners sugar
1 cup nuts, chopped

Mix all filling ingredients together. When bread is cold, unroll, fill with filling, re-roll. Freeze, wrapped with wax paper and foil.

Melanie C. Hughes
Birmingham, Alabama

BROCCOLI BREAD

4 eggs
1 small carton cottage cheese
1 box 8½ ounce corn meal muffin mix
½ teaspoon salt
½ cup margarine, melted

2 tablespoons onions, finely chopped
1 10 ounce box frozen chopped broccoli, cooked and drained

Beat eggs well. Add cottage cheese and mix well. Add muffin mix, salt, and margarine. Mix well. Add broccoli and onion. Stir gently. Pour into greased 8x10 baking dish. Bake for 30 minutes at 375 degrees.
Yield: 8 servings.

Pat King
Pinckard, Alabama

AUNT ADELAIDE'S NUT BREAD

1   cup sugar
1   egg
1¼ cup milk
3   cups self-rising flour or 3 cups
    all-purpose flour plus 3
    tablespoons baking powder
    with a pinch of salt

1   cup walnuts, chopped

Mix sugar, egg, and milk together. Gradually add flour and mix well. Add nuts. Pour batter into large, greased loaf pan. Bake at 350 degrees for 50 minutes. (Pecans may be substituted for walnuts.)
Note: May be topped with softened cream cheese.

Winser Hayes

GINGY'S OLD FASHIONED WAFFLES AND PANCAKES

2   cups all purpose flour, sifted
4   teaspoons baking powder
¼   teaspoon salt
2   tablespoons sugar
2   eggs, separated
1¼ cups milk

6   tablespoons melted butter,
    margarine, or cooking oil
1   teaspoon of your favorite
    flavoring
Optional items: fruit, nuts,
    coconut, chocolate chips, etc.

Beat egg yolks until thick and lemon colored. Add melted butter, milk and egg yolks to sifted dry ingredients. In a separate bowl, beat egg whites until stiff peaks form and carefully fold into batter. Cook according to your waffle iron or griddle.

Laura Frances Mathison
Montevallo, Alabama

BRIDES ROLLS

2 cups boiling water
1 cup shortening
1 cup sugar
2 teaspoons salt

2 eggs, beaten
2 ¼ ounce packages yeast
1½ cups warm water
7 to 10 cups self-rising flour

Pour boiling water over shortening in a large mixing bowl. Add sugar and salt. Blend and cool. Add eggs. Dissolve yeast in water, add to egg mixture. Add sifted flour. Knead until smooth and refrigerate. Make into rolls 1-2 hours before baking. Either roll out batter and cut out rolls or hand roll clover leaf rolls. Bake at 400 degrees for 10 to 12 minutes.
Yield: 4 dozen medium rolls.
Note: Mixture may be kept in refrigertor up to one week using just amount desired at each cooking. Makes best as clover leaf rolls.

Zell S. Copeland (Mrs. Jimmy)
Similar recipe submitted by Mrs. Alice Jones

DR. JIMMY'S BRAN YEAST ROLLS

1 cup wheat bran cereal
¾ cup margarine, softened
¾ cup sugar
1 tablespoon salt
1 cup water, boiling
2 packages yeast

1 cup lukewarm water
2 eggs, beaten
6 cups all-purpose flour
Margarine, melted, enough to
   cover bottoms of pans

Combine cereal, margarine, sugar, and salt. Pour one cup boiling water over this and stir. Dissolve yeast in one cup lukewarm water. When first mixture is cool, add beaten eggs and yeast mixture. Mix gently. Stir in approximately 6 cups flour. Don't knead. Cover with greased waxed paper and let rise. Melt margarine or butter in the bottom of pans—enough to cover bottoms. Lightly knead dough on floured surface. Roll out and cut with floured biscuit cutter. Place rolls in cake pans (refrigerate if you wish.) Let rise a second time. Preheat oven to 400 degrees. Reduce heat to 350 degrees and bake 20 to 25 minutes.
Yield: 4 dozen rolls.

Betty Lou Camp

Two teaspoons of vinegar added to one cup of milk will make a good substitute for buttermilk.

HOMEMADE YEAST ROLLS
"Easy, delicious homemade rolls."

½ cup shortening
⅓ cup sugar
1 teaspoon salt
½ cup hot water

1 egg
1 package dry yeast, dissolved
   in ½ cup warm water
3 cups all-purpose flour

Cream shortening, sugar and salt. Add hot water and egg. Add yeast mixture. Add flour until the right consistency. Let rise in a warm place for 2 hours (or until doubled). Make into cloverleaf rolls (roll 3 balls and put into a muffin tin). Bake at 375 degrees for 15 to 20 minutes.
Yield: 12 servings.

Mrs. Mike Baker (Joni)
Similar recipe submitted by *Mrs. John W. Bryant (Mary Carson)*

OLD FASHION CORNBREAD
"The way Grandma used to make it."

2 cups plain white cornmeal
1 teaspoon soda
1 teaspoon baking powder
1 teaspoon sugar

1 teaspoon salt
3 cups buttermilk
3 eggs
¼ cup oil

Sift dry ingredients. In a large bowl, beat buttermilk and eggs with mixer. Add dry ingredients and mix until moistened. Warm ¼ cup oil in skillet over medium heat. Pour mixture in 10-inch iron skillet when oil is hot. Bake at 450 degrees for 30 minutes or test by inserting knife in center of cornbread.

Mrs. Susan S. Booth

VIRGINIA SPOON BREAD

4 cups milk
1 tablespoon butter, melted
1 teaspoon sugar
1 cup yellow corn meal

1 teaspoon salt
2 egg yolks, beaten
4 egg whites, stiffly beaten

In a saucepan, warm milk; add butter, sugar, meal, and salt. Bring to a boil and cook 5 minutes stirring constantly. Remove from heat. Stir in beaten egg yolks. Then carefully fold in egg whites and bake in greased 9x14 inch casserole dish for about 40 minutes in 350 degree oven. Serve immediately.

Ms. Nell J. Fears
Madison, Georgia
Similar recipe submitted by *Mrs. Marion H. Sims (Ginny)*

PUNCH OUT BREAD

1	16 ounce box hot roll mix	2 to 3	teaspoons garlic salt
½	cup Parmesan cheese	1	teaspoon Italian seasoning
1	tablespoon instant minced onion	1	teaspoon paprika
		3	teaspoons butter

Grease 9x5 inch loaf pan. Prepare basic recipe on hot roll box mix. Cover, let rise. Combine Parmesan cheese, minced onion, garlic salt, Italian seasoning and paprika. On well-floured surface, toss dough until no longer sticky. Roll out to a 12x7 inch rectangle. Brush with 1½ teaspoons melted butter. Sprinkle all except 1 tablespoon cheese filling over dough. Starting with shorter side, roll up tightly, sealing after each roll. Place loaf in pan, brush with 1½ teaspoons melted butter and sprinkle with remaining cheese filling. Cover; let rise again. Bake at 375 degrees for 25 to 35 minutes until golden brown. Cool 10 minutes in pan before removing.

Mrs. Glen Gaines (Laura)

COLONIAL BREAD

½	cup yellow cornmeal	2	packages dry yeast
⅓	cup brown sugar	½	cup lukewarm water
1	tablespoon salt	½	cup whole wheat flour
2	cups boiling water	½	cup rye flour
¼	cup cooking oil	4½	cups unbleached flour

Thoroughly combine cornmeal, brown sugar, salt, boiling water, and oil. Let cool to lukewarm, about 30 minutes. Soften yeast in ½ cup lukewarm water; stir into the cornmeal mixture. Add whole wheat and rye flour, mixing well. Stir in unbleached flour to make a moderately stiff dough. Turn out on floured surface and knead well for about 5 minutes. Place in greased bowl, let rise until doubled in bulk, punch down dough and divide in half. Let rest 10 minutes. Form each half into a loaf and place in greased loaf pans. Bake at 375 degrees for 45 minutes.

Mrs. George Sims (Sylvia)

Desserts

CHERRY CHEESECAKE
"This cheesecake is very light and tasty."

1   8 ounce package of cream
    cheese
½   cup sugar
1   3 ounce package whipped
    topping mix

½   cup milk
½   teaspoon vanilla extract
1   graham cracker crust

Blend together cream cheese and sugar until smooth. Whip up one package of whipped topping mix with ½ cup milk and vanilla extract (lemon extract may be added if preferred). Beat together cream cheese, sugar, and whipped topping. Pour into graham cracker crust

Glaze:
1   16 ounce can cherries in juice
¼   cup sugar

1   tablespoon of cornstarch
A few drops of red food coloring

Mix cherry juice, sugar, and cornstarch together and heat over stove until thickened and has a clear look. Add cherries to juice. Add a couple of drops of red food coloring to make cherries look pretty. Let cool and then add to top of pie.

Cathy Fuller

NO BAKE CHEESECAKE

1   package lemon gelatin
1   cup hot water
1   8 ounce package cream
    cheese
1   cup sugar

1   12 fluid ounce can evaporated
    milk, chill 24 hours
1   teaspoon vanilla

Dissolve gelatin in hot water and cool in refrigerator until syrupy. Cream cheese and beat in sugar until smooth. Combine gelatin and cheese mixture. In large bowl, whip evaporated milk and vanilla until milk is light and fluffy. Fold in gelatin and cheese mixture. Beat until creamy. Pour into crumb crust. Chill until ready to serve. Keep refrigerated.

Crust:
15   whole graham crackers,
     crushed

½   cup sugar
½   cup butter, melted

Mix crushed graham crackers, sugar, and butter into 9x13x2 inch pan. Save ⅔ cup to sprinkle on top.
Yield: 16 servings.

Mrs. Harvey Hendrix (Laura)

LEMON GLAZED CHEESECAKE

2 cups graham cracker crumbs
6 tablespoons butter, melted
2 tablespoons sugar
3 8 ounce packages cream
  cheese, softened
¾ cup sugar

3 eggs
¼ cup lemon juice
2 teaspoons lemon rind, grated
2 teaspoons vanilla
2 cups sour cream
3 tablespoons sugar
1 teaspoon vanilla

Preheat oven to 350 degrees. Combine first three ingredients thoroughly. Press crust evenly onto bottom and sides of buttered 9x3 springform pan. Bake 5 minutes, cool. Beat cream cheese until soft. Add sugar blending thoroughly. Add eggs one at a time, beating well after each addition. Mix in lemon juice, rind, and vanilla. Blend well. Turn into springform pan. Bake 35 minutes. While cake is baking, blend sour cream, sugar, and vanilla. Remove cake from oven. Gently spread sour cream mixture over top. Return to oven and bake 12 minutes. Cool on rack 30 minutes in pan. Spread with lemon glaze. Chill several hours or overnight before removing sides of pan. May garnish with lemon strips, strawberry, and mint leaves.

Lemon Glaze:

½ cup sugar
1½ tablespoons cornstarch
¼ teaspoon salt
¾ cup water

⅓ cup lemon juice
1 egg yolk
1 tablespoon butter
1 teaspoon lemon rind, grated

In a heavy 1 quart saucepan, mix sugar, cornstarch, and salt. Combine water, lemon juice, and egg yolk; add to sugar mixture. Cook over low heat, stirring constantly, until mixture comes to a slow boil. Add butter and lemon rind. Spread on cheesecake before glaze sets.
Yield: 10 to 12 servings.

Mrs. J. Milton Coxwell, Jr. (Kathi)

MARBLED CHEESECAKE

Chocolate Crumb Crust:

1½ cups chocolate chip cookie   ¼ cup butter or margarine,
    crumbs   melted
½ teaspoon ground cinnamon

Combine all ingredients. Press firmly into the bottom of a greased 8-inch springform pan and chill.

Cheesecake:

12 ounces cream cheese,   2 eggs
    softened   1½ cups sour cream
½ cup sugar   ⅔ cup, semi-sweet chocolate
1 teaspoon lemon rind, grated   morsels, melted

Combine first three ingredients in a medium bowl. Beat at medium speed until smooth. Add eggs one at a time. Add sour cream and beat until mixed. Combine 1 cup of the cheesecake mixture and melted chocolate. Mix well and set aside. Pour remaining cheesecake mixture into prepared crust. Pour chocolate mixture over the top. Gently swirl with a knife. Bake at 325 degrees for 30 to 35 minutes. Cool on a rack for 1 to 2 hours. Chill 8 hours. Yield: One 8 inch cheesecake.

Mrs. Jerry Studdard (Margaret)

NEW YORK CHEESECAKE

4 8 ounce packages of cream   3 tablespoons all-purpose flour
    cheese, room temperature   1 stick butter, melted
4 eggs, room temperature   1 teaspoon vanilla
1½ cups sugar   1½ tablespoons lemon juice
1 teaspoon salt   1 pint sour cream
3 tablespoons cornstarch

Beat cream cheese until soft. Add eggs. Add sugar, salt, cornstarch, and flour to cream cheese mixture. Next add melted butter, vanilla, and lemon juice. Beat until smooth. Pour into ungreased 8 to 10 inch springform pan with waxed paper liner in bottom. Bake at 350 degrees for 1 hour and 15 minutes. Should be a light golden brown on top when done. After baking leave oven door ajar and allow cake to remain in oven until it reaches room temperature. Then refrigerate overnight. Spread sour cream on top. *Note:* Could be topped with blueberry pie filling.

Vicki Wirt Hultzapple

RICH CHOCOLATE CHEESECAKE

Chocolate Wafer Crust:

1¼ cups chocolate wafers, ⅓ cup butter, melted
crumbs crushed

Combine crumbs and butter, mixing well. Firmly press crumb mixture into bottom of springform pan.

Chocolate Cheesecake:

1 12 ounce package semi-sweet chocolate morsels
4 8 ounce packages cream cheese, softened
2 cups sugar
4 eggs
1 tablespoon cocoa
2 teaspoons vanilla flavoring
1 16 ounce carton sour cream

Place chocolate morsels in top of a double boiler, bring water to a boil. Reduce heat. Cook until chocolate melts. In a large bowl, beat cream cheese until light and fluffy. Gradually add sugar. Add eggs one at a time, beating well after each. Stir in melted chocolate, cocoa, and vanilla, beat until blended. Stir in sour cream. Pour cheesecake mixture on top of crust. Bake for 1 hour and 40 minutes at 300 degrees. Garnish with whipped topping and fresh strawberries.

Note: It makes more than the pan can handle, so have a smaller pan ready to make a small cheesecake.

Mrs. Rick Barber (Tracey)

WHITE CHOCOLATE CHEESECAKE
WITH MANDARIN ORANGES

"A very elegant, special occasion dessert."

1½ cups graham cracker crumbs	2 8 ounce packages cream cheese, softened
¼ cup pecans, finely chopped	½ cup sour cream
¼ cup plus 1 tablespoon margarine, melted	¼ cup sugar
1 pound white chocolate, coarsely chopped	3 eggs
	1 teaspoon vanilla

Combine first 3 ingredients, stirring until blended. Press mixture into bottom and 1 inch up the side of a 9 inch springform pan. Place white chocolate in top of a double boiler; bring water to a boil. Reduce heat to low; cook until chocolate melts (stir occasionally). Let cool slightly. Combine cream cheese and sour cream in a large mixing bowl. Beat at medium speed of electric mixer until fluffy. Add sugar and beat. Add eggs, one at a time, beating after each addition. Add vanilla and chocolate, stirring just until blended. Pour filling into prepared pan. Bake at 300 degrees for 50 to 60 minutes or until cheesecake is almost set. Turn oven off, and partially open oven door. Leave cake in oven 30 minutes then cool on a wire rack. Chill.

Topping:

1 11 ounce can mandarin oranges, undrained	½ cup orange juice (from can of mandarin oranges)
¼ cup orange-flavored liqueur	1 tablespoon plus 1 teaspoon cornstarch
⅓ cup sugar	

Drain mandarin oranges, reserving ½ cup liquid. Combine mandarin oranges and orange-flavored liqueur. Stir gently. Set aside. Drain liqueur from oranges; reserving the liqueur. Set oranges aside. Combine reserved ½ cup orange juice, reserved orange-flavored liqueur, sugar, and cornstarch in pan. Stir well. Cook over medium heat until thickened, stirring constantly. Cool slightly. Remove outer rim of springform pan and place cheesecake on serving plate. Arrange mandarin oranges in center and around outer edge of cheesecake. Spoon glaze over top. Chill.

Mrs. James Barnett (Lynn)

CRUSTY POUND CAKE

1½ cups butter, softened	½ tablespoon vanilla extract
3 cups sugar	½ teaspoon lemon extract
6 eggs	3 cups all purpose flour

Cream butter well in a large mixing bowl. Add sugar gradually, mixing until texture is fine and mealy. Add eggs, one at a time, beating after each addition. Add flavorings and beat again. Stir flour into mixture, beating just until flour is moistened. Do not overbeat. Pour into a greased and floured fluted pan. Bake at 325 degrees for 1½ hours or until toothpick comes out clean when inserted. Cool in pan 10 minutes. Turn right side up and out of pan to cool completely.

Patti Reaves Burch
Baton Rouge, Louisiana

SNO-BALL CAKE

1 3 ounce box strawberry gelatin	1 large angel food cake
1 pint strawberries, sliced	1 12 ounce container frozen whipped non-dairy topping
½ cup sugar	½ cup plus 3 tablespoons canned coconut
⅛ teaspoon salt	
¾ cup pecans, chopped	

Mix gelatin by directions on box, place in refrigerator and let thicken, but not gel. Mix strawberries, sugar, salt, and pecans together by hand. Place in refrigerator and let chill. Tear cake into small pieces. When gelatin is thick, mix in ½ container of whipped topping, add strawberry mixture and mix well. Place a layer of cake in bottom of large serving bowl, spoon a layer of gelatin mixture, alternate, ending with gelatin mixture on top. Spread remaining whipped topping on top and sprinkle with coconut. Refrigerate before serving.

Mrs. Ronnie Busby (Kay)

AUNT LILLIAN'S POUND CAKE

"An old family recipe, never before published."

2⅓ cups sugar
1¼ cups cooking oil
2 cups all-purpose flour
1 cup self-rising flour

4 eggs
1½ teaspoons flavoring (vanilla or lemon)
Cinnamon

Grease and flour bundt cake pan. Beat sugar and oil. Add flour about 1 cup at a time. Add one egg at a time. Beat after each addition until fluffy. Add flavoring. Pour ½ of batter mixture into greased bundt pan. Sprinkle cinnamon on top of mixture. Add remaining batter. Bake at 325 degrees, approximately 1 hour and 15 minutes.

Glaze:

2 cups confectioners sugar
2 teaspoons margarine

1 teaspoon flavoring (vanilla or lemon)

To make glaze, beat all ingredients until well blended, pour over warm cake.

Gail Joiner (Mrs. Doyle)
Similar recipe submitted by *Mrs. J.B. Boykin (Evelyn)* and
Patti Reaves Burch, Baton Rouge, Louisiana

ANNIE'S SOUR CREAM POUND CAKE

1 cup shortening
3 cups sugar
6 eggs
3 cups all-purpose flour
¼ teaspoon soda

1 teaspoon salt
1 8 ounce carton sour cream
1 teaspoon vanilla extract
½ teaspoon almond extract

Cream shortening and sugar. Add eggs one at a time, beating well between additions. Combine flour, soda, and salt. Add sour cream and flour mixture alternately. Beat well. Add flavorings. Bake at 325 degrees for 1½ hours, in a greased and floured pan.

Linda McCardle
Recipe of the late *Annie McCardle*
Similar recipe submitted by *Judy B. Vinyard*

BROWN SUGAR POUND CAKE

"Great for bridge night."

1 cup butter	3½ cups all-purpose flour
½ cup shortening	½ teaspoon baking powder
1 16 ounce box plus 1 cup brown sugar	1 cup milk
5 eggs	1¼ teaspoon vanilla

Cream butter, shortening, and brown sugar. Add eggs and beat. Sift flour and baking powder; add alternately with milk to creamed mixture. Add vanilla and blend. Pour into a well-greased tube pan lined with wax paper. Bake in a 350 degree oven for 1½ hours. Cool and turn cake out.

Topping:

½ cup butter	1 teaspoon vanilla
1 cup pecans, chopped	Milk as needed
1 box confectioners sugar	

Combine ½ cup butter and pecans. Cook until brown. Remove from heat and add remaining ingredients. Add enough milk to spread. Spread over cooled cake.

Angela H. Dempsey

BUTTERSCOTCH POUND CAKE

1 cup margarine	3 cups all-purpose flour
3 cups sugar	1 6 ounce package butterscotch morsels
½ cup shortening	1 cup nuts, chopped
5 eggs	
1 8 ounce package cream cheese, room temperature	

Beat margarine, sugar, and shortening together. Add eggs one at a time. Add cream cheese. Add flour. Stir in butterscotch morsels and nuts. Bake in a greased and floured tube pan at 350 degrees for 1 hour 40 minutes or until cake tester inserted in the center of the cake comes out clean. When done, cool for one hour before removing from pan.
Yield: 16 servings.

Mrs. Rick Barber (Tracey)

CARAMEL POUND CAKE

1	cup butter	1	teaspoon baking powder
½	cup shortening	3	cups all-purpose flour
1	16 ounce box light brown sugar	1	5¾ ounce can evaporated milk
½	teaspoon salt	2	teaspoons vanilla
1	cup granulated sugar	1½	cups nuts, chopped
5	large eggs		

Cream butter, shortening, brown sugar, and salt. Add granulated sugar, cream well. Add eggs one at a time, beating well after each. Mix baking powder and flour; add alternately with milk to creamed mixture. Add vanilla. Grease and flour tube pan. Sprinkle nuts over bottom of pan. Cook 1-1½ hours at 325 degrees.

Frosting:

1	cup light brown sugar	⅓	cup milk
½	cup butter	2	cups confectioners sugar

Bring sugar, butter, and milk to boiling. Cook 2 minutes. Remove from heat and cool a few minutes. Add confectioners sugar and beat. Spread on cake.

Doris Munroe

CHOCOLATE WHIPPING CREAM POUND CAKE

1	cup shortening	2½	cups sifted self-rising flour
3	cups sugar	½	cup sifted cocoa
6	large eggs	1	cup whipping cream
1	tablespoon vanilla extract		

Cream shortening and sugar. Add eggs one at a time, beating one minute after each. Add vanilla and beat. Combine flour and cocoa. Add flour mixture and whipping cream to mixture alternately, beginning and ending with flour. Beat 5 minutes at medium speed. Pour into large greased tube pan. Bake at 300 degrees for 1½ hours.
Note: To make *plain* pound cake, omit cocoa and add ½ cup flour and ½ teaspoon lemon extract.

Marion Molliston
Similar recipe submitted by *Sharon Killough*

COCONUT POUND CAKE

1½ cups shortening
2½ cups sugar
1 cup milk
½ teaspoon baking powder
¼ teaspoon salt

3 cups all-purpose flour
5 large eggs
1 tablespoon coconut flavoring
1 3½ ounce can coconut

Cream shortening and sugar. Add milk. Sift together baking powder, salt, and flour. Alternately add dry ingredients and eggs to creamed mixture, beating well after each addition. Add coconut flavoring and blend well. Fold in can of coconut. Place cake mix into greased tube pan. Place in a cool oven. Bake at 300 degrees for 2 hours. Cover with foil when taken from oven. Let cake completely cool in pan.

Mrs. Marty Phillips (Pam)

MAPLE-PECAN POUND CAKE

1 cup butter
3 cups sugar
6 egg yolks
3 cups all-purpose flour
½ teaspoon baking soda

1 cup sour cream
1 cup nuts, chopped
1½ teaspoons maple flavorings
6 egg whites, stiffly beaten

Cream butter and sugar well. Add egg yolks one at a time, beating well after each addition. Sift together flour and soda. Add to sugar mixture alternating with sour cream. Blend in nuts. Fold in flavoring and egg whites. Pour in greased and paper lined tube pan. Bake at 300 degrees for 1½ hours.

Mildred Goodpasture
Oak Ridge, Tennessee

ROSEMARY'S EASY CHOCOLATE CHIP CAKE

1 package Devils food cake mix
1 8 ounce carton sour cream
1 4 ounce box instant
   chocolate pudding
4 eggs

½ cup warm water
½ cup oil
1½ cup chocolate chips
Confectioners sugar

Mix all above ingredients *except* chocolate chips and confectioners sugar. Fold in chocolate chips. Bake in bundt pan which has been greased and dusted with flour. Bake 50 to 60 minutes at 350 degrees. Let cool in pan 15 minutes. Turn on plate and dust with confectioners sugar.

Mrs. A.O. Yoe, Jr. (Marion)

CHOCOLATE CHIP CAKE

1   4 ounce bar German
    chocolate, grated
1   18½ ounce box yellow cake
    mix
1   4 ounce box instant vanilla
    pudding
4   eggs

¾   cup oil
¾   cup water
1   6 ounce package semi-sweet
    chocolate chips
1   teaspoon vanilla
Confectioners sugar

Grate bar of German chocolate and reserve ¼. Mix together cake mix and pudding. Add ¾ grated chocolate. Add eggs, one at a time. Add oil, water, chips, and vanilla. Mix well. Pour into 13x9 inch greased pan. Bake at 325 degrees for 45 minutes. Remove from oven when done and sprinkle with remaining grated chocolate. When cool, sprinkle with confectioners sugar.

Mrs. Cathy Glow

CHOCOLATE DREAM CAKE

1   cup milk
4   tablespoons all-purpose flour

1   18½ ounce box chocolate
    cake mix

Put milk and flour in saucepan and cook until thick. Cover. Set aside to cool for later use. Bake cake according to directions on box in two 9 inch pans. Cool 20 minutes and remove from pans. Split layers.

Filling:
½   cup margarine
½   cup shortening

1   cup sugar
1   teaspoon vanilla

Whip filling ingredients until together light and fluffy. Add milk and flour mixture from above and beat until well blended. Put filling between layers of cake.

Icing:
½   cup margarine
4   tablespoons cocoa

6   tablespoons milk
1   box confectioners sugar

Melt margarine, add cocoa and milk and bring to a boil. Pour over sugar and beat until right consistency for spreading. Add a few drops of milk if it is too thick. Frost top and sides of cake.

Mrs. JoAnn Mullins

CHOCOLATE ZUCCHINI CAKE

1½ cups margarine, softened
½ cup vegetable oil
1¾ cups sugar
2 eggs
1 teaspoon vanilla
1½ cups sour milk
4 tablespoons cocoa

½ teaspoon baking powder
1 teaspoon baking soda
½ teaspoon cinnamon
½ teaspoon cloves
2½ cups all-purpose flour
2 cups zucchini, diced
¼ cup chocolate chips

Cream margarine, oil and sugar well. Add eggs, vanilla, and sour milk. Sift together all dry ingredients. Stir in diced zucchini. Bake in greased and floured 9x12 inch pan. Cook at 325 degrees about 40 minutes. Sprinkle chocolate chips on top before baking.
Yield: 24 servings.

Winser D. Hayes

JANIE'S MISSISSIPPI FUDGE CAKE

½ cup butter or margarine
2 tablespoons cocoa
1 cup sugar
2 eggs

¾ cup self-rising flour
Pinch of salt
1 cup pecans, chopped
1 cup miniature marshmallows

Melt butter or margarine and blend with cocoa. Beat sugar and eggs together until well blended and add to butter and cocoa mixture. Add flour, salt, and pecans and blend well. Pour into a greased 6x10 inch pan. Bake 350 degrees for 45 minutes. Top with marshmallows while *still hot*.

Frosting:
2 tablespoons butter or margarine
5 tablespoons milk
2 cups confectioners sugar

¼ cup cocoa
1 teaspoon vanilla

Bring butter and milk to a boil. Sift together sugar and cocoa and add slowly to butter and milk, stirring constantly. Add vanilla and beat until creamy. Spread over marshmallows. Cut into squares when cool.

Mrs. Janis McCardle

Nuts will not settle to the bottom of the cake batter if they are first heated in the oven and then dusted with flour before adding to the batter.

$100 CHOCOLATE CAKE
"This cake got RAVE reviews!"

Cake:
1 cup butter
2 cups sugar
2 teaspoons baking powder
¼ teaspoon salt
3 cups all-purpose flour

1⅓ cups milk
2 eggs
2 squares unsweetened chocolate
1 teaspoon vanilla

Cream butter. Sift all dry ingredients. Add butter alternately with milk. Beat eggs to lemon color, add to mixture. Melt chocolate in double boiler with vanilla. Add to batter. Grease and flour three 9 inch cake pans. Bake at 350 degrees for 25 to 30 minutes.

Filling:
2 cups pecans, chopped
8 tablespoons butter
6 tablespoons cream

3 cups confectioners sugar
1 dash salt
2 teaspoons vanilla

Sauté pecans in butter, stirring constantly. Remove from heat. Mix all other ingredients and combine with pecans. Spread between layers of cake.

Icing:
2 cups sugar
2 tablespoons white corn syrup
1 cup heavy cream

2 tablespoons cocoa
¼ teaspoon salt

Mix thoroughly and let stand for 15 minutes. Cook over low heat until soft ball is formed. Beat and cover top and sides of cake before icing hardens.

Althea J. Dennis
Albertville, Alabama

For easy removal of cake layers, place the pans on a damp cloth immediately after taking the pans from the oven.

APRICOT LOAF CAKE

1½ teaspoons baking powder
1 teaspoon baking soda
2 cups all-purpose flour
1 cup sugar
½ cup margarine, softened
3 eggs

1 8 ounce carton sour cream
2 teaspoons vanilla
1 cup pecans, chopped
1 cup (6 ounce) dried apricots, chopped

Preheat oven to 350 degrees. Grease and flour 9x5 inch loaf pan. In a large bowl, mix baking powder, baking soda, flour, and sugar. Cut in margarine until mixture resembles coarse crumbs. Stir in eggs, sour cream, and vanilla, just until flour mixture is moistened. Add pecans and apricots. Spoon batter evenly into pan. Bake 1 hour and 15 minutes or until toothpick inserted in middle comes out clean. Cool 15 minutes in pan. Remove.
Yield: 10 servings

Melba Hagan
Alexander City, Alabama

CHOICE PINEAPPLE CAKE

Cake:
2 eggs
1 20 ounce can crushed pineapple, undrained
2 cups all-purpose flour

1 cup sugar
1 cup brown sugar
2 teaspoons baking soda
1 cup nuts, chopped

In large mixing bowl, beat 2 eggs until light and fluffy. Add pineapple, flour, sugar, brown sugar, and soda. Mix well *by hand* — not electric mixer. Stir in nuts. Pour into greased 13x9x2 inch pan. Bake at 350 degrees for 40 to 45 minutes or until toothpick comes out clean. Let cool. Frost with Cream Cheese Ginger Frosting.

Cream Cheese Ginger Frosting:
1 3 ounce package cream cheese, softened
¼ cup butter
1 teaspoon vanilla

1¾ cups confectioners sugar
½ teaspoon ground ginger

Beat together with mixer: cream cheese, butter, and vanilla. Then gradually add confectioners sugar and ginger. Beat until frosting has smooth consistency.
Note: Chopped nuts may be sprinkled on top of frosting as a garnish.

Mrs. Mike Riley (Pam)

DUSKY DELIGHT CAKE

⅔ cup shortening
1¾ cups sugar
3 eggs
½ cup cocoa
½ cup water

2¼ cups all-purpose flour, sifted
1 teaspoon soda
1 teaspoon salt
¾ cup buttermilk
Icing according to taste

Cream shortening and sugar until fluffy; add eggs, one at a time. Blend together cocoa and water. Add to creamed mixture. Sift together flour, soda, and salt. Add flour mixture alternately with buttermilk. Pour batter into 3 greased and floured 9 inch cake pans. Bake at 350 degrees for 20 to 25 minutes. When cool, remove from pans. Ice cake with your favorite icing. Yield: 1 3-layer cake.

Charlotte Washam

FRESH PEACH CAKE

Cake:
1 18 to 19 ounce package white cake mix
½ cup milk
1 3 ounce package peach-flavored gelatin

½ cup coconut
4 eggs
½ cup vegetable cooking oil
½ cup fresh peaches, mashed
½ cup pecans, chopped

Icing:
1 16 ounce box confectioners sugar, sifted
½ cup fresh peaches, mashed
½ cup pecans, chopped

½ cup butter, softened
½ cup coconut

Mix well all cake ingredients in a large bowl. Pour into a greased and floured 13x9 inch sheet cake pan. Bake at 350 degrees for 30 to 45 minutes or until cake tester inserted in the center of the cake comes out clean. While cake is baking, mix together all icing ingredients. When cake is done, remove from oven and poke holes in cake with ice pick. Pour icing immediately over cake while in the pan. Cover and refrigerate until ready to serve. Yield: 12 servings.
Note: This cake should be prepared 24 hours ahead and refrigerated until time to serve. The longer it stays refrigerated, the better it is.

Denise Murray
Montgomery, Alabama

DRIED PRUNE CAKE

Cake:

1 cup oil
2 cups sugar
3 eggs
2 cups all-purpose flour
1 teaspoon salt
1 teaspoon soda
1 teaspoon cinnamon

1 teaspoon allspice
1 teaspoon nutmeg
1 cup buttermilk or sourmilk*
1 cup prunes, cooked and finely chopped**
1 cup nuts, chopped

Cream together oil and sugar. Add eggs one at a time. Sift together flour, salt, soda, cinnamon, allspice, and nutmeg. Alternating, add dry sifted ingredients and buttermilk. Fold in cooked prunes and nuts. Bake in 13x9 inch pan at 350 degrees for 40 minutes. Ice when cool.

Icing:

1 cup sugar
½ cup buttermilk

½ cup butter

In a saucepan combine ingredients and boil until thickened. The mixture should be runny. Punch holes in cake and drizzle icing over cake.

Note: *To make sourmilk when you don't have buttermilk use 1 cup milk and 1 tablespoon vinegar.

**½ cup prunes equals 1 cup cooked prunes. If you use pitted prunes, put a little water in saucepan and allow prunes to come to a boil and then drain.

Ann McKinney (Mrs. Grady)

CHRISTMAS CAKE

1 pound butter (not margarine)
2 cups sugar
6 eggs
1 ounce lemon flavoring

4 cups all-purpose flour, sifted
1 pound candied pineapple
1 pound candied cherries
1 quart pecans, chopped

Cream butter and sugar until like whipped cream. Add eggs one at a time; beat well after each. Add flavoring and 2 cups flour. Chop cherries, pineapple, and nuts. Dredge in remaining cups of flour. Pour batter over nuts and fruit mixture. Mix well until all is well coated with batter. Pour into greased and floured tube pan. Bake at 325 degrees for 30 minutes. Reduce oven to 300 degrees for 1 hour, then reduce to 275 degrees for 15 minutes.

Mrs. Rick Barber (Tracey)

FUNNY CAKE

"You will be delighted with this cake in a pie."

1	cup sugar	½	cup shortening
½	cup cocoa	2	cups all-purpose flour
1	cup water	2	teaspoons baking powder
1	teaspoon vanilla	1	cup milk
3	frozen pie shells	2	eggs
2	cups sugar	1	teaspoon vanilla

In saucepan, stir together 1 cup sugar, cocoa, water, and 1 teaspoon vanilla. Cook over medium heat for 10 minutes, stirring frequently. Pour cocoa mixture into three frozen pie shells, dividing equally. In large bowl, combine remaining ingredients, mixing well. Pour batter on top of each cocoa filling. Bake at 350 degrees for 40 to 45 minutes or until done.
Note: Delicious when served warm with ice cream or whipped topping.

April Edmiston

HUMMINGBIRD CAKE

3	cups all-purpose flour	1½	teaspoon vanilla
2	cups sugar	1	8 ounce can crushed pineapple
1	teaspoon salt		
1	teaspoon soda	1	cup pecans or walnuts, chopped
1	teaspoon ground cinnamon		
3	eggs, beaten	2	cups bananas, mashed
1½	cups cooking oil		

Combine flour, sugar, salt, soda, and cinnamon. Add eggs and oil. Stir until all ingredients are moistened, but do not beat. Stir in vanilla, pineapple, nuts, and bananas. Bake in three 9 inch greased and floured round pans at 350 degrees for 25 to 30 minutes. Cool on racks before icing.

Icing:

1	cup butter, softened	1	cup nuts, chopped
4	3 ounce packages cream cheese, softened	2	teaspoons vanilla
1½	16 ounce boxes confectioners sugar		

Combine all ingredients and beat until smooth.

Karan K. Bush
Birmingham, Alabama

54

JIFFY CAKE
"You can make it in a jiffy."

Cake:
3   eggs
1½ cups sugar
1½ teaspoons vanilla
1½ cups all-purpose flour

1½ teaspoons baking powder
1   teaspoon salt
¾   cup milk
1½ teaspoons butter

Beat eggs until thick. Gradually add sugar and vanilla. Sift flour, baking powder, and salt and add to egg mixture. Heat milk and butter to boiling point and add to batter. Pour into greased and floured 9x12 inch pan. Bake at 375 degrees for 30 minutes.

Icing:
4½ tablespoons butter
3   tablespoons cream or
    evaporated milk

7½ tablespoons brown sugar
¾   cup dry coconut

Mix all ingredients in a small saucepan. Boil for 5 minutes. Pour over hot cake and place under broiler until light brown, usually about 2 minutes.

Marvel Winser Babcook (Mimi)
Sloatsburg, New York

KENTUCKY WONDER CAKE
"This cake has a 'wonderful' flavor."

2   cups sugar
1½ cups oil
4   egg yolks
2½ cups self-rising flour
1½ teaspoons cinnamon
1½ teaspoons nutmeg

3¾ tablespoons hot water
1   8 ounce can crushed
    pineapple, drained
1½ cups nuts, chopped
1   cup raisins
4   egg whites, beaten

Cream together sugar, oil, and egg yolks. Mix well. Sift together flour, cinnamon, and nutmeg. Alternately mix flour mixture to sugar mixture adding water and pineapple. Add nuts and raisins. Mix well. Beat egg whites until stiff and fold into batter. Cook in greased and floured tube pan for 1 hour at 350 degrees.

Gail Joiner (Mrs. Doyle)

LEMON CHIFFON CAKE

1   18¼ ounce box lemon cake   1   cup water
    mix with pudding   4   eggs
½   cup cooking oil

Combine cake ingredients in the above order. Mix well at medium speed of mixer. Pour into greased and floured tube pan. Bake 45 to 50 minutes at 350 degrees. After removing cake from oven use ice pick to put holes all over the cake. Leave cake in pan.

Icing
½   cup orange juice   2   cups confectioners sugar
2   tablespoons butter, melted

Mix all ingredients and pour over the cake, allowing it to soak for several hours or overnight. Then remove cake from pan.
Yield: 16 servings.
Note: Can use regular lemon cake mix and add one box of instant lemon pudding to it.

Mrs. Bobby Lumpkin (Beth)

OATMEAL COCOA CAKE
*"This cake turns out perfect — even for a
novice baker."*

½   cup vegetable oil   1   teaspoon baking powder
1½ cups boiling water   1   teaspoon soda
1   cup sugar   ½   teaspoon salt
½   cup brown sugar   1   cup oatmeal
2   eggs, beaten   1   6 ounce package chocolate
1½ cups all-purpose flour   morsels

Mix together oil, water, sugars, and eggs. Sift together flour, baking powder, soda, and salt. Add all above to oatmeal. Mix and beat well, Pour into greased 9x13 inch cake pan. Sprinkle chocolate morsels over top. Bake 40 minutes at 350 degrees.

Topping:
½   cup margarine, softened   ½   cup sweetened condensed milk
1   cup brown sugar   1   cup coconut, flaked

Mix together and spread over warm cake, place back in oven for 5 minutes.

Mrs. Harvey Hendrix (Laura)

OATMEAL CAKE
"This cake was the hit of the club meeting."

1½ cups boiling water
1 cup oatmeal
½ cup margarine
1 cup white sugar
1 cup brown sugar
2 egg yolks

1½ cup all-purpose flour
1 teaspoon soda
½ teaspoon cinnamon
½ teaspoon nutmeg
1 teaspoon vanilla
¼ teaspoon salt

Pour water over oatmeal and set aside to cool. Blend margarine, sugars, and egg yolks. Add oatmeal mixture, then dry ingredients. Pour into 13x9 inch pan. Bake 20 to 25 minutes at 350 degrees.

Topping:
½ cup margarine
1 cup brown sugar
1 cup flaked coconut

1 cup nuts, chopped
2 egg whites, unbeaten

Cream brown sugar and margarine. Add coconut, nuts, and egg whites. Spread on top of partially cooked cake and bake 15 additional minutes. Cut in squares.

Susan Holdridge
Alexander City, Alabama

ORANGE PARTY CAKES

1 18½ ounce box yellow cake mix
3 oranges
3 lemons

2 16 ounce boxes confectioners sugar, sifted
Rind from 2 oranges, grated
Rind from 2 lemons, grated

Mix the cake mix according to directions on the box and cook in greased miniature cupcake pans. While cakes are baking, squeeze juice from 3 oranges and 3 lemons. Grate rind from 2 oranges and 2 lemons. Add the rind to the juice. Sift 2 boxes of confectioners sugar and add to the juice. When cakes are done, drop immediately into the juice mixture. Remove and cool.
Yield: 30 or more servings
Note: These may be frozen.

Rhonda Lewis

PINEAPPLE DELIGHT CAKE

1   18½ ounce box yellow butter cake mix
4   eggs
½   cup cooking oil
1   11 ounce can mandarin oranges, undrained
1   8 ounce can crushed pineapple, well drained, reserve juice

1   3¾ ounce package instant vanilla pudding
1   13 ounce carton frozen whipped non-dairy topping
½   cup nuts, chopped
½   cup coconut

Preheat oven to 375 degrees. Grease and flour 2 round 9 inch cake pans. Mix cake mix, eggs, oil, and oranges (with juice). Pour into pans and bake 30 minutes. Cool. Stir together crushed pineapple, vanilla pudding, whipped topping, nuts, and coconut. Make holes with an ice pick on top of cake layers. Drizzle a small amount of pineapple juice over cake layers. Let soak in a few minutes. Ice each layer with frosting. Leave in refrigerator overnight or several hours before serving.
Note: Keep refrigerated.

Mrs. Ronnie Busby (Kay)

PLUM CAKE

Cake:
2   cups self-rising flour
2   cups sugar
1   teaspoon cinnamon
1   teaspoon ground cloves

1   cup oil
3   eggs
2   jars strained plum baby food
1   cup nuts, chopped (optional)

Mix all ingredients and bake for 55 minutes at 325 degrees in a greased bundt pan.

Glaze:
1   3 ounce package cream cheese
1   cup pecans, chopped (optional)

2   tablespoons confectioners sugar
1   tablespoon milk

Mix and pour on hot cake.

Alternate Glaze:
1 cup confectioners sugar with enough milk or lemon juice to make it smooth and creamy. Pour over hot cake.

Mrs. Matt Mihelic (Ree)

OLD WITCHES MAGIC NUT CAKE
"A true treat at Halloween, or any time."

3	eggs	1½	teaspoon baking soda
1	16 ounce can pumpkin	1¼	teaspoon salt
¾	cup vegetable oil	¾	teaspoon nutmeg
½	cup water	¾	teaspoon cinnamon
2½	cups all-purpose flour	1	cup yellow raisins
2¼	cups sugar	½	cup nuts, chopped

Beat together the first four ingredients. Add other ingredients that have been sifted; except raisins and nuts. Then add raisins and nuts. Bake in 13x9 inch pan at 350 degrees until toothpick comes out clean.

Frosting:

1	8 ounce package cream cheese	2	teaspoons vanilla
		1	box confectioners sugar
6	tablespoons butter	½	cup nuts, chopped

Beat together cream cheese and butter. Add vanilla and confectioners sugar and beat until creamy. Spread over cooled cake. Sprinkle nuts over top.

Melba Hagan
Alexander City, Alabama

GOLDEN CAKE

½	pound whipped, lightly salted butter	2	teaspoons vanilla
		½	teaspoon orange extract
½	cup shortening	3	cups cake flour, sifted
2	cups sugar	½	cup buttermilk
5	eggs		

Cream butter with shortening, gradually add sugar until like whipped cream. Add eggs, one at a time, beating well each time. Add flavoring. Add flour and milk alternately, beginning and ending with flour. Pour in greased 10 inch tube pan, bake at 300 degrees for 1¼ hours.

Icing

¼	cup margarine	1½ - 2	cups sifted confectioners sugar
½	cup brown sugar		
3	tablespoons milk		

Melt margarine and brown sugar. Cook over low heat two minutes. Add milk, bring to boil, but *do not* allow to boil. Cool ten minutes. Add sifted confectioners sugar to desired thickness.

Zell S. (Mrs. Jimmy) Copeland

CHOCOLATE ICING

3 cups sugar	1 cup margarine
3 tablespoons all-purpose flour	1¼ cups evaporated milk
½ cup cocoa	1 teaspoon vanilla flavoring

Combine sugar and flour in heavy saucepan. Add cocoa and stir to blend well. Add softened margarine and evaporated milk. Cook to softball stage (230 degrees), stirring constantly. Remove from heat, and add vanilla. Beat with an electric mixer until icing loses its shiny color, approximately 5 minutes. Spread on cake immediately, as icing hardens quickly.
Yield: Icing for a 2 or 3 layer 9 inch cake.

Charlotte Washam

NEVER FAIL CHOCOLATE ICING

2 cups sugar	½ cup margarine
2 tablespoons cocoa	1 teaspoon vanilla
½ cup milk	

Mix all ingredients in sauce pan. Boil rapidly for 2 minutes. Cool.

Pat Thompson
Alexander City, Alabama

MADELEINES

1¼ cup all-purpose flour, sifted
½ teaspoon baking powder
¼ teaspoon salt
3 eggs
1 teaspoon vanilla

⅔ cup sugar
2 teaspoons lemon rind, grated
¾ cup butter, melted and cooled
Madeleine pan

Sift flour with baking powder and salt. Set aside. Beat 3 eggs until light, add vanilla, gradually beat in sugar. Continue beating until volume has increased to about 4 times the original amount. Fold in lemon rind. Gradually fold in flour mixture. Stir in melted and cooled butter. Brush pans with additional melted butter and spoon about 1 tablespoon batter into each shell. Bake in preheated 350 degree oven, 10 to 12 minutes. Remove cookies to wire rack and sift confectioners sugar over the tops.
Yield: 3 dozen.
Note: Store in closed container.

Mrs. W. A. Davis (Mona)

GRANDMA'S TEA CAKES

1 cup sugar
1 cup butter or margarine
3 eggs

1 teaspoon vanilla extract
3½ cups self-rising flour

Cream butter and sugar. Add eggs and vanilla. Beat until blended, approximately 5 to 8 minutes on high speed. Add flour slowly while running mixer on low speed. The flour may form dust in the kitchen if mixed too fast. Chill dough, (can be kept in refrigerator for 2 days before baking). On floured cloth or paper, knead until dough can be rolled to approximately ¼ inch thick. Cut with cutters. Bake at 350 degrees for 10 minutes. Do not overbake. Remove cookies from oven as edges begin to show signs of browning. Carefully remove with a spatula while cookies are warm, to prevent overcooking.
Yield: 4 to 5 dozen.
Note: Can be iced with your favorite icing. We prefer them plain with milk or lemonade.

A lady's age can be revealed with a plate of these cookies. If she calls these "sweet cakes," she's over 80, "tea cakes" over 60, "why, that's a plate of cookies," well under 40. This is a quote passed down from Southern farm cooks.

Mrs. Carl R. Reaves (Joyce)
Similar recipe submitted by *Rachel Munroe*

DROP SUGAR COOKIES

1½ cups margarine
2¾ cups sugar
4 eggs
1½ teaspoons vanilla flavoring
1½ teaspoons lemon flavoring

1½ teaspoons orange flavoring
½ teaspoon salt
1½ teaspoons cream of tartar
1½ teaspoons soda
6 cups all-purpose flour

Cream margarine and sugar well. Add all other ingredients. Mix well and put in refrigerator to chill for several hours. Shape into balls about the size of a walnut. Grease your hands slightly if dough sticks to your fingers. Roll balls in granulated sugar and place on greased cookie sheet. Press down with bottom of glass dipped in sugar. Bake on greased cookie sheet at 350 degrees for about 12 minutes or until they start to turn slightly brown. Yield: 5 to 6 dozen.

Mrs. Robert M. Wikle (Berniece)

SHORT BREAD COOKIES

¼ cup butter or margarine, softened
1 8 ounce cream cheese, softened

1 egg
¼ teaspoon vanilla
1 package yellow cake mix

Cream butter, cheese, blend in egg and vanilla. Add cake mix ⅓ at a time. This makes a stiff dough. Drop by teaspoons on ungreased cookie sheet. Press end of fork crosswise on mound of dough. Cook 8 to 10 minutes at 375 degrees. Cool slightly before removing from pan.

Marvel Babcook
Sloatsburg, New York

MOLASSES COOKIES

1½ cups margarine, melted
2 cups sugar
½ cup molasses
2 eggs

3 teaspoons baking soda
1 teaspoon vanilla
½ teaspoon salt
4 cups all-purpose flour

Mix all ingredients well. Let stand in refrigerator overnight. Roll in ball size of walnut, dip in granulated sugar, and place on greased cookie sheet; press down with bottom of glass dipped in sugar. Bake in 350 degree oven until done.
Yield: 4 to 5 dozen.

Mrs. Robert M. Wikle (Berniece)

RANCH COOKIES

1 cup butter or margarine
1 cup sugar
1 cup brown sugar
2 cups all-purpose flour
1 teaspoon baking soda
½ teaspoon baking powder
2 eggs, unbeaten

1 cup quick cooking oatmeal, uncooked
1 cup crispy rice cereal
1 cup coconut, shredded
1 cup pecans, chopped
1 teaspoon vanilla

Preheat oven to 350 degrees. With electric mixer, cream butter and sugars. Beat in flour, soda, and baking powder. Add eggs and mix well. Add oatmeal, crispy rice cereal, coconut, and pecans. Mix well, using a spoon. Then add vanilla. Chill dough. Roll into marble-sized balls and bake on slightly greased cookie sheet at 350 degrees about 7 minutes.
Yield: 200 small cookies.

Mrs. A. H. Meacham (Odessa)

OLD FASHIONED OAT COOKIES

1 cup raisins
½ cup boiling water
2 cups quick or old fashioned oats
⅔ cup oat bran
1 cup walnuts or pecans, chopped
1⅓ cups all-purpose flour

2 teaspoons pumpkin pie spice
½ teaspoon baking soda
½ teaspoon salt
1 cup margarine, not whipped
1 cup brown sugar, packed
1 teaspoon vanilla extract
2 large eggs

Grease 2 cookie sheets. Soak raisins in boiling water. Toast oats, oat bran, and nuts on cookie sheet in oven until lightly browned. Cool. Mix flour, spice, baking soda, and salt. Beat margarine, sugar, and vanilla in mixer bowl until light. Beat in eggs one at a time. Stir in flour mixture. Drain raisins and add to batter with oat mixture. Stir until blended. Drop dough by teaspoonsful onto cookie sheets. Bake 10 to 12 minutes at 350 degrees until golden brown and tops feel dry.
Yield: 5 dozen.

Mrs. Doyle Joiner (Gail)

Place a slice of bread in cookie jar to keep cookies soft.

CHOCOLATE CHIP AND OATMEAL COOKIES

2 cups butter
2 cups sugar
2 cups light brown sugar
4 eggs
2 teaspoons vanilla
4 cups all-purpose flour
5 cups oatmeal, blended in a blender to a fine powder

1 teaspoon salt
2 teaspoons baking powder
2 teaspoons baking soda
1 24 ounce bag chocolate chips
1 8 ounce chocolate bar, grated
3 cups pecans, chopped

Cream butter and both sugars. Add eggs and vanilla. Mix together with flour, oatmeal, salt, baking powder, and baking soda. Add chips, candy, and nuts. Roll into balls and place 2 inches apart on a cookie sheet. Bake for 6 minutes at 375 degrees.
Yield: 9 dozen cookies.

Mrs. George Montgomery (Andrea)

CHOCOLATE OATMEAL NUT BROWNIES

¾ cup quick cooking rolled oats
1 6 ounce package semisweet chocolate morsels
6 tablespoons butter or margarine
½ cup packed brown sugar

2 eggs
1 teaspoon vanilla
¾ cup all-purpose flour
½ cup nuts, chopped
¼ teaspoon baking soda
¼ teaspoon salt

Sprinkle 2 tablespoons of the oats over bottom of greased 9x9x2 inch baking pan; set aside. In saucepan melt chocolate and butter over low heat; stir constantly. Remove from heat; blend in sugar. Beat in eggs and vanilla. Stir together flour, remaining oats, nuts, soda, and salt; stir into chocolate mixture. Spoon into prepared pan. Bake at 325 degrees about 30 minutes. Cool; cut into bars.
Yield: 16 servings.

Laine Austin Randall
Greensboro, North Carolina

Cookies that soften during storage will become crisp again by placing in 300 degree oven for five minutes.

CHOCOLATE PEANUT SQUARES

¼ cup butter or margarine
1 6 ounce package semi-sweet
  chocolate pieces
1½ cups rolled oats
½ cup peanut butter
1 8 ounce package cream
  cheese, softened

¼ cup sugar
1 teaspoon vanilla
½ cup milk
1 cup whipping cream
¼ cup peanuts, chopped

In saucepan heat together butter or margarine and ¼ cup of the chocolate pieces over low heat just until melted. Stir in oats until coated. Press into the bottom of 8x8x2 inch pan; chill. In small saucepan heat and stir peanut butter and remaining chocolate together over low heat until melted. Cool slightly. In mixer beat cream cheese, sugar and vanilla until fluffy. Beat in peanut butter mixture (mixture will be quite stiff). Blend in milk. Whip cream just to soft peaks. Fold into peanut butter mixture. Turn into pan. Sprinkle peanuts atop. Cover; chill well.
Yield: 9 to 12 servings.

Mrs. Dan Kearley (Frances)

TEDDY'S FAVORITE BROWNIES

1 package yellow cake mix
1 cup peanut butter
½ cup melted margarine
2 eggs
1 12 ounce package semi-sweet
  chocolate chips

1 15 ounce can condensed milk
2 tablespoons margarine
½ teaspoon salt
1 cup pecans, chopped
2 teaspoons vanilla

Stir cake mix, peanut butter, margarine, and eggs until it holds together; press ⅔ batter in bottom of ungreased 9x13 inch pan. In heavy saucepan combine semi-sweet chocolate chips, condensed milk, margarine, and salt. Melt over low heat, stirring constantly. Remove from heat and add pecans and vanilla; spread over batter. Crumble remaining ⅓ batter on top and press lightly. Bake at 325 degrees for 20 to 25 minutes.

Mrs. Dan Kearley (Frances)

FANTASTIC MINT BROWNIES

1   21½ ounce box chewy
    brownie mix
1   16 ounce can of vanilla
    frosting

2   6 ounce boxes of foil
    wrapped chocolate mints

Prepare brownie mix as recipe on box suggests. Bake and cool. Spread with vanilla frosting mix. Melt the 2 boxes of mints in the top of double boiler (or melt in microwave), then spread on top of vanilla frosting. Cool about 15 minutes, then cut into squares. Refrigerate after cutting. Cover until ready to serve.
Note: In place of canned frosting, you can make your own vanilla frosting.

Mrs. Paul A. Bingham, Jr. (Sally Barber)
Athens, Georgia

CREME FILLED CHOCOLATE SANDWICH COOKIES

Cookies:
1   18½ ounce box dark
    chocolate cake mix
½   cup margarine or butter,
    melted

1   egg, slightly beaten

In a large bowl, combine all cookie ingredients; mix well. Firmly shape dough into 1 inch balls. Place 2 inches apart on ungreased cookie sheets. Bake at 350 degrees for 9 to 13 minutes or until set. Cool 1 minute; remove from cookie sheets. Cool completely.

Filling:
2   cups confectioners sugar
¼   cup shortening

½   teaspoon vanilla
1   egg white

In small bowl, combine ½ cup of the confectioners sugar, shortening, vanilla, and egg white; blend well. Add remaining confectioners sugar; beat until smooth and creamy. Spread a heaping teaspoon of filling between 2 cookies; repeat with remaining cookies.
Yield: 24 sandwich cookies.
Variations: Add nuts to cookie mixture; change cake mix to yellow, lemon, white, or butter pecan.

Melba Sirmon
Munford, Alabama

ROUND CRACKER TREATS

"Serve these sensations soon."

1	cup dates, chopped	3	ounce package cream cheese, softened
1	15 ounce can sweetened condensed milk	¼	cup margarine, softened
1	cup pecans, chopped fine	2	cups confectioners sugar
1	box round buttery crackers	1	teaspoon vanilla

Cook dates and condensed milk in boiler over medium heat until very thick. Add nuts and stir well. Spread small amount on top of cracker (like peanut butter on cracker). Bake in 350 degree oven for 6 to 8 minutes. Cool completely. Beat cream cheese, margarine, sugar and vanilla until creamy. Put a dollop of this mixture on top of cooled crackers. Refrigerate until needed. *Note:* Freezes well.

Kaye Spears

VANILLA WAFER FRUIT LOGS

1	14 ounce can sweetened condensed milk	1	8 ounce package dates, chopped
½ to 1 pound candied cherries, chopped		1	16 ounce box vanilla wafers, crumbled
2	cups pecans, chopped		

In a large mixing bowl, pour sweetened milk over cherries, pecans, and dates. Fold in wafer crumbs, and roll into 3 or 4 logs. Roll each log in additional crumbs. Refrigerate overnight. Slice each log before serving.

Judy Griffin

NELDA'S FUDGE

4	cups sugar	1	7 ounce jar marshmallow cream
1	14½ ounce can evaporated milk	3	6 ounce packages milk chocolate morsels
½	cup margarine	4	cups pecans, chopped
1	teaspoon vanilla		

Boil sugar and evaporated milk for 10 minutes after first bubbles appear. Then add other ingredients and stir until chocolate is melted. Drop on wax paper and cool.

Pat Thompson
Alexander City, Alabama

TOFFEE

2¼ cups sugar
½ cup water
1 teaspoon salt
1¼ cups butter (no substitutes)
1½ cups blanched almonds, chopped and divided

1 cup pecans, finely chopped and divided
1 teaspoon vanilla
1 6 ounce package semi-sweet chocolate morsels

Combine sugar, water, salt and butter in a 3 quart saucepan. Bring to a boil over medium high heat. Stir in ¾ cup almonds. Stirring constantly, cook to a hard crack stage (300 to 310 degrees). Remove from heat and stir in remaining ¾ cup almonds, ½ cup pecans and vanilla. Quickly, pour onto a buttered jellyroll pan and spread evenly. Sprinkle chocolate morsels over warm toffee to soften morsels and spread evenly. Sprinkle with remaining pecans. Cool completely. Break into pieces. Cover and store in refrigerator.
Yield: 2 pounds

Pat S. Pike
Lincoln, Alabama

MILLIONAIRE CANDY

Filling:
1 14 ounce bag caramels
2 tablespoons evaporated milk

2 cups pecans, chopped

Melt caramels and milk in small saucepan stirring constantly. Stir in nuts after caramels have melted. Drop by spoonfuls onto waxed paper to harden.

Chocolate Dip:
½ bar paraffin wax

10 1½ ounce chocolate candy bars

Melt wax and candy over low heat. Dip hardened candy caramels into melted chocolate then place back onto waxed paper.
Yield: 100 pieces of candy.
Note: Chocolate may need to be reheated during dipping process.

Mrs. Mike Riley (Pam)

FAYE'S BANANA CREAM PIE

Crust:

70 vanilla wafers   ⅔ cup butter, melted

Blend wafers, one-fourth at a time, until finely crumbled in a covered blender. Preheat oven to 375 degrees. Mix crumbs and melted butter in medium bowl. Set aside 3 tablespoons for garnish. Press mixture to bottom and side of two 9 inch pie pans with back of spoon, making a small rim. Using another pie pan, place on top and press down. Bake at 375 degrees for 8 minutes. Remove crust to wire rack to cool.

Filling:

3 heaping tablespoons flour   1 tablespoon vanilla flavoring
2 cups sugar   4 bananas
3 egg yolks, beaten   ½ cup pecans, chopped
1 can evaporated milk   2 pints whipping cream
2 cups milk   4 tablespoons sugar
3 tablespoons butter, melted

Mix flour and sugar until smooth. Mix yolks with evaporated milk and milk. Slowly combine flour and sugar mixture with egg and milk mixture until smooth. Place mixture into deep bowl and add butter and vanilla flavoring. Place in microwave oven. Cook on high about 12 minutes, or until thick, stirring every four minutes. Allow to cool. Refrigerate for at least one hour. Slice bananas and place in bottom of two prepared pie shells. Sprinkle ¼ cup chopped pecans on top of each pie shell. Pour half of refrigerated pudding mixture into each pie shell. Whip each carton of whipping cream with 2 tablespoons sugar. Spread onto pies and garnish with wafer crumbs or pecans.
Yield: Two 9 inch pies.

Mrs. Marty Phillips (Pam)

FRESH BLUEBERRY COBBLER

4 cups (1¼ pounds) fresh blueberries, rinsed	1 tablespoon all-purpose flour
	1 teaspoon cinnamon

Preheat oven to 425 degrees. Grease a shallow 2 or 2½ quart baking dish. Mix ingredients. Pour into prepared dish.

Topping:

1½ cups all-purpose flour	¾ cup milk
½ cup sugar	1 large egg, slightly beaten
2 teaspoons baking powder	½ cup butter or margarine,
¼ teaspoon salt	melted

Mix flour, sugar, baking powder, and salt in bowl. Add remaining ingredients, stir to blend. Drop by heaping tablespoons over blueberry mixture. Bake 35 to 40 minutes until golden brown. Serve hot.
Yield: 10 servings.

Melba Hagan
Alexander City, Alabama

COCONUT CREAM PIE

¾ cup sugar	2 tablespoons butter or
⅓ cup cornstarch	margarine
¼ teaspoon salt	1 teaspoon vanilla extract
2 cups milk	1 cup flaked coconut
3 egg yolks	1 9 inch pastry shell, baked

Combine sugar, cornstarch and salt in a heavy 2 quart saucepan. Gradually stir in milk. Cook over medium heat, stirring constantly until thick and bubbly. Cook one minute. Beat egg yolks, gradually stir hot mixture into yolks. Return to heat. Cook 30 seconds, stirring constantly. Remove from heat. Add butter, vanilla and coconut. Pour into pastry shell. Bake at 350 degrees for 30 minutes.

Meringue:

3 egg whites	4 tablespoons sugar

Beat egg whites until stiff, gradually beating in the sugar. Cover baked pie with meringue. Return to 350 degree oven and bake until meringue is brown.
Note: May be garnished with toasted coconut.

Melba Hagan
Alexander City, Alabama

QUICK LIMEADE PIE

1   14 ounce can sweetened
    condensed milk
1   4 ounce frozen whipped non-
    dairy topping
1   6 ounce can frozen limeade,
    thawed

½   tablespoon fresh lime juice
3   drops green food coloring
1   8 inch graham cracker pie
    crust

Mix condensed milk into non-dairy topping. Stir in limeade, lime juice, and food coloring. Pour mixture into pie crust and refrigerate for several hours until firm.

"Tee" Albright
Plant City, Florida

SPECIAL PEACH PIE

1½ cups self-rising flour
½   cup butter flavored shortening
⅓   cup milk
1½ cups sugar

2   cups hot water
½   teaspoon lemon juice
½   cup margarine
2   cups peaches, sliced

Mix first three ingredients. Blend until soft dough forms. Turn onto floured surface and roll out dough. Mix sugar, water, and lemon juice. Stir until sugar is dissolved. Set aside. Melt margarine and spread over dough. Spread peaches on top of margarine. Roll dough, as for jelly roll, and cut in ¾ inch to 1 inch slices. Place in 13x9x2 inch baking dish. Pour sugar mixture over fruit and pastry, being sure to cover each roll. Bake at 350 degrees for 55 minutes. Serve warm.

Mrs. Dewayne Clark (Marion)

GRATED SWEET POTATO PIE

3 cups raw sweet potato, grated	1 teaspoon vanilla
1 cup sugar	¼ teaspoon salt
1 cup milk	½ cup coconut or raisins
4 eggs, slightly beaten	(optional)
¼ cup butter or margarine, melted	

Combine all ingredients and stir well. Spoon into a greased shallow 2 quart baking dish. Bake uncovered at 350 degrees for 30 minutes. Stir and bake an additional 15 minutes, or until a knife inserted in center comes out clean.

Grace Neighbors
Alexander City, Alabama

PUMPKIN ICE CREAM PIE

"Great with Thanksgiving dinner."

1 pint vanilla ice cream	1 teaspoon pumpkin pie spice
2 to 3 tablespoons crystallized ginger, finely chopped	½ teaspoon ginger
1 graham cracker pie crust	½ teaspoon salt
1 cup canned or mashed pumpkin, cooked	½ cup nuts, chopped
¾ cup sugar	1 cup whipping cream, whipped

Soften ice cream, quickly fold in crystallized ginger and spread in pie crust, freeze. Stir pumpkin, sugar, spices, and nuts together. Fold in whipped cream. Pour over ice cream in pie crust. Freeze.

Andrea K. Montgomery

"EGGCEPTIONAL" EGG CUSTARD

1¾ cups milk	4 eggs, beaten
¾ cup sugar	1 9 inch deep dish pie shell,
1 tablespoon butter or margarine	unbaked
1 teaspoon vanilla	Nutmeg

Heat (not boil) milk, sugar, butter, and vanilla. Pour into beaten eggs and mix well. Pour into unbaked pie shell. Sprinkle nutmeg on top. Bake at 400 degrees for 10 minutes then 350 degrees for 25 minutes or until firm.

Jimmie Holdridge
Fort Payne, Alabama

BERRY NUTTY PIE

Crust:

3   egg whites, at room
    temperature
¾   cup sugar
½   teaspoon baking powder
¾   cup semi-sweet minichocolate
    morsels

½   cup pecans, crushed
1   cup buttery flavored crackers,
    crushed
1   teaspoon almond extract

In a small, deep bowl beat egg whites until soft peaks form. Combine sugar and baking powder; gradually adding to egg whites, beating until stiff peaks form. Set aside 2 tablespoons each of chocolate morsels and pecans. Combine cracker crumbs, chocolate pieces, and pecans. Fold egg whites and almond extract into cracker mixture. Spread in a greased baking dish. Bake at 350 degrees for 25 minutes. Cool completely.

Filling:

1   cup whipping cream
2   tablespoons confectioners
    sugar

½   teaspoon vanilla flavoring

Whip cream to soft peaks. Add confectioners sugar and vanilla. Spread over crust.

Topping:

1   pint strawberries, sliced

Top pie with strawberries. Sprinkle reserved chocolate and pecans to garnish. Refrigerate before serving.

Jody Parker

STRAWBERRY YOGURT PIE

1   12 ounce frozen whipped
    non-dairy topping
1   10 ounce frozen sliced
    strawberries

1   8 ounce carton strawberry
    yogurt
1   graham cracker pie shell

Mix all ingredients in a bowl. Spread mixture in the pie shell and freeze until set, about 30 minutes. Remove and keep refrigerated.

Nancy Hare
Montgomery, Alabama

STRAWBERRY PIE

1	cup water	1	pint fresh strawberries (sliced)
1	cup sugar	1	9 inch pie shell, baked
3	tablespoons cornstarch		Frozen whipped non-dairy
4	tablespoons strawberry		topping
	gelatin		Garnish each slice of pie with
	Red food coloring		whole strawberry (optional)

Cook water, sugar, and cornstarch on medium heat until it is thick and the mixture clears. (May substitute flour for cornstarch.) Add the gelatin and a few drops of red food coloring. Place in the refrigerator and leave until the mixture begins to gel. Arrange strawberries in the baked, cooled pie shell. Pour partially gelled mixture over the strawberries and return to the refrigerator to gel until firm. Top with whipped non-dairy topping and a strawberry before serving, if desired.
Yield: 6 to 8 servings.

Elizabeth Campbell Garrison

DELICIOUS TROPICAL PIE

1	14 ounce can sweetened condensed milk	1	12 ounce carton frozen whipped non-dairy topping
½	cup lemon juice	2	9 inch pie shells, baked
½	cup coconut, flaked		Frozen whipped non-dairy
1	8 ounce can crushed pine-apple, well drained		topping, optional
1	banana, cut in small pieces		Fresh strawberries, optional
1	10 ounce package frozen strawberries		

In a large bowl, blend together the sweetened condensed milk, lemon juice, coconut, pineapple, and banana. Add frozen strawberries. Mix all ingredients well. Fold in the 12 ounces of frozen whipped non-dairy topping. Put mixture in baked, cooled pie shells. Chill approximately one hour before serving. May garnish pie with frozen whipped non-dairy topping and fresh strawberries before serving.
Yields: 16 servings.
Note: May substitute 1 can of strawberry pie filling for frozen strawberries.

Mrs. Robert M. Wikle (Berniece)

FESTIVE FRUIT PIE

½   cup margarine
2   eggs, slightly beaten
1   cup sugar
½   cup raisins (white raisins makes prettier pie)

½   cup pecans, chopped
½   cup coconut
1   tablespoon vinegar
1   unbaked pie shell

Melt margarine, then add all other ingredients; but be sure to add the vinegar last! Pour into unbaked pie shell and bake at 300 degrees for 40 minutes.

Ruby Richardson
Tuscaloosa, Alabama

TROPICAL CHIFFON PIE

Crust:
1   cup graham cracker crumbs
⅓   cup coconut, flaked

¼   cup butter or margarine, melted

In small bowl combine crumbs and coconut; stir in butter until blended. Press mixture onto sides and bottom of 9 inch deep dish pie pan. Freeze.

Filling:
1   20 ounce can crushed pineapple in juice
2   envelopes unflavored gelatin
1   15 ounce can cream of coconut

2   large eggs, separated
⅓   cup orange juice
1   cup heavy cream
¼   cup sugar

Drain pineapple, reserve juice. Sprinkle gelatin over juice in saucepan. Let stand 5 minutes to soften. Over low heat cook 3 to 5 minutes, stirring constantly until gelatin is dissolved. In another non-aluminum pan combine cream of coconut and beaten egg yolks; cook over low heat 5 minutes stirring constantly until mixture is very hot but not simmering. Remove from heat. Stir into gelatin mixture. Add orange juice and reserved pineapple. Spoon mixture into large bowl. Chill at least 1 hour. With electric mixer beat until foamy. Beat heavy cream to stiff peaks. Fold into gelatin mixture. Beat egg whites until foamy. Add sugar gradually, beat stiff. Fold into gelatin mixture. Add to crust. Refrigerate until set and firm. Decorate as desired.
Yield: 8 to 10 servings.
Note: Can double crust recipe to make 2-9 inch pies.

Lera Jenkins

PETITE PECAN PIES

Crust:

1	3 ounce package cream cheese	½	cup butter
		1	cup sifted all-purpose flour

Mix cream cheese and butter. Add flour and chill 1 hour. Divide into 24 small balls. Using small tins, place ball in each and press with finger to make smooth crust.

Filling:

1	egg	1	teaspoon vanilla
¾	cup brown sugar		Dash of salt
1	tablespoon butter, softened	⅔	cup nuts, chopped

Beat all ingredients (except nuts) until smooth. Add nuts. Place filling in crusts. Cook 25 minutes at 325 degrees.
Yield: 24 petite pies.

Nancy Hopewell

PECAN CREAM CHEESE PIE

2	3 ounce packages cream cheese, softened	1¼	cups pecans, chopped
½	cup sugar	3	eggs
1	egg	¾	cup light or dark corn syrup
1	teaspoon vanilla	3	tablespoons sugar
¼	teaspoon salt	3	tablespoons margarine, melted
1	9 inch deep dish pie shell, unbaked	1	teaspoon vanilla

Beat cream cheese until smooth. Add ½ cup sugar, one egg, one teaspoon vanilla, and salt. Mix well. Spread cream cheese mixture in the bottom of pie shell. Sprinkle pecans on top of cream cheese mixture. Beat the remaining eggs (3) until yolks and white are combined. Add syrup, 3 tablespoons sugar, margarine, and vanilla. Slowly pour syrup mixture over pecans. Bake on lower rack of oven at 375 degrees for 40 minutes. Wrap a piece of foil around edge of pan if crust appears to be getting too brown. Pie is completely baked when center is firm to touch.
Yield: 8 servings.

Mrs. Robert M. Wikle (Berniece)

CRUSTLESS PECAN PIE

3   egg whites
½   teaspoon baking powder
½   teaspoon salt
1   cup sugar
1   cup graham cracker crumbs

1   cup pecans, chopped
2   teaspoons vanilla
Sweetened whipped cream or
other whipped topping

Beat egg whites, baking powder, and salt until peaks are formed. Slowly add sugar, blend in crumbs, pecans, and vanilla. Pour in greased 8 inch pie pan. Cook at 350 degrees for 30 minutes. Cool 4 hours before serving. Serve with whipped topping.

Vivian Davis
Florence, Alabama

PEANUT BUTTER PIE

1   4 ounce package butterscotch
    instant pudding mix
2   cups milk
2   graham cracker crusts
1   3 ounce package cream
    cheese

1   cup confectioners sugar
½   cup crunchy peanut butter
1   16 ounce container frozen
    non-dairy whipped topping

Mix pudding with milk and pour into two crusts. Blend cream cheese, confectioners sugar, and peanut butter with mixer. Blend in frozen non-dairy topping. Put mixture on top of pudding in crusts. Refrigerate for 1 hour.

Jenni Griffin

CHOCOLATE COCONUT PIE

3   cups sugar
6   tablespoons cocoa
4   eggs
½   cup margarine, melted

1   12 ounce can evaporated milk
1   teaspoon vanilla extract
2   cups coconut
2   unbaked pie shells

Mix ingredients as listed. Beat well. Pour into 2 unbaked pie shells. Bake 35 to 40 minutes at 350 degrees.

Mrs. Ricky Lawson (Teresa)

BROWNIE PIZZA

Crust:

¾ cup light or dark corn syrup
⅓ cup heavy or whipping cream
1 8 ounce package semi-sweet chocolate morsels or 2 4 ounce packages of German sweet chocolate squares
½ cup butter
½ cup sugar

2 eggs
½ teaspoon vanilla
¾ cup all-purpose flour, unsifted
½ teaspoon salt
½ cup walnuts, coarsely chopped

Grease and flour 12x½ inch pizza pan (or two 9 inch layer cake pans). In a 3 quart saucepan, bring corn syrup and cream to a boil over medium heat, stirring occasionally. Add chocolate; stir until melted. Set aside ½ cup of chocolate sauce. Add butter and sugar to remaining sauce, stir until butter melts. Remove from heat. Stir in eggs and vanilla. Gradually stir in flour, salt, and nuts. Pour into pan. Bake at 350 degrees for 20 minutes or until firm. Cool on rack.

Topping:

½ gallon ice cream (any flavor), slightly softened
Fresh fruit (such as strawberries and bananas), sliced

Remaining chocolate sauce
1 cup nuts, chopped

Smooth ice cream over brownie crust. Freeze until ready to serve. Just before serving, arrange sliced fruit on top of pizza. Drizzle sauce over top. Sprinkle chopped nuts over pizza. Serve immediately.
Yield: 12 servings.

Mrs. Larry Edmiston (Donna)

To measure syrup, grease cup in which it is to be measured.

CHOCOLATE CHIP PIE

½ cup margarine	1 teaspoon vanilla
1 cup sugar	2 eggs, beaten
½ cup self-rising flour	½ cup pecans, chopped
1 cup chocolate morsels	1 9 inch deep dish pie crust

Melt margarine and cool. Mix together sugar and flour. Add remaining ingredients, except pie crust. Mix with the cooled margarine. Pour into an unbaked 9 inch deep dish crust and bake for one hour at 300 degrees. Cool or chill before cutting.

Mrs. Moody Scroggins (Joan)
Similar recipes submitted by *Barbara D. Sweat* and *Connie Barnes*

$1,000 FRENCH SILK CHOCOLATE PIE

Crust:

1 cup all-purpose flour	⅓ cup shortening
½ teaspoon salt	2 to 3 tablespoons cold water

Sift together flour and salt. Cut in shortening until particles are size of small peas. Sprinkle cold water over mixture. Toss lightly with fork and form into a ball. Roll out and put in pie pan, prick with fork. Bake at 450 degrees for 10 to 12 minutes.

Filling:

½ cup butter	1 teaspoon vanilla extract
¾ cup sugar	2 eggs
1 square unsweetened chocolate	Whipped cream
	Chopped nuts (optional)

Cream butter, adding sugar gradually until creamed well. Blend in melted and cooled chocolate and vanilla. Add eggs, one at a time, beating 5 minutes after each addition (use medium speed). Pour into cooled, baked shell. Chill 1 to 2 hours. Top with whipped cream and nuts (optional) before serving. Yield: 8 servings.

Winser Hayes

MUD PIE
"When calories are no object."

28	chocolate sandwich cookies, crushed	1	5 ounce can evaporated milk
¼	cup butter, slightly softened	2	squares semi-sweet chocolate
½	gallon ice cream (chocolate chip mint, coffee, or your favorite), softened	3	tablespoons butter
		1	teaspoon vanilla
1	cup sugar	1	12 ounce container frozen whipped non-dairy topping
		1	cup pecans, chopped

Crush cookies and combine with ¼ cup butter. Press into a 9x13 inch pan and freeze until firm (about one hour). Spread ice cream onto crust; freeze until firm (about 1½ hours). Over medium heat, combine sugar, milk, chocolate, and 3 tablespoons butter; bring to a boil. Remove from heat; stir in vanilla. Cool mixture completely and pour over ice cream. Freeze at least one hour until firm. Spread whipped topping and sprinkle pecans on top. Garnish with chocolate shavings.

Jody Parker

CHOCOLATE CHESS PIE

1	cup sugar	½	cup butter, melted
3	tablespoons cornmeal	½	cup light corn syrup
3	tablespoons cocoa	1	teaspoon vanilla
3	eggs, beaten	1	unbaked 9 inch pie crust

Mix sugar, cornmeal, and cocoa in a bowl. Add the rest of the ingredients. Mix well. Pour into unbaked pie crust. Bake at 350 degrees for 45 minutes.

Note: May serve with spoon of whipped topping or whipped cream on each slice.

Mrs. John Coleman, Jr. (Ginny)

ANGEL SQUARES
"How heavenly."

½ cup all-purpose flour, sifted
¼ cup brown sugar
½ cup pecans, chopped
½ cup margarine, melted
2 egg whites
⅔ cup sugar

1 10 ounce package frozen strawberries, partially thawed
2 tablespoons lemon juice
1 cup whipping cream, whipped
Whole strawberries, optional

Stir together first four ingredients. Spread evenly in shallow 13x9 inch pan. Bake at 350 degrees for 20 minutes, stirring occasionally. Sprinkle ⅔ of crumbs in bottom of 13x9x2 inch casserole dish. Combine egg whites, sugar, berries, and lemon juice in large mixing bowl. Beat at high speed with electric mixer until stiff peaks form. Fold in whipped cream. Spoon mixture over crumbs. Top with remaining crumbs and freeze 6 hours or overnight. Cut into 10 to 12 squares.
Note: May garnish each square with a whole strawberry.

Mrs. Erskine Murray (Betty)
Montgomery, Alabama

FROZEN CARAMEL CRUNCHY DELIGHT
"A very attractive and wonderful dessert."

1½ cups all-purpose flour
1 cup 3-minute oatmeal
½ cup brown sugar
1½ cup nuts, chopped
1 cup butter, melted

1 6 ounce jar caramel topping (may use 2 jars if you like more caramel flavor)
½ gallon vanilla ice cream, slightly softened

Combine flour, oats, brown sugar, and nuts; stir in melted butter. Spread a thin layer on a cookie sheet and bake at 350 degrees for 20 minutes or until brown. Cool and crumble. Put one-half of the crumbs in a 13x9 inch pan. Spoon caramel topping over crumbs (may need to heat caramel.) Slice softened ice cream over topping. Top with remaining crumbs and caramel topping, if desired. Freeze until firm. Cut in squares to serve.
Yield: 12 servings.
Note: Can mix warm caramel with crumbs for each layer.

Mrs. Jim Preuitt (Rona)

ASSIMINA'S BAKLAVA

4	cups pecans	$\frac{1}{8}$	teaspoon ground cloves
$2\frac{1}{4}$	cups almonds	2	pounds butter, melted
3	tablespoons sugar	$1\frac{3}{4}$	pounds phyllo
$\frac{1}{2}$	tablespoon ground cinnamon		

Grind pecans and almonds very fine and mix with sugar and spices. Grease 17x12x2½ inch pan with melted butter. Place 8 phyllo in pan, brushing each with melted butter. Sprinkle with thin layer of nut mixture. Cover with 2 phyllo, brushing with melted butter. Cut pastry into small squares to aid in baking. Bake at 275 degrees for 30 minutes or until lightly browned. Cover with aluminum foil and bake 1 hour at 200 degrees. Remove from oven and cool.

Syrup:

4	cups sugar	1	jigger brandy, whiskey, or
3	cups water		cognac
$\frac{1}{2}$	lemon	4	tablespoons honey
1	stick cinnamon		

Mix all syrup ingredients. Bring to a boil and boil for about 10 minutes, to medium consistency. A spoon will stick to a plate when the right consistency is reached. Remove lemon and cinnamon stick. Top cooled baklava with hot syrup.

Mrs. Assimina P. Hontgas
Similar recipe submitted by *Winser Hayes*

CHEESECAKE TARTS

2	8 ounce packages cream cheese, softened	2	teaspoons vanilla
2	eggs		Vanilla wafers
$\frac{1}{2}$	cup sugar		Cherry pie filling

Mix cream cheese, eggs, sugar, and vanilla. Place a vanilla wafer on the bottom of cup cake liner. Fill each ½ way with filling. Bake at 375 degrees for 10 minutes. Cool. Top with cherry pie filling or any other pie filling desired. Yield: 18 cheesecake tarts.

Jeannie Hill

CHOCOLATE ANGEL DELIGHT

1   12 ounce package semi-sweet chocolate chips
2   tablespoons water
3   eggs, separated
Pinch salt
3   tablespoons sugar

1½ cups (1 pint) whipping cream
1   tablespoon vanilla
1   13 ounce Angel food cake mix, prepared
Peppermint ice cream (optional)

Melt chocolate chips and water in top of double boiler. Beat egg yolks, and add to chocolate—let cool. Add salt. In another bowl, beat egg whites until stiff, add sugar, then stir them into cooled chocolate, blend well. Whip cream, add vanilla and fold into chocolate mixture. Break the cake into bite size pieces and place in 9x14 inch dish. Cover the cake with chocolate sauce. Chill in refrigerator at least 6 hours before serving. (Can be made the day before serving.) Cut in squares and serve cold, with dip of peppermint ice cream served on top, if desired.
Yield: 10 to 12 servings.

Arazell R. Barnes

DELICIOUS CHOCOLATE ICE BOX DESSERT
"Quite rich."

1   16 ounce package semi-sweet chocolate chips
3   tablespoons boiling water
4   eggs, separated
2   tablespoons confectioners sugar

½ to ¾ cup pecans or walnuts, chopped
1   cup whipping cream, whipped
12 lady fingers, split or 1 box thin chocolate wafers

In top of a double boiler melt chocolate chips stirring with wooden spoon. Blend in water and stir until shiny. Remove from heat and stir in egg yolks one at a time. Beat vigorously until well blended. Add sugar and nuts; stir in well. Beat egg whites until stiff in a medium sized bowl. Whip cream in another bowl. Fold the chocolate mixture and whipped cream alternately into the egg whites until all all are mixed (mixture may be a bit soupy.) Line bottom and sides of 9x9 inch or 10x11½ inch glass baking dish with lady fingers or wafers. Pour mixture in. Cover with plastic wrap and chill 24 hours before serving.
Yield: 9 servings.

Mrs. Marion H. Sims (Ginny)

PRALINE CRACKER CRUNCH

½ cup butter
½ cup margarine
1 cup sugar

1 cup pecans, chopped
1 box rectangular buttery crackers

Melt butter and margarine in saucepan. Add sugar and cook over medium heat until sugar dissolves. Break crackers into small rectangles and place large cookie sheet, close to each other but not touching. Sprinkle pecans over the crackers. Pour butter and sugar mixture over crackers. Bake at 350 degrees for 8 to 10 minutes or until golden. Remove from cookie sheet immediately.

Kaye Spears

HEAVENLY GERMAN CHOCOLATE DESSERT

Crust:

3 egg whites
½ teaspoon vanilla
½ teaspoon almond extract
¾ cup sugar
1 teaspoon baking powder

1 4 ounce bar German sweet chocolate, grated
1 cup round buttery crackers, crushed
½ cup pecans, chopped

Crust: Beat egg whites with vanilla and almond flavoring to soft peaks. Combine ¾ cup sugar and baking powder, gradually add to egg whites, beating to stiff peaks. Reserve 2 tablespoons grated chocolate. Fold remainder of chocolate gently into egg whites along with cracker crumbs and pecans. Spread in lightly greased 9 inch pie pan, shaping like a pie crust. Bake at 350 degrees for 25 minutes or until done. Cool completely.

Filling:

1 cup whipping cream
2 tablepoons sugar

½ teaspoon vanilla
½ teaspoon almond extract

Filling: Whip cream with sugar and flavorings. Spread over cooled meringue. Chill six hours before serving for best flavor.

Gloria Hughes
Birmingham, Alabama

CRACKER CAKE

Cake:
6 egg whites	32 soda crackers, crushed
1 teaspoon cream of tartar	2 cups pecans, chopped
2 cups sugar	

Beat egg whites with cream of tartar and sugar. Add crackers and pecans. Bake in a 13x9 inch pan at 350 degrees for 25 minutes or until light brown.

Topping:
1 12 ounce carton frozen non-dairy topping	1 7 ounce can coconut
1 20 ounce can crushed pineapple, drained	

Spread non-dairy topping on cake. Next layer with pineapple and top with coconut. Refrigerate until ready to serve. It is better to let it set overnight. Yield: 8 servings.
Note: Will keep in refrigerator for several days.

Mrs. Billy Mills (Faye)
Similar recipe by *Susan Holdridge*
Alexander City, Alabama

CHERRY FLUFF
"Delicious and attractive."

1 14 ounce can sweetened condensed milk	1 12 ounce carton frozen whipped non-dairy topping
1 21 ounce can cherry pie filling	1⅓ cups coconut
1 16 ounce can crushed pineapple, undrained	1 cup miniature marshmallows
	1 cup pecans, chopped

Mix all ingredients in large bowl. Chill and serve. Can be served frozen. Yield: 12 or more servings.
Note: May be served as a salad or as a dessert.

Mrs. Mike Riley (Pam)

PUNCH BOWL TRIFLE
"Serve this in a punch bowl."

1	18½ ounce box yellow cake mix	2	cups hot water
2	5½ ounce package vanilla instant pudding mix	1	16 ounce carton frozen strawberries
1	20 ounce can pineapple chunks, drained	1	12 ounce carton frozen whipped non-dairy topping
1	6 ounce box strawberry flavored gelatin		Fresh strawberries, optional

Bake cake according to package directions. Cool and remove from pans. Break cake into small pieces and cover bottom of a large punch bowl. Mix pudding according to package directions. Blend pineapple chunks with pudding, then spread over cake. Mix gelatin with 2 cups hot water and add frozen strawberries. Spread gelatin mixture over pineapple layer in punch bowl. Top gelatin mixture with whipped non-dairy topping. Garnish with fresh strawberries.
Yield: 24 or more ½ cup servings.
Note: Can substitute vanilla instant pudding with another flavoring.

Mrs. Jackie Stephens (Elaine)

FRUIT DISH

1	large package instant vanilla pudding	2	bananas, diced
3	tablespoons orange flavored powdered breakfast drink	1	large apple, peeled and diced
1	small can mandarin oranges	1	quart fresh strawberries, sliced
1	15¼ ounce can pineapple tidbits		

Mix pudding and breakfast drink powder with juices drained from pineapple and mandarin oranges. Combine all fruits. Stir in above sauce. Refrigerate overnight for best flavor.
Note: May add nuts and grapes.

Anita Stokes

FRUIT PIZZA
"Such a pretty treat."

1   roll refrigerated sugar cookie dough
1   8 ounce package cream cheese
½   cup confectioners sugar
Assorted fruits of choice—(pineapple, peaches, grapes, strawberries, blueberries, kiwi, mandarin oranges)

1½   cups orange juice
3   tablespoons cornstarch
6   tablespoons sugar

Spread cookie dough into bottom of a 12 inch pizza pan. Cook 8 to 10 minutes at 350 degrees, or until slightly brown. Cool. Mix cream cheese and confectioners sugar together until smooth. Spread over cooked crust. Top with assorted fruits. To make glaze, mix orange juice, cornstarch, and sugar. Cook over low heat until thick, stirring constantly. Cook slightly. Drizzle over fruit. Chill.
Yield: 8 to 10 servings.

Mrs. James Barnett (Lynn)

LEMON DELIGHT FREEZE

Crust
1   cup flour
½   cup margarine

2   tablespoons sugar

Mix crust ingredients together in 9 inch square pan. Bake at 375 degrees for 20 minutes, stirring several times during cooking. Reserve ½ cup for topping. Cool.

Filling
1   14 ounce can sweetened condensed milk
3   large eggs, separated

Juice of 3 lemons
½   cup sugar
Non-dairy whipped topping

Mix milk, egg yolks, and juice. Beat egg whites and add sugar. Fold together and pour over crust. Sprinkle reserved crumbs on top. Freeze at least 6 hours or overnight (take out of freezer a few minutes before serving). Top with non-dairy topping.

Mary Catherine Harris

FROSTY STRAWBERRY DESSERT

1 cup all-purpose flour	2 cups fresh strawberries, sliced
¼ cup brown sugar, packed	(or 1 package frozen)
½ cup walnuts or pecans,	2 tablespoons lemon juice
chopped	1 cup whipping cream, whipped
½ cup butter, melted	Fresh strawberries for garnish,
2 egg whites	sliced
1 cup sugar	

Stir together flour, sugar, nuts, and butter. Sprinkle crumbly mixture onto a cookie sheet. Bake at 350 degrees for 20 minutes or until golden brown, stirring during baking to break up crumbs. Whip egg whites until frothy. Add 1 cup sugar. Gradually beat until sugary. Add strawberries and lemon juice, beat at high speed about 10 minutes until very light and fluffy. Fold in whipped cream. Sprinkle ⅔ of crumbs into a 13x9 inch pan. Spread with strawberry mixture. Top with rest of crumbs. Cover and freeze 4 hours or longer until firm.

Mrs. Larry Edmiston (Donna)

CARAMEL FLAN

Caramel:

½ cup water	½ cup sugar

Combine water and sugar in 1 pint glass container. Stir well until dissolved. Microwave on high for 10 to 12 minutes, until light but rich brown. Pour into 1½ quart casserole dish and rotate to coat bottom. Let cool.

Custard:

¼ cup sugar	2 cups milk, scalded
3 eggs	½ teaspoon vanilla extract
1 pinch salt	

Beat eggs, sugar, and salt. Slowly add scalded milk (to scald milk, microwave on high for 2 to 3 minutes.) Add vanilla and pour custard over caramel. Place casserole in pan of hot water and bake at 350 degrees for 1 hour until knife inserted in center comes out clean. Chill.
Yield: 4 servings.

Muffett Robbs Conover

GRECIAN PEARS WITH LACE COOKIES

Grecian Pears
6   fresh camico or aujou pears
    (only)
4½ cups sugar
2   cups water

1   stick cinnamon
3 to 4 whole cloves
1   8 ounce container sour cream
Mace

Peel pears and core from blossom, leaving stems on. Combine sugar and water in a large saucepan. Cook over low heat, stirring until sugar is dissolved. Place pears in syrup and boil gently about 15 minutes or until tender. Remove from heat. Add cinnamon stick and cloves. Refrigerate several hours. Place chilled pears upright in individual compotes. Add 1 to 2 tablespoons syrup. Spoon sour cream around pears. Sprinkle with mace. Serve with lace cookies.
Yield: 2 to 4 servings.

Lace Cookies:

½   cup butter or margarine,
    melted
1   cup sugar

1   cup oatmeal
1   egg
½   teaspoon vanilla

Mix all ingredients and drop by ¼ teaspoonful on ungreased foil placed on cookie sheet. Bake at 350 degrees until brown (about 10 minutes.) Let stay on foil until completely cool. Remove by gently punching from under foil.
Yield: 100 or more cookies.

Betty Lou Camp

SWEET POTATO SURPRISE DESSERT

1   40 ounce can sweet potatoes,
    mashed
1   cup honey
1   cup coconut

1   cup pecans, chopped
1   8 ounce can crushed
    pineapple, drained

Mix all ingredients together, pour into a greased 2 quart casserole dish. Bake at 325 degrees for 35 minutes.

Norma Bowden

EASY BLITZ TORTE

½ cup butter or margarine
½ cup sugar
4 eggs, divided

1 cup all-purpose flour
1 teaspoon baking powder
3 tablespoons milk

Mix ½ cup butter, sugar, 4 egg yolks. When smooth, add flour, baking powder and milk. Beat well. Divide batter into two greased 9 inch cake pans.

Topping:

½ teaspoon cream of tartar
½ teaspoon baking powder
¾ cup sugar

1 container whipping cream,
   whipped
Strawberries, sliced

Beat to stiff peaks: 4 egg whites, cream of tartar, and baking powder. Gradually add sugar, beating well. Spread meringue on top of batter mixture. (1 tablespoon sugar and cinnamon with ½ cup chopped nuts may be sprinkled on top of meringue.) Bake 30 minutes at 350 degrees. When the cake is cooled, put layers together with whipped cream. Strawberries may be added to the top.

Jane B. Davis
Tuscaloosa, Alabama

CHOCOLATE PRALINE TORTE

*"Surprise your family and guests with this
special treat."*

1½ cups pecans, chopped
1½ cups vanilla wafer crumbs
1 cup firmly packed brown
   sugar
1 cup margarine, melted

1 18½ ounce box devils food
   cake mix without pudding
1 16 ounce container frozen
   non-dairy topping

Combine first four ingredients. Sprinkle ¾ cup mixture in each of 4 well greased 9 inch cake pans. Press lightly into pans. Prepare cake mix according to package directions. Pour over nut mixture in pans. Bake at 325 degrees for 15 to 20 minutes. Remove layers from pans immediately and cool completely on rack. Place one layer nut side up on serving plate. Spread with refrigerated whipped topping. Repeat layers ending with whipped topping. Chill for several hours.

Patti Reaves Burch
Baton Rouge, Louisiana

RICE PUDDING

2 cups cooked rice, drained
1½ cups sugar
3 eggs, beaten

1½ cups milk
1 tablespoon vanilla flavoring
½ cup butter, sliced into squares

Mix together rice, sugar, eggs, milk, and vanilla flavoring. Mix well. Pour into greased 13x9 inch casserole dish. Cut butter into squares and put on top of rice mixture. Bake at 350 degrees for one hour.
Yield: 10 servings.

Viola Hatcher

FROZEN LEMON MOUSSE

4 egg yolks
½ cup fresh lemon juice
¼ cup sugar
1½ tablespoons lemon rind, grated
4 egg whites

⅛ teaspoon cream of tartar
Pinch of salt
¼ cup sugar
1½ cup whipping cream
½ cup sugar

Combine yolks, lemon juice, ¼ cup sugar, and lemon rind in mixer bowl and beat until lemon colored. Beat egg whites until foamy, add cream of tartar and salt. Continue beating and gradually add ¼ cup sugar—beat until stiff. Whip cream with ½ cup sugar until soft peaks form. Fold all together and freeze for 8 hours.
Yield: 8 servings.
Note: This is pretty served in parfait or wine glasses. Garnish with twist of lemon peel.

Mrs. Allen Gray McMillan, Jr. (Jean)

LEMON ICE CREAM

1 pint whipping cream, do not whip
1 cup sugar
⅓ cup fresh squeezed lemon juice

2 tablespoons lemon rind, grated

Stir all ingredients together. Pour into quart container. Place in freezer for several hours or overnight. Serve in parfait glasses.
Yield: 6 servings.

Holly H. Gilbert
Homewood, Alabama

STRAWBERRY ALMOND BOMBE

1 quart vanilla ice cream, slightly softened
1 16 ounce package frozen strawberries with sugar, thawed
1 14 ounce can sweetened condensed milk
1½ cups toasted almonds, sliced and crushed
1 cup whipping cream, whipped
¼ teaspoon almond extract

Chill 2 quart bowl, mold, or loaf pan in freezer 30 minutes. Working quickly, line dish with ice cream using back of large spoon or hands (whichever is easier for you) to form an even layer (entire bottom and sides of pan must be covered.) Return bowl to freezer. Thoroughly drain strawberries, reserving juice for sauce. In large bowl, combine condensed milk, strawberries, and crushed almonds. Fold in whipped cream and chill 1 hour. Stir and pour into ice cream lined bowl. Cover and freeze overnight or up to two weeks. To serve, dip mold briefly into warm water. Loosen edges with knife and invert onto chilled serving dish. If not serving immediately, return to freezer. Slice and garnish with sauce and almonds.
Yield: 10 to 12 servings.

Strawberry Almond Sauce:
1 16 ounce package frozen sliced strawberries with sugar, thawed
Strawberry juice reserved from Bombe recipe
1 tablespoon cornstarch
¼ cup amaretto (optional)
¼ cup toasted almonds, sliced

In large saucepan, heat just to boiling, the package of strawberries. Mix reserved juice and cornstarch together and stir into heated strawberries. Cook and stir until mixture is slightly thickened, about 3 minutes. Cool, then cover and refrigerate up to 3 days. Just before serving, stir in ¼ cup amaretto to blend thoroughly. Sprinkle almonds on top of each slice as a garnishment.

Wanda Embry

SILVER CREAM
"Elegant."

12 macaroons (coconut or almond)	1 24 ounce jar whole bing cherries, drained
½ cup orange liqueur (or almond)	1 quart vanilla ice cream

Crumble and soak macaroons in the orange liqueur 30 minutes. Place silver bowl in freezer for at least 10 minutes. Remove from freeezer and, with ice cream scoop, place several scoops of ice cream on bottom. Sprinkle soaked crumbs and a few cherries. Repeat with another layer starting with ice cream and ending with crumbs and cherries. Cover with plastic wrap and place in freezer. When ready to serve, pass bowl with large silver spoon for each guest to serve themselves.
Yield: 10 to 12 servings.

Betty M. Martin
Lincoln, Alabama

OLD FASHIONED VANILLA ICE CREAM

6 eggs	Pinch of salt
1 tablespoon all-purpose flour	1 12 ounce can evaporated milk
2 cups sugar	Milk
1 tablespoon vanilla flavoring	

Separate eggs and beat whites until thick. In large bowl, beat yolks; add flour, sugar, and flavoring; beating until creamy. Add salt and evaporated milk. Fold egg whites into mixture. Pour into freezer. Fill to full line with milk and freeze as usual. Serve immediately or remove dasher and pack until ready to serve.
Note: Use a four quart electric freezer.

Mary Ellen Hayes

Similar recipe by *Zell S. Copeland (Mrs. Jimmy)*

PEACH TEASE

Peaches to make 1 quart pulp (9 large)
Juice of 2 lemons
⅛ teaspoon salt
½ teaspoon almond extract
2 cups sugar
2 quarts whole milk

Peel peaches and remove seeds. Place in blender until pulp is soft with no lumps and there is one quart. Dump into cold can of ice cream freezer. Pour juice of lemons over pulp. Add salt, almond extract, and sugar. Add milk. *Do not stir!* Put can in freezer. Freeze until firm. Remove dasher, leaving can in freezer. Cover with ice and let sit for an hour to improve taste. Yield: Approximately 3 quarts.
Note: Leftovers can be stored in freezer.

Eleanor H. Johnson (Mrs. Joe)

COCONUT CREAM CHEESE RING

1 cup pineapple juice
2 packages unflavored gelatin
2 8 ounce packages cream cheese at room temperature
2 cups cream of coconut
1 16 ounce package frozen non-dairy topping

Dissolve gelatin in pineapple juice. In a saucepan, bring gelatin and juice to a boil, stirring constantly. Cool. Beat cream cheese until light and creamy. Add pineapple mixture and cream of coconut. Let partially congeal in refrigerator (until syrupy). Fold in whipped topping. Spray ring mold with non-stick cooking spray. Pour mixture into mold and refrigerate several hours or overnight. Unmold. Decorate with fruit if desired.
Note: Cream of coconut can be found in the soft drink section of your grocery.

Mrs. A. D. Wellbaum (Clara)

Entrees

AUNT GEORGIA MAE'S ROAST

1   eye of roast (any size)   Italian seasoning
Cooking oil

Wash roast and pat dry. Using your hands and/or paper towels, grease roast with cooking oil. Then sprinkle roast with Italian seasoning. Use your hands to pat seasoning so it will stick to roast. Bake uncovered in a foil-lined baking pan at 325 degrees for 45 minutes per pound. Slice thinly to serve. Good hot or cold. Makes delicious roast sandwiches.

Mrs. Marty Phillips (Pam)

BEEF BURGUNDY

2   pounds beef sirloin, cut into   1½ cups Burgundy
    pieces   1   cup mushrooms, sliced
1   10 ounce can golden   1   package dry onion soup
    mushroom soup

Mix all ingredients and bake covered for 1½ hours at 350 degrees. Bake uncovered an additional 1½ hours. Serve over rice or noodles.

Kathryn Rogers
Stone Mountain, Georgia

HUNGARIAN GOULASH

2   pounds stew meat   1   bay leaf
3   tablespoons oil   1   clove garlic
1   large onion, sliced in rings   ½   teaspoon salt
3   tablespoons all-purpose flour   3   beef bouillon cubes
1   16 ounce can tomatoes   Dash of thyme
1   8 ounce can tomato sauce   Rice
1   cup celery, chopped

Brown meat in 3 tablespoons oil. Remove meat. Cook onions in oil until clear. Add 3 tablespoons flour. Return meat to pan and add remaining ingredients. Cook over low heat for 1½ hours or until meat is tender. Serve over hot rice.
Yield: 8 servings.

Barbara D. Sweat

MARINATED BEEF CUBES

"They will think these came off the grill
at your favorite steakhouse."

½	cup salad oil	2	pounds lean beef round or
¼	cup vinegar		chuck, cut in 1½ inch cubes
¼	cup onion, chopped	2	green peppers, cut in 1 inch
1	teaspoon salt		squares
1	teaspoon coarsely ground or	2	fresh tomatoes, cut in wedges
	cracked pepper	2	onions, cut in wedges
2	teaspoons Worcestershire or		
	steak sauce		

In deep bowl, combine oil, vinegar, chopped onion, salt, pepper, and Worcestershire sauce, mix well. Add meat to marinade and stir to coat. Refrigerate overnight or let stand at room temperature 2 to 3 hours, turning meat occasionally. Fill skewers with meat cubes alternating with tomatoes, green peppers, and onions. Grill until done.

Florence Kaylor

ROAST BEEF SUPREME

1	3 to 4 pound beef roast	2	tablespoons steak sauce
1	10¾ ounce can mushroom	½	cup butter or margrine,
	soup		melted
1	package dry onion soup mix		
2	tablespoons Worcestershire		
	sauce		

Place roast on foil. Combine remaining ingredients and spoon mixture over roast. Wrap foil loosely around roast. Roast will make its own gravy. Bake 3½ hours on 350 degrees.
Note: You may wish to cook potatoes with it.

Mrs. Raymond Shepherd (Margie)
Starkville, Mississippi

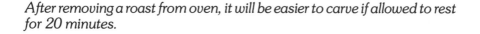

After removing a roast from oven, it will be easier to carve if allowed to rest for 20 minutes.

BEEF STROGANOFF

2 pounds lean beef strips
½ cup margarine
¼ cup onion, chopped
2 tablespoons chili sauce
1 tablespoon vinegar
1 teaspoon salt
¼ teaspoon pepper

1 2½ ounce jar sliced
mushrooms
1 10¾ ounce can cream of
chicken soup
1 soup can milk
1 8 ounce carton sour cream

Brown beef in margarine. Add remaining ingredients except sour cream and simmer 1½ hours. Remove from heat. Stir in sour cream. Serve over rice or noodles.
Yield: 4 to 6 servings.

Hyland Camp (Mrs. Jeffry)

GREEN PEPPER STEAK

1 pound chuck roast or round
steak, fat trimmed
¼ cup soy sauce
1 clove garlic (optional)
1½ teaspoon grated fresh ginger
or ½ teaspoon ground ginger
¼ cup salad oil

1 cup onion, thinly sliced
1 cup green peppers, cut in
strips
2 stalks celery, thinly sliced
2 tomatoes, cut into wedges
1 cup water (as needed)

Cut beef across grain into ⅛ inch strips. Combine soy sauce, garlic, ginger; add beef. Toss and set aside. Heat oil in frying pan or wok. Add beef and toss over high heat until browned. Test meat. If it is not tender, cover and simmer for 20 minutes over low heat. Turn heat up and add onion, peppers, and celery; stir until vegetables are tender but crisp. Add tomatoes and heat through.
Yield: 4 servings.
Note: If you half the recipe you might need to add additional water. For eight servings, double the ingredients, add about 1¾ cup water. If you wish to thicken, you may add 1 teaspoon cornstarch to water. May be served over rice.

Gladys G. Barton

PEPPER STEAK WITH RICE

1½ pounds sirloin steak, cut in ¼ inch strips	2 green peppers, cut in strips
1 tablespoon paprika	2 large fresh tomatoes, diced
2 cloves garlic, crushed	1 cup water
2 tablespoons butter or margarine	¼ cup water
	2 tablespoons cornstarch
1 cup onion, sliced	2 tablespoons soy sauce
	3 cups cooked rice

Sprinkle steak with paprika, set aside. Brown garlic in butter; add steak, onions, and peppers. Cook until vegetables are wilted. Add tomatoes and 1 cup water, simmer about 15 minutes. Blend ¼ cup water, cornstarch and soy sauce. Stir into steak. Cook until thick. Serve over 3 cups cooked rice. Yield: 6 servings.

Melba Hagan
Alexander City, Alabama

MARINATED FLANK STEAK

½ cup vegetable oil	½ teaspoon ginger
¼ cup soy sauce	1 clove garlic, minced
¼ cup sherry	1 flank steak
2 teaspoons Worcestershire sauce	

Combine all ingredients except the flank steak. Pour over the steak in a freezer bag and freeze. When thawed, remove the steak from the marinade and grill or broil 8 to 12 minutes per side.
Note: If you wish to serve steak without freezing it, you should marinate the steak at least 3 hours.

Susan Nicholls Reeves (Mrs. Mike)
Beaumont, Texas

Similar recipe submitted by *Diane Grosiak Vita*, West Patterson, New Jersey

ROULADES OF BEEF WITH
CRABMEAT STUFFING

4 pounds sirloin steak, sliced thin and cut into 24 rectangles-¼ inch thick	1 cup dry bread crumbs
½ cup tomato juice	2 tablespoons parsley, chopped
2 eggs, beaten	4 tablespoons butter
2 tablespoons lemon juice	1 10½ ounce can beef broth
½ teaspoon salt	1½ cup dry white wine
½ teaspoon Worcestershire sauce	1 teaspoon salt
2 7½ ounce cans crabmeat, drained and flaked	2 tablespoons parsley, snipped
	2 cloves garlic
	2 bay leaves
	1 pint fresh mushrooms
	2 tablespoons cornstarch

Pound beef to ⅛ inch thickness. Combine tomato juice, eggs, lemon juice, ½ teaspoon salt and Worcestershire sauce. Add crabmeat, crumbs, and 2 tablespoons parsley. Mix well. Place a heaping tablespoon of mixture on each rectangle. Roll up and secure with a toothpick or string. Refrigerate, covered well until 2 hours before serving. Melt 4 tablespoons butter in a large skillet. Brown rolls, turning quickly. Transfer to two 13x9 inch baking dishes. To juice in skillet, add beef broth, wine, 1 teaspoon salt, 2 tablespoons parsley, garlic, and bay leaves. Bring to a boil, scraping sides of skillet. Pour ½ liquid over each pan of rolls. Cover tightly with foil. Bake at 350 degrees for 1½ hours. Cook mushrooms in butter. Add water to juice to make 3 cups. Blend in cornstarch. Stir until blended. Serve over roulades. *Note:* Roulades may be assembled and refrigerated the night before. Serve with brown rice or wild rice.

Jean Barton Hendrickson
Birmingham, Alabama

STEAK AND MADEIRA WINE SAUCE

1 or 2 beef sirloin steaks,
cut 1 to 1½ inches thick

Salt to taste
Pepper to taste

Place steak on rack in broiler pan 2 to 3 inches from heat. When one side is browned; season, turn and finish cooking on the second side. Season. Steak cut 1 inch thick requires 18 to 20 minutes for rare; 20 to 25 minutes for medium. Steak cut 1½ inches thick requires 25 to 30 minutes for rare; and 30 to 35 minutes for medium.

Wine Sauce:

2   tablespoons butter
1   cup mushrooms
½   cup green onions, sliced
¼   cup water

2   teaspoons cornstarch
¼   teaspoon salt
½ cup Madeira Wine

Cook mushrooms and onions in butter; stirring occasionally (about 4 minutes). Combine water, cornstarch and salt. Add to mushrooms and onions. Stir in wine and cook slowly four minutes, stirring occasionally. Yield: 1 cup.
To serve: Slice steak ½ to 1 inch, pour wine sauce over steak or serve wine sauce on the side.

Norma Bowden

BEEF GOULASH

2   pounds ground beef
1   10¾ ounce can chicken
    noodle soup
1   10¾ ounce can mushroom
    soup
1   15 ounce can Spanish rice
½   cup green pepper, chopped

1   16 ounce can bean sprouts,
    drained
½   cup Worcestershire sauce
1   teaspoon black pepper
1   3 ounce can chow mein
    noodles

Brown ground beef and drain. Add all other ingredients except chow mein noodles. Bake 1 hour, fifteen minutes in covered 9x13 inch baking dish at 275 degrees. Sprinkle noodles on top. Bake for an additional 30 minutes at 400 degrees uncovered.
Yield: 8 servings.

Nancy Hopewell

SAUERBRATEN WITH GINGERSNAP GRAVY
"Well worth the trouble."

3 to 3½ pounds eye of round roast
1 teaspoon salt
½ teaspoon peppercorns
4 bay leaves
8 whole cloves
2 medium onions, sliced

Parsley (optional)
1 small carrot, minced
1 stalk celery, chopped
1½ cups red wine vinegar
2½ cups water
¼ cup butter

Rub meat with 1 teaspoon salt and ½ teaspoon pepper. Place meat in large deep glass casserole with all spices and vegetables. Heat the vinegar and water to boiling point and pour hot over meat. Let cool. Cover tightly and refrigerate. Let marinate at least 48 hours, turning meat twice a day. When ready to cook, remove meat from marinade and dry with paper towels (save marinade). Melt ¼ cup butter in Dutch oven and brown meat all over. Cover with tight fitting lid. Let simmer slowly 2½ to 3 hours until tender. Remove meat, slice and serve on platter. Parsley could be used as garnish.

Gingersnap Gravy:
2 tablespoons sugar
½ cup water

¾ cup gingersnaps, crushed
(Optional-½ cup sour cream)

Melt 2 tablespoons sugar in iron skillet, stir until golden brown. Strain 1½ cups marinade and heat with ½ cup water. Gradually add hot marinade and water to sugar. Add ¾ cup gingersnap crumbs. Stir constantly. Cook until gravy thickens (add sour cream if you like). Salt to taste.

Note: Ladle some gravy over Sauerbraten and pass remainder in bowl.

Hattie Wallace Coker

Add a small, grated, raw potato to each pound of ground meat for juicy hamburgers.

CAVATINI CASSEROLE

1 pound ground beef (may substitute 1 pound ground turkey or ground chuck)
1 onion, chopped
1 bell pepper, chopped (optional)
1 8 ounce package spiral noodles
1 32 ounce jar prepared spaghetti sauce
1 2½ ounce jar mushrooms (optional)
1 package pepperoni
10 ounce mozzarella cheese, shredded

Preheat oven to 350 degrees. Brown ground beef, pepper, and onion. Cook noodles according to directions. Layer noodles, ground beef, spaghetti sauce, and mushrooms in 9x12 inch dish. Stir together. Arrange pepperoni on top. Top with shredded mozzarella. Bake until cheese bubbles, approximately 15 to 20 minutes, at 350 degrees.

Susan Holdridge
Alexander City, Alabama

COMPANY MEATLOAF
"This will dazzle your guests."

2 pounds ground round or chuck
2 eggs, beaten
¾ cup bread crumbs
½ cup tomato juice
2 tablespoons parsley, dry or fresh
½ teaspoon oregano, crushed
¼ teaspoon salt
¼ teaspoon lemon pepper salt
1 teaspoon garlic salt
8 thin slices boiled ham, luncheon meat style
1½ cups mozzarella cheese, shredded
2 or 3 tomatoes, peeled and thinly sliced
3 slices mozzarella cheese

Combine first 9 ingredients and mix well. Pour on wax paper and shape into a 12x10 inch rectangle. Arrange ham on top of meat mixture-leaving ½ to 1 inch margin on edge. Sprinkle with shredded cheese. Top with sliced tomatoes. Gently roll like jelly roll, using wax paper to help lift. Remove paper. Place seam side down in pan. Bake at 350 degrees for 1 hour and 15 minutes. Remove from oven and place sliced cheese on top. Bake for 15 more minutes.
Yield: 6 servings.

Dorothy Parker

HAMBURGER CRUNCH

1	pound ground beef	3	tablespoons soy sauce
1	medium onion, chopped	½	cup rice, uncooked
1	tablespoon margarine	1	dash pepper
1	10¾ ounce can cream of mushroom soup	1	3 ounce can chow mein noodles
1	10¾ ounce can cream of chicken soup	1½	cups Cheddar cheese, shredded

Sauté beef and onion in margarine until meat loses red color. Add soups, soy sauce, rice, and pepper. Pour into greased 9x13 inch dish and bake for 50 minutes at 350 degrees. Add noodles then cheese on top. Heat about 10 minutes or until cheese melts.
Yield: 6 servings.

Mrs. Jeannie Hill

HAM BEEF MEAT LOAF A LA PECHE

Meat Loaf:

		⅛	teaspoon pepper
1	pound ready-to-cook ham	½	cup milk
1	pound ground chuck	¼	cup peach syrup
2	eggs	1	jar pickled peaches; drained, reserving syrup
1	cup soft bread crumbs		

Mix together ham, ground chuck, eggs, bread crumbs, pepper, milk, and peach syrup. Shape into round meat loaf pan. Bake at 350 degrees for 45 minutes.

Sauce:

¼	cup brown sugar	1	tablespoon cornstarch
Remainder of peach syrup		1	tablespoon water
2	teaspoons prepared mustard		

Cook brown sugar, remainder of peach syrup, and mustard over medium heat in saucepan. Mix water and cornstarch; blend with sugar/mustard mixture. Cook until thick, then add peaches. When meat is done, place peaches around the meat on platter and serve with sauce.

Mrs. Al Yoe

DELICIOUS LASAGNA

1   8 or 10 ounce package lasagna noodles, cooked and drained

1   pound mozzarella cheese slices

Meat Sauce:

1½ pounds ground beef
1   medium onion, chopped
1   clove garlic, minced
1   tablespoon fresh parsley
1   teaspoon basil

1   tablespoon oregano
1   16 ounce can tomatoes
1   6 ounce can tomato paste
1   tablespoon chili powder

Brown beef and onion, drain grease. Add remaining ingredients. Cover and simmer 20 minutes.

Cottage Cheese Mixture:

1   24 ounce carton cottage cheese
2   eggs, beaten
2   teaspoons salt

½   teaspoon pepper
2   tablespoons parsley
½   cup Parmesan cheese

Combine cottage cheese with eggs. Add remaining ingredients.

Preheat oven to 350 degrees. Using a greased, 9x13 inch pan, layer ingredients in this order: ½ cooked noodles, ½ cottage cheese mixture, ½ mozzarella cheese slices, and ½ meat sauce. Repeat layers. Cook at 350 degrees for 30 minutes.

Mrs. Samuel Earl Yates (Heidi)

Add 1 to 2 tablespoons of oil to the water when cooking pasta to prevent it from sticking or boiling over.

MACETTE
"Fix ahead and serve to guests."

1	pound ground round	1½	cups water
1	large onion, chopped	1	teaspoon oregano
1	small bell pepper, chopped	1	tablespoon chili powder
2	teaspoons garlic powder	1	5 ounce package egg noodles
1	10¾ ounce can cream of mushroom soup	1	10 ounce package sharp Cheddar cheese, shredded
1	10¾ ounce can tomato soup		

Brown meat, onion, and bell pepper. Add garlic powder. Drain excess grease. Add mushroom soup, tomato soup, water, oregano, and chili powder. Simmer 20 minutes. Cook egg noodles according to package directions. When noodles are done, drain and mix with meat mixture. Place in a 3 quart casserole dish. Bake for 25 minutes in a 350 degree oven. Sprinkle cheese on casserole and put back in oven to melt cheese. Serve hot.

Joyce Howard

PEG'S STUFFED MANICOTTI

1	8 ounce box manicotti noodles	3	slices moist bread, crumbled
1	tablespoon olive oil	½	cup milk
1½	pounds ground chuck	1	6 ounce can tomato paste
1	egg, slighly beaten	½	teaspoon salt
½	pound mozzarella cheese, shredded	½	teaspoon pepper
		½	teaspoon parsley
		1	15 ounce jar spaghetti sauce

Cook manicotti according to package directions. Add olive oil to keep noodles from sticking together. Run cold water over noodles to drain. Mix uncooked ground chuck, egg, cheese, bread, milk, tomato paste, salt, pepper, and parsley. Stuff noodles with meat mixture. Grease 9x13 inch pan. Place noodles in dish, cover with spaghetti sauce. Bake at 325 degrees for 45 minutes.
Yield: 6 servings.

Mrs. Steve Turner (Peggy)
Birmingham, Alabama

HOMEMADE PIZZAS

Crust:

2 packages active dry yeast	3 tablespoons cooking oil
1 cup lukewarm water	3½ to 4 cups all-purpose flour
1 teaspoon salt	

Dissolve yeast in lukewarm water. Stir in salt, oil, and enough flour to make a stiff dough. Let dough rise in a warm place for 10 minutes. Divide dough in half. Pat half of the dough on the bottom and up sides of a greased 12 inch pizza pan with greased hands. Repeat with other half of dough in another pizza pan.

Topping:

1 pound ground beef	1 cup tomato sauce
1 teaspoon garlic powder	1 cup pizza sauce
1 teaspoon salt	1 cup onion, chopped
½ teaspoon black pepper	1 cup green pepper, chopped
1 teaspoon oregano leaves	½ cup celery, chopped
1 cup tomato paste	4 cups (1 pound) mozzarella
Cheese, shredded	

While dough is rising, brown 1 pound ground beef. Add the garlic powder, salt, pepper, and oregano. In another container, combine the tomato paste, tomato sauce, and pizza sauce. Set aside. Spread each pizza dough with half of the tomato sauce mixture. Spoon half of the meat mixture over sauce on each pizza. Top each pizza with half of the onions, pepper, celery, and cheese. Bake at 450 degrees for 15 to 20 minutes.

Mrs. George Sims (Sylvia)

SOUR CREAM ENCHILADA CASSEROLE
"Your guests will rave over this dish."

1 cup water	1 teaspoon garlic powder
2 tablespoons picante sauce	¾ cup ripe olives, sliced
12 corn tortillas	¼ cup picante sauce
2 pounds ground beef	½ cup margarine
1 medium onion, chopped	2 tablespoons all-purpose flour
1 to 1½ teaspoon salt	1½ cups milk
⅛ teaspoon black pepper	1 16 ounce carton sour cream
2 teaspoons ground cumin	2 cups Cheddar cheese,
1 tablespoon chili powder	shredded

Combine water and 2 tablespoons picante sauce in large shallow dish. Place tortillas in picante mixture; let stand 5 minutes. Drain. Cook beef and onion in skillet until brown. Drain. Stir in next (7) seven ingredients. Simmer meat mixture 5 minutes. In medium saucepan melt margarine. Add flour, stirring until smooth. Cook 1 minute, stirring constantly. Gradually stir in milk, cooking over medium heat until thickened and bubbly. Remove from heat; add sour cream and stir until blended. Place half of tortillas in 13x9x2 inch baking dish. Pour half of sour cream over tortillas; then half the meat mixture, spreading evenly. Sprinkle half of cheese over this layer. Make another layer using same directions with remaining ingredients. Place in 375 degree oven and bake for 25 minutes.
Yield: 8 servings.

Mrs. Rex Killough (Sharon)

TACO CASSEROLE

1 16 ounce can refried beans	1 16 ounce can tomatoes
½ cup taco sauce	1 cup tortilla chips, crushed
1 pound ground beef, browned	1 cup Cheddar cheese,
2 tablespoons taco seasoning	shredded
1 cup pre-cooked rice	

In greased 2 quart casserole dish, spread refried beans, top with taco sauce, add browned beef, sprinkle with taco seasoning. Cook rice in juice of tomatoes (1 cup liquid) until tender. Chop tomatoes and mix with rice. Place rice over beef. Layer crushed tortilla chips on top. Cover with shredded cheese. Bake in 350 degree oven for 10 minutes or until heated through. Microwave instruction: Cook on high for 5 minutes until heated through.
Yield: 6 servings.

Mrs. Robert Kline (Marilyn)
Childersburg, Alabama

MEXICAN MEAL

1½ pounds ground chuck
1 package dry chili mix
1 28 ounce can of tomatoes
2 5 ounce packages of
seasoned yellow rice
1 11 ounce can Cheddar
cheese soup

½ cup milk
Chopped tomatoes
Diced onion
Shredded lettuce
Taco sauce
Shredded cheese
Corn chips

Brown meat and drain. Add chili mix and tomatoes to meat and simmer 20 minutes. Cook rice according to directions. Layer rice and meat in casserole. Make sauce of soup and milk and heat. Pour over top of casserole. Cook at 350 degrees for 10 to 15 minutes or until bubbly hot. Serve with tomatoes, onions, lettuce, taco sauce, and grated cheese. Sprinkle crushed corn chips over individual servings.
Note: This freezes well.

Faye P. Cooley

TACO PIE

1 pound ground beef
1 medium onion, chopped
1¼ ounce package taco
seasoning mix
¾ cup water
1 16 ounce can refried beans
1 8 ounce jar taco sauce

1 9 inch deep dish pie shell,
baked
2 cups Cheddar cheese,
shredded
1 cup corn chips, crushed
Shredded lettuce
Chopped tomato

Cook ground beef and onion until meat is browned, stirring to crumble meat. Drain. Add taco seasoning and water, stirring well. Bring to a boil. Reduce heat and simmer 20 minutes, stirring occasionally. Combine refried beans and ⅓ cup taco sauce. Spoon half of the bean mixture into pastry shell. Top with meat, cheese, and chips. Repeat layers. Bake at 400 degrees for 20 to 25 minutes. Top with lettuce and tomato. Serve with remaining sauce. Yield: 6 servings.

Melba Hagan
Alexander City, Alabama

MEXICAN CASSEROLE

*"You can prepare this the night before
your supper club comes for dinner."*

2 pounds ground chuck
1 large onion, chopped
1 10 ounce can tomatoes and green chilies
1 12 ounce package frozen chopped spinach, thawed and squeezed dry
1 teaspoon salt
Pepper to taste
1 10¾ ounce can cream of mushroom soup
1 10¾ ounce can golden mushroom soup
1 8 ounce carton sour cream
¼ cup milk
¼ teaspoon garlic powder
16 corn tortillas
¼ cup margarine
2 4 ounce cans chopped green chilies; drained
½ pound longhorn or Monterey Jack cheese, shredded

Brown meat with onion and drain fat. Stir in tomatoes, spinach, salt, and pepper. Combine soups, sour cream, milk, and garlic powder in a bowl. Dip half the tortillas in melted margarine to soften. Line bottom of 13x9x2 inch dish with softened tortillas. Spread with 1 can chopped chilies. Top with half of the meat mixture, then half of soup mixture. Sprinkle with half of the cheese. Make another layer of all ingredients and top with remaining cheese. Cover and refrigerate overnight. Bake uncovered for 45 minutes at 325 degrees or until cheese is melted and bubbly.
Yield: 12 servings.

Mrs. Glen Gaines (Laura)

SHEPHERD'S PIE

1 pound ground beef
1 onion, chopped
1 10¾ ounce can tomato soup
1 15 ounce can mixed vegetables, drained
¼ cup ketchup
Salt to taste
5 potatoes, peeled, cooked, and mashed
1 cup cheese, shredded

Brown beef and onion. Drain well. Add soup, vegetables, and ketchup. Salt to taste. Heat well. Pour in 2 quart casserole. Spread mashed potatoes over top. Top with cheese. Heat in 375 degree oven or microwave at 70% until heated thoroughly and bubbling.
Yield: 4 servings.

Mrs. Mike Riley (Pam)

BUTTERBEAN PIE

"A meal in a casserole."

1	pound ground beef	1	16 ounce can tomato wedges
1	onion, chopped	1	15 ounce can butterbeans or
1	8 ounce can tomato sauce		frozen lima beans, cooked
½	teaspoon pepper	8½	ounce package cornbread mix
1	teaspoon salt		for topping, prepare batter
1	teaspoon garlic powder		according to package
1	10½ ounce can whole kernel		direction
	corn		

Brown beef and onion, drain. Prepare 2 quart casserole with non-stick vegetable spray. Stir hamburger, onion, tomato sauce, pepper, salt, and garlic powder together. Layer casserole with meat mixture, corn, tomato wedges, and butterbeans. Top with thin layer of uncooked cornbread batter. Bake 25 minutes on 350 degrees or until brown.

Hilda Fannin

SICILLIAN MEAT ROLL

2	eggs, beaten	¼	teaspoon salt
¾	cup soft bread crumbs	¼	teaspoon pepper
½	cup tomato juice	2	pounds lean ground beef
2	tablespoons snipped parsley	8	thin slices boiled ham
½	teaspoon dried oregano,	1½	cup (6 ounces) mozzarella
	crushed		cheese, shredded
1	small clove garlic, minced	3	slices mozzarella cheese

Combine first eight (8) ingredients. Add beef, mix well. On foil, pat meat to 12x10 inch rectangle. Arrange ham on top. Top ham with shredded cheese. Starting from short end, carefully roll up meat, using foil to lift; seal edges and ends. Place, seam side down, in 13x9x2 inch baking dish. Bake in 350 degree oven for 1¼ hours. Half cheese diagonally; place atop roll. Return to oven until melted.
Yield: 8 servings.

Mrs. John Morris (Gail)

GRILLED HAM WITH GLAZE

3 ham steaks (any ham steak
may be used)

Glaze:

2 tablespoons oil
½ cup brown sugar
¼ cup lemon juice

2 tablespoons horseradish
2 tablespoons mustard

Start grill and let burn for 10 minutes or until hot. Put ham on hot grill. Mix glaze ingredients and baste. Ham usually takes about 10 minutes on each side to cook. Continue to baste 3 to 4 minutes until done.

Melanie Hughes
Birmingham, Alabama

MARINATED PORK ROAST

1 center cut pork loin roast
(have butcher cut bone to
make carving easier)

½ cup honey
¼ cup brandy
1 teaspoon ground ginger

Bake roast in 325 degree oven for 35 minutes per pound, marinating every 15 minutes with mixture of honey, brandy, and ginger.

Mrs. Marty Phillips (Pam)

BAKED PORK CHOPS

6 1 inch thick loin pork chops
3 tablespoons brown sugar
¾ cup ketchup or chili sauce

6 slices onion
6 slices lemon

Place chops in baking pan in single layer; salt and pepper to taste. Spread 2 teaspoons brown sugar and 2 tablespoons ketchup on each chop. Top with slice of onion and slice of lemon. Add enough water to reach a level halfway up on chops. Bake, covered, at 350 degrees for 2½ to 3 hours. Uncover last half hour of cooking.
Yield: 6 servings.

Mrs. Al Kline (Naomi)

COMPANY PORK CHOPS

2 tablespoons vegetable oil
4 ¾ inch thick center cut pork chops
1 small onion, sliced and separated into rings
1 clove garlic, minced
½ cup orange juice
1½ tablespoons cider vinegar

1 teaspoon paprika
1 teaspoon honey
⅛ teaspoon salt
⅛ teaspoon pepper
1 cup chicken broth, divided
2 tablespoons all-purpose flour
Chopped parsley and orange slices (optional for garnish)

Heat oil in large heavy skillet. Brown pork chops on both sides. Add next 8 ingredients and ½ cup chicken broth. Bring to a boil. Cover and reduce heat; simmer one hour. Remove chops to serving platter and keep warm. Gradually stir remaining ½ cup chicken broth into flour. Stir mixture into drippings in skillet. Cook, stirring constantly until thickened. Serve with pork chops. Garnish with parsley and orange wedges if desired.
Yield: 4 servings.

Mrs. A. H. Meacham (Odessa)

REVOLUTIONARY RIBS

3 pounds very lean country-style pork ribs
5 tablespoons sugar
3 tablespoons brown sugar
3 tablespoons soy sauce

2 tablespoons catsup
1 teaspoon salt
1 cup hot chicken broth or 1 bouillon cube and 1 cup hot water

Place ribs in baking dish just large enough to hold meat in single layer. Combine remaining ingredients and pour over ribs; allow to marinate 2 or more hours (in refrigerator if longer than 2 hours). Turn to coat top of ribs about once an hour. Bake at 300 degrees uncovered about 2 hours. Baste occasionally with sauce. Cover for last 20 minutes of cooking if ribs appear too dry.
Yield: 4 servings.

Mrs. Glen Gaines (Laura)

Bake hams about 20 minutes per pound.

BARBECUED BEEF BRISKET
"Flavorful favorite."

1 4 or 5 pound beef brisket, trim fat	2 tablespoons liquid smoke
½ teaspoon onion salt	¼ cup plus 2 tablespoons Worcestershire sauce
½ teaspoon celery salt	¾ cup commercial barbecue sauce
¼ teaspoon garlic powder	

Sprinkle beef with onion salt, celery salt, and garlic powder; place in a shallow baking dish. Mix liquid smoke and Worcestershire sauce and pour over the meat. Cover with foil. Refrigerate several hours or overnight, turning once. Bake, covered at 300 degrees for 4 to 4½ hours or until tender. Pour commercial barbecue sauce over beef and bake, uncovered an additional 30 minutes.
Yield: 8 to 10 servings.

Mrs. Raymond Shepherd
Starkville, Mississippi

VENISON BURGUNDY
"This is delicious! No one will ever know it is venison."

2 pounds boneless venison, trimmed of all fat and cut into ¾ inch cubes	1 pound fresh mushrooms, sliced
½ cup fresh bacon drippings	4 tablespoons all purpose flour
1 cup canned beef consommé	A generous pinch of thyme and marjoram
1¾ cup *good* California burgundy	Fresh ground pepper to taste
3 medium onions, peeled and sliced thin	Salt to taste
	Hot cooked noodles

Sauté onions in ¼ cup bacon drippings in a 4 quart dutch oven. Remove onions and reserve. Brown meat in small batches, adding more drippings as needed. Return browned meat to the dutch oven. Sprinkle flour over meat and stir. Add wine, consommé, mushrooms and seasonings. Cover and simmer gently for 3 hours, stirring occasionally. Serve over hot buttered noodles.
Yield: 8 to 10 servings.

Drue D. Gravlee
Fayette, Alabama

ESCALOPES DE VEAU VALLEE D'AUGE
(Veal Scallops)

12 very small white onions
6   2 ounce veal scallops

Salt and pepper to taste
3   tablespoons butter

Cook onions in boiling salted water until tender (approximately 20 minutes); drain and set aside. Sprinkle veal scallops with salt and pepper and pound with meat mallet to flatten and tenderize. In a large skillet, cook the scallops in the butter over medium heat for 30 seconds on each side or until they are cooked through but not browned. Transfer the scallops with a slotted spatula to a heated serving dish and keep them warm, covered with buttered wax paper.

Sauce:
4   large mushrooms, quartered
1   cup heavy cream

2   tablespoons apple brandy
Parsley (optional garnish)

Increase the heat under the skillet to medium high. In the fat remaining in the pan, sauté the mushrooms until they are golden. Add the white onions and cream. Deglaze the pan, scraping up the brown bits clinging to the pan. Reduce liquid, stirring until it is thickened. Add 2 tablespoons apple brandy and simmer sauce for three minutes. Season the sauce with salt and pepper to taste, pour it over the veal (after draining any juice from serving dish), and garnish with parsley.
Yield: 6 small servings.

Gladys G. Barton

INDONESIAN SHISH KABOB

½   cup soy sauce
1   teaspoon dark molasses
1   teaspoon ground cayenne
    pepper
¾   cup hot water
⅔   cup peanut butter

1   clove garlic, minced
Juice of 1 lemon
3   pound leg of lamb, well
    trimmed, boned, and cut into
    1 inch cubes

Mix soy sauce and molasses. Combine with remaining ingredients except lamb in saucepan. Bring to a boil and stir until smooth. Cool to room temperature. Pour half the sauce over the lamb cubes. Mix well and let stand for approximately 1 hour. Arrange lamb on skewers. Cook to desired doneness on grill or under preheated broiler. Serve with remaining sauce.

Muffett Robbs Conover

CHICKEN ALFREDO

1	12 ounce package fettucine	1	cup frozen peas
¼	pound fresh mushrooms, quartered	2½	cups cooked chicken pieces (about 1 pound), deboned
¼	cup onion, chopped	½	teaspoon salt
2	tablespoons butter or margarine	½	teaspoon black pepper
1	cup heavy cream	½	cup Parmesan cheese, grated

Cook fettucine according to package directions, drain, and transfer to large serving dish. Over medium heat, sauté mushrooms and onions in butter in medium size skillet until tender. Add cream and bring to boil. Lower heat and cook gently, uncovered, about 5 minutes. Add peas, chicken, salt, and pepper. Cook, stirring constantly until hot. Pour over fettucine. Sprinkle with cheese. Toss to mix well.
Yield: 8 servings.

Melba Hagan
Alexander City, Alabama

FRENCH CHICKEN BAKE

⅔	cup butter	4	cups milk
1	pound mushrooms, sliced	4	cups cooked chicken, diced
1	cup celery, chopped	8	ounces egg noodles, cooked and drained
¼	cup cornstarch	¼	cup white wine
2	teaspoons salt	1	cup fine dry bread crumbs
¼	teaspoon white pepper		
1	teaspoon dried thyme leaves		

Heat 6 tablespoons of butter over medium heat. Add mushrooms and celery; sauté 5 minutes. Strain and set aside, reserving juices. In saucepan, mix next 4 ingredients. Gradually stir in reserved juices and milk until smooth. Bring to boil over medium heat, stirring constantly; boil 1 minute. Remove from heat. Stir in next 3 ingredients. Pour into 3 quart casserole dish. Melt remaining butter; stir in bread crumbs. Sprinkle over top. Bake for 20 minutes at 400 degrees.
Yield: 8 to 10 servings

Mrs. Michael G. Helton (Lynda)

CHICKEN CASSEROLE
"Dinner's almost complete in this one dish."

½ cup mayonnaise or salad dressing
2 tablespoons Worcestershire sauce
1 10 ounce can cream of chicken soup
2 cups cooked rice
2 cups cooked chicken, chopped
1 medium onion, chopped
1 cup celery, chopped
2 boiled eggs, chopped
1 8½ ounce can English peas, drained
Toasted cracker crumbs

Mix first three ingredients and set aside. Beginning with rice and ending with peas, place ingredients in layers in 9x13 inch baking dish. Dollop sauce mixture on top layer and smooth to sides of dish. Top with toasted cracker crumbs. Bake at 350 degrees about 30 minutes or until bubbly hot.

Lucile L. Sharpley

CHICKEN A LA KING

1 cup green olives, chopped
1 4 ounce can mushrooms, sliced and drained
½ cup margarine, melted
½ cup all-purose flour
2 teaspoons salt
¼ teaspoon black pepper
2 cups chicken broth
2 cups half-and-half
2 cups cooked chicken, diced
2 4 ounce jars chopped pimento
1 8½ ounce can water chestnuts, sliced
2 10 ounce packages frozen pastry shells, baked

Sauté olives and mushrooms in margarine in large skillet or Dutch oven. Combine flour, salt and pepper; add to mushroom and olive mixture, stirring until smooth. Cook 1 minute, stirring constantly. Gradually add chicken broth and half-and-half. Cook over medium heat, stirring constantly, until thickened and bubbling. Stir in chicken, pimento and water chestnuts. Cook until throughly heated. Divide filling among patty shells. Cook approximately 30 minutes.
Yield: 12 servings.
Note: May also be served over rice or noodles.

Martha Williams

COMPANY CREAMY CHICKEN
"Great make ahead dish"

1	3 pound chicken	1	onion, quartered
6	cups water	1	chicken bouillon cube
2	stalks celery, broken into pieces		

Cook all the above in covered Dutch oven until chicken is tender, about an hour. Remove chicken. Cool and debone into small pieces. Strain broth into another pan and set aside.

6	tablespoons margarine	1½	cups milk
1½	stalks celery, diced	1	2 ounce can mushrooms, sliced and drained
1	medium onion, diced		
⅜	cup all-purpose flour	½	2 ounce jar sliced pimento, drained
1½	cups chicken broth		
1	cooked chicken		Salt and pepper to taste

Using the Dutch oven, sauté celery and onions in half of the margarine. Add remaining margarine and melt. Remove from heat and blend in flour. Gradually stir in broth. Return to heat. Add chicken, milk, mushrooms, and pimento, stirring until mixture thickens. Add salt and pepper to taste. May be prepared in advance and refrigerated or frozen. Reheat to serve. Serve in chafing dish on cooked rice, heated pastry shells or cooked egg noodles. Yield: 12 servings.

Mrs. Jack R. Wood (Jackie Smith)
Heflin, Alabama

CHICKEN SURPRISE

4	large chicken breasts	1	10¾ ounce cream of mushroom soup
1	medium onion, cut in four slices		Salt to taste
2	medium potatoes, each cut in four slices		Pepper to taste

Place breasts in shallow 2 quart casserole dish. Put one onion slice and 2 potato slices on top of each breast. Spread soup over potatoes. Salt and pepper as desired. Cover with aluminum foil. Bake at 325 degrees for 2 hours.

Mrs. Ray Edmiston (Kara)

118

EASY CHICKEN PIE

1 medium chicken, stewed and boned
1½ cup chicken broth
1 10¾ ounce can cream of chicken soup

1 medium onion, chopped
1 20 ounce can mixed vegetables, drained
1 boiled egg, chopped (optional)

Mix all ingredients and place in a large casserole dish.

Crust:
1 cup self-rising flour
1 cup milk

½ cup margarine, melted

Mix, pour over chicken mixture. Bake 1 hour at 350 degrees.

Mrs. Hugh M. Parker (Mary Frances)

Similar recipe submitted by *Mrs. Erskine Murray (Betty),* Montgomery, Alabama and *Mrs. Robert Kline (Marilyn),* Childersburg, Alabama

EASY CHICKEN "N" DUMPLINGS

"Your family will think you have been cooking all day!"

1½ pounds boneless chicken breasts
½ tablespoon salt
2 cups milk

2 cups water
2 5 ounce cans butter-flavored biscuits
Pepper to taste

Rinse and skin chicken and place in a casserole dish after adding salt and pepper. Cover and microwave on high for approximately 15 minutes. While chicken is baking in microwave, take a large double boiler and bring milk and water to a boil. Take biscuits, roll out, and slice in strips. Add biscuit strips to boiling liquid and boil for a few minutes. Cut chicken in bite size pieces and add to dumpling mixture, boiling all ingredients for approximately 15 minutes or until biscuit dough is completely done. Add pepper along while cooking.
Yield: 6 to 8 servings.

Mrs. Gary Highfield (Dona)

ZESTY CHICKEN CASSEROLE
"Great meal in a jiffy."

1 chicken, skinned and deboned
1 10¾ ounce can cream of celery soup
1 10¾ ounce can cream of mushroom soup

1 soup can full of chicken broth, (heated)
1 soup can full of minute rice (uncooked)
1 2.8 ounce can onion rings

Cook chicken — dice and save chicken broth. Combine soups, broth, and rice. Stir well. Add chicken. Pour ingredients into a greased 2 quart casserole dish. Bake at 325 degrees covered for 15 minutes. Remove from oven and top with onion rings. Bake uncovered an additional 15 minutes at 325 degrees. Serve hot.
Yield: 4 to 6 servings.

Joyce Hutchinson

CHICKEN DRESSING CASSEROLE

1 chicken
½ cup margarine
1 8 ounce package seasoned dressing mix
1 10¾ ounce can cream of mushroom soup

1 10¾ ounce can cream of chicken soup
2 cups chicken broth

Boil chicken in salted water. Cool and debone. Reserve broth. Cut chicken into bite size pieces. Melt margarine and mix with dressing mix. Put ¾ of crumbs into 9x13 inch casserole dish. Put chicken pieces over crumbs. Mix soups with 2 cups broth and pour over chicken. Top with remaining crumbs. Cook 20 to 25 minutes at 350 degrees.

Faye P. Cooley

To keep juices in and grease out, soak chicken in salt water before flouring.

CHICKEN KELLY

4   large chicken breast fillets, cut
    into bite sized pieces
2   eggs, beaten
1   cup bread crumbs
1   tablespoon parsley
1   teaspoon garlic powder
Oil

1   tablespoon margarine
¾   pound fresh mushrooms,
    sliced
Slices of Muenster cheese
2   cubes bouillon dissolved in
    1 cup water

Marinate chicken bits in beaten eggs at least 2 hours or overnight. Mix crumbs, parsley, and garlic powder in paper bag. Add chicken and shake until thoroughly coated. Brown chicken in oil. Drain on paper towel. Melt margarine in 13x9 inch pan or casserole dish, preferably rectangular shape. Add chicken, layer of sliced mushrooms and cover with cheese slices. Pour chicken bouillon liquid over casserole. Cover and bake at 350 degrees for 45 minutes.
Note: May make day before and bake before serving. Don't add bouillon liquid until ready to bake.

Judy Cobb

PLUM CHICKEN

6   large chicken breast halves or
    thighs
2   tablespoons butter or oil
1   teaspoon or more curry
    powder

1   teaspoon seasoned salt
1   20 ounce can red plums or
    plum jelly
½   cup dry or cream sherry
1   lemon, thinly sliced

In a skillet, brown chicken in butter or oil. Transfer chicken to a greased 7½x11 inch casserole dish. Stir curry powder into pan juices. Pour juice into casserole dish. Sprinkle seasoned salt over chicken. Add plums or jelly, sherry, and lemon slices. Bake uncovered at 350 degrees for 35 to 40 minutes depending on size of chicken. Baste several times until the amount of juice is reduced. It should be thick and yummy.
Yield: 6 servings.

Mrs. John Coleman (Mary Dowdell)

RED CHICK
"It's not barbecued; it's better."

Chicken pieces	2 tablespoons brown sugar
½ cup onion, sliced	2 tablespoons prepared
½ cup bell pepper, chopped	mustard
½ teaspoon garlic powder	2 tablespoons Worcestershire
1 bay leaf	sauce
½ teaspoon oregano	¼ teaspoon pepper
1 8 ounce can tomato sauce	¼ cup vinegar
1 tomato sauce can of water	

Place chicken pieces side by side in 13x9 inch casserole dish. Mix together remaining ingredients and pour over chicken. Cook at 350 degrees for 1½ hours. Turn pieces midway through the cooking time.
Yield: 4 to 6 servings.

Mrs. Glen Gaines (Laura)

QUICK SKILLET BARBECUE CHICKEN
"When you have little time, but want great taste!"

6 pieces of chicken	1 cup cola beverage
Salt, pepper, and flour	1 cup barbecue sauce
2 tablespoons of vegetable oil	

Salt, pepper, and lightly flour chicken. Brown chicken in vegetable oil in large skillet. Pour cola beverage and barbecue sauce over chicken. Reduce heat to simmer, cover and cook for 30 to 45 minutes.

Mary Virginia Avery

APRICOT CHICKEN

1 chicken, cut into parts	1 8 ounce jar apricot preserves
1 package dry onion soup mix	1 8 ounce jar Russian dressing

Place chicken in 13x9 inch baking dish. Mix remaining ingredients and pour over chicken. Bake uncovered at 350 degrees for 1 to 1½ hours.
Yield: 6 servings.
Note: May substitute 4 chicken breasts for chicken parts.

Mildred Goodpasture
Oak Ridge, Tennessee

SWEET 'N SOUR CHICKEN

1　pound boneless chicken, cut
　　in cubes
2　tablespoons oil
1　garlic clove, minced
1　cup green pepper, cut in strips
1　cup carrots, sliced
1¼ cups chicken bouillon

¼　cup soy sauce
2　tablespoons sherry (optional)
3　tablespoons vinegar
3　tablespoons brown sugar
½　teaspoon ginger
1　8 ounce can chunk pineapple
　　in juice
1½ cups minute rice, cooked

Brown chicken in oil. Add garlic, green peppers, and carrots — sauté briefly. Add bouillon, soy sauce, sherry, vinegar, brown sugar, ginger, and pineapple with juice. Bring to a full boil. Stir in rice. Cover, remove from heat and let stand 5 minutes. Stir before serving.
Yield: 4 servings.

Mrs. James C. Rogers (Marian)

CHICKEN AND NUTS

2　tablespoons sesame oil
3　cloves garlic, minced
¾　teaspoon red pepper flakes
1　cup broccoli florets
10 to 12 Chinese pea pods
1　10 ounce can bamboo shoots
1　7 ounce can sliced water
　　chestnuts
4　scallions, sliced

4　boneless chicken breasts,
　　sliced
1　15¼ ounce can of chicken
　　broth
2　tablespoons arrowroot,
　　chopped
2　tablespoons soy sauce
¾　cup mixed nuts

Heat oil to medium in wok, add garlic and red pepper. Cook, stirring, for 1 minute. Add broccoli, pea pods, bamboo shoots, water chestnuts, scallions, and chicken then stir fry until chicken is done. Stir in chicken broth, arrowroot, and soy sauce. Cover and simmer 5 minutes. Sprinkle with nuts. Serve over angel hair pasta or rice.
Yield: 4 to 6 servings.

Leigh Hardwick Hardy

CHICKEN JAMBALAYA

1	3 pound fryer	2	cloves garlic, chopped
	Salt, black pepper, red pepper to taste	¼	bell pepper, chopped
	Flour to coat chicken	2	cups rice, washed
3	tablespoons oil	1	can beer
3	large onions, chopped	2½	cups water
5	stalks celery, chopped	2	tablespoons salt

Cut chicken into serving pieces. Season with salt, black pepper, and red pepper. Coat chicken with flour. Heat oil in a large skillet or wok. Fry chicken until brown, then remove from skillet. To the oil, add the onins, celery, garlic, and bell peppers. Cook until wilted. Put the chicken back in the skillet and cover. Cook slowly until the chicken is tender, about 30 minutes. Add rice to chicken. Stir thoroughly for 2 or 3 minutes. Pour beer and water over the mixture and stir thoroughly. Add salt and cook slowly, about 30 minutes, until rice is cooked. Serve with salad and French bread.

Linda B. Miller

SPICY COMPANY CHICKEN

6 to 8 chicken breasts, deboned, cut into small pieces	1	10¾ ounce can golden mushroom soup
Paprika	1	14½ ounce can stewed tomatoes
1 4 ounce bottle olive oil	1	tablespoon all-purpose flour
1½ large onions, chopped	1	pound fresh mushrooms, sliced
1 or 2 large bell peppers, chopped	1	teaspoon salt
1 10¾ ounce can tomato soup		

Coat chicken with paprika. Sauté in olive oil until white. Take chicken out; sauté onion and add pepper. Add ½ of onion and pepper mixture to top of chicken in 5 quart casserole dish. Mix tomato soup and mushroom soup and spread over chicken. Drain tomatoes and thicken juice with 1 tablespoon flour. Return to tomatoes. Add to casserole. Add mushrooms to other ½ of peppers and onions with salt. Add this to casserole. Bake at 350 degrees for 1 hour. Refrigerate overnight. Bake again for 1½ hours at 350 degrees. Serve over brown rice.

Mrs. John Haskell (Peggy)

CHICKEN WITH RED WINE

1 cup red wine
¼ cup soy sauce
3 tablespoons salad oil
2 tablespoons water
1 clove garlic, minced

1 teaspoon ginger
¼ teaspoon oregano
1 tablespoon brown sugar
6 chicken breast halves

Mix all ingredients and marinate chicken 24 hours in a baking dish covered with aluminum foil. Bake for 1½ hours in a 350 degree oven, uncovering for the last 15 minutes. Pan juices may be used for gravy.
Yield: 4 to 6 servings.

Judy Elliott (Mrs. Joel)

MEXICAN CHICKEN SALAD

⅓ cup salad oil
4 8 inch flour tortillas
3 cups iceberg lettuce, shredded
1 ripe avocado, peeled and sliced
¼ cup red or green onion, chopped
2 tomatoes, cut into eighths

2 cups chicken breasts, cooked and shredded
1 cup Cheddar cheese, shredded
½ cup sour cream
¼ cup black olives, chopped
Salsa fresca (recipe follows)

Heat oil in skillet. Add tortillas one at a time and fry about one minute per side until crisp and golden brown. Divide lettuce among the four fried tortillas, piling it evenly on top. Arrange avocados, onion, and tomatoes on lettuce. Top with chicken and sprinkle with cheese. Add dollops of sour cream. Sprinkle with chopped olives. Serve individual bowls of the salsa fresca to spoon over the tostada as it is eaten.

Salsa Fresca

2 to 3 medium tomatoes, peeled and chopped
3 tablespoons canned green chilies, diced

2 tablespoons onion, minced
1 teaspoon oil
1 teaspoon white vinegar
½ teaspoon salt

Mix ingredients. Cover and refrigerate to chill and blend flavors.
Yield: 4 servings.

Mrs. Larry Edmiston (Donna)

CHICKEN MEXICANA

6	chicken breasts		Pepper to taste
3	tablespoons vegetable oil	1	tablespoon chili powder
2	large onions, sliced	1	16 ounce can tomatoes,
2	bell peppers, sliced		undrained
2	tablespoons all-purpose flour		Hot cooked rice
1	teaspoon salt		

Wash and dry chicken with cloth. Brown both sides of chicken in oil. Remove to 9x13 inch casserole dish. In a skillet sauté onion and bell pepper. Top chicken with onion and bell pepper. With the oil and liquid from onion and bell pepper, add flour and seasoning, making a paste. Add tomatoes to paste. Cook to make a smooth sauce. Pour over chicken. Cover casserole with foil. Cook for 1 hour and 15 minutes at 350 degrees. Serve over hot rice. Yield: 6 servings.

Doris Munroe

CHICKEN WITH LIME BUTTER

6	chicken breast halves, skinned		Juice of 1 lime
½	teaspoon salt	8	tablespoons butter
½	teaspoon pepper	½	teaspoon chives
⅓	cup cooking oil	½	pound mushrooms, sliced
		½	teaspoon dill weed

Sprinkle chicken on both sides with salt and pepper. In a large skillet, place oil and heat to medium temperature. Add chicken and sauté about 4 minutes or until lightly browned. Turn chicken over, cover and reduce heat to low. Cook 12 to 15 minutes or until fork can be inserted in chicken with ease. Remove chicken and keep warm. Drain off oil and discard. In same skillet, add juice of one lime and cook over low heat until juice begins to bubble. Add butter, stirring until butter become opaque and forms thickened sauce. In saucepan, sauté chives and mushrooms. Add sautéed mixture and dill weed to sauce. Spoon sauce over chicken.
Yield: 6 servings.
Note: Could use chopped green onions rather than chives.

Mrs. Jim Preuitt (Rona)

TURKEY AND RICE SALAD WITH GREEN PEPPERCORN DRESSING

"Very colorful."

3   cups cooked long grain rice, preferably warm
1   cup smoked or roasted turkey, diced
½   cup zucchini, diced

½   cup red or yellow sweet pepper, diced
½   cup cheddar cheese, shredded
½   cup black olives, chopped
¼   cup parsley, minced

Dressing:

3   tablespoons red wine vinegar
1   teaspoon dijon mustard
1   tablespoon green peppercorns, drained

9   tablespoons olive oil

Combine cooked rice, turkey, zucchini, pepper, cheese, olives, and parsley. Toss to combine. In blender combine vinegar, mustard and peppercorns. Process on high speed until well mixed. While blender is still running, add oil in a steady stream and blend until emulsified. Taste and adjust seasoning. Pour over rice mixture and toss to coat. Serve at room temperature or chilled.
Yield: 4 main dish servings.

Laine Austin Randall
Greensboro, North Carolina

BROCCOLI AND CHICKEN CASSEROLE

4   chicken breasts
2   10 ounce packages of frozen broccoli
2   tablespoons butter
1   10¾ ounce can cream of chicken soup

½   teaspoon garlic salt
¼   cup milk
½   cup sour cream
1   cup cheese, shredded

Boil or bake chicken. Pull meat off in strips. Cook broccoli, drain and place in large casserole dish. Dot with butter. Put chicken strips on top of broccoli. Mix soup, garlic salt, milk and sour cream. Pour over chicken and broccoli. Sprinkle cheese on top. Cook in 350 degree oven until it bubbles.
Variation: Add slivered almonds and mushrooms to the sauce.

Mrs. Ronnie Busby (Kay)
Similar recipe by Mrs. Janet Haywood

CHICKEN BOG

6	cups water	1	cup long grain rice
1	tablespoon salt	½ to 1 pound smoked sausage,
1	medium onion, finely		sliced
	chopped	2	tablespoons herb seasoning
3 pound chicken (or 3 or 4 whole	1	package "chicken and herb"
	chicken leg quarters)		seasoning

Measure 6 cups water, salt, onion, and chicken. Boil until tender. (About 1 hour.) Remove chicken, let cool and remove bones. Chop meat in bite-size pieces. Skim off fat from juice. Measure 3½ cups of this broth into a six quart saucepan. Add rice, chicken pieces and smoked sausage, herb seasoning, and "chicken and herb" seasoning. Cook these ingredients for 30 minutes. Let come to a boil and turn to low, keeping covered the entire time. If rice mixture is too juicy, cook uncovered until desired consistency. Yield: 6 servings.

Mrs. Claxton Ray
Conway, South Carolina

CRAB-STUFFED CHICKEN BREAST

6	chicken breasts, deboned and	½	cup herb seasoned stuffing
	skinned		mix
Salt and pepper to taste	2	tablespoons flour
½	cup onion chopped	½	teaspoon paprika
½	cup celery, chopped	6	tablespoons butter
3	tablespoons butter	1	recipe Hollandaise sauce
3	tablespoons white wine	2	tablespoons white wine
1	cup crabmeat, drained	½	cup Swiss cheese, shredded

Pound chicken to flatten, sprinkle with salt and pepper. Cook onion and celery in butter until tender. Remove from heat and add wine, crabmeat, and stuffing mix. Blend well. Divide among chicken breasts. Secure with toothpicks. Mix flour and paprika; coat chicken. Place in glass baking dish and dot with melted butter. Bake uncovered in 375 degree oven for one hour. Place on serving platter. Add wine and Swiss cheese to Hollandaise sauce and pour over chicken.
Yield: 6 servings.

Betty M. Martin

OLD FASHIONED CORNBREAD DRESSING
WITH GRAVY
"A must for the holidays."

1 large cake of cornbread	2 small onions, chopped
2 to 3 pound chicken	3 to 4 eggs
½ loaf white bread, toasted	Sage to taste
5 stalks celery, diced	Black pepper to taste

Salt chicken and boil it in skin. Remove chicken and debone, removing skin. Reserve at least 1½ quarts of broth. Add celery and onion to broth and boil until vegetables are tender. In a large bowl, crumble cornbread and toasted white bread. Beat eggs and add to bread. Add sage and pepper to taste. Stir in broth, reserving 2 cups for gravy. Mixture should be soupy. Pour into 13x9 inch pan. Bake at 325 degrees until brown. Do not overcook or it will be dry.

Gravy:

2 cups chicken broth   Small amount of cornstarch
1 or 2 hard boiled eggs, grated

Thicken remaining broth with cornstarch. Grate eggs into gravy.
Note: Diced chicken may be added to dressing before cooking or it can be served separately.

Linda McCardle

DILLED FISH STEAKS

4	6 ounce fish steaks	½	cup lemon juice
2	tablespoons butter or	1	clove glaric, minced
	margarine, melted	½	teaspoon pepper
¼	cup snipped fresh dill or	½	cup onion, thinly sliced
	1 tablespoon dried dill weed	4	tomato slices
1	teaspoon salt		

Brush both sides of fish steaks with butter, and place each steak on a piece of heavy aluminum foil and drizzle with remaining butter. Sprinkle with lemon juice, dill, salt, garlic and pepper. Top each with onion and tomato slices. Seal fish steaks securely in foil. Grill over hot coals for 25 to 30 minutes, turning every 10 minutes.
Yield: 4 servings.
Note: This can also be broiled in a conventional oven.

Linda D. Taconis
Charlotte, North Carolina

YANKEE CLAM CHOWDER

4	slices bacon, chopped coarse	½	teaspoon salt
1	onion, chopped	¼	teaspoon dried whole thyme
2	stalks celery, chopped	2	6½ ounce cans minced clams,
1	garlic clove, minced		undrained
2	cups water	2	tablespoons cornstarch
2	cups potatoes, diced		
1	28 ounce can whole tomatoes, undrained and chopped		

Cook bacon in a Dutch oven until lightly browned. Add onion, celery and garlic, sauté until tender. Add next 5 ingredients. Cover and cook over medium heat for 20 minutes or until potatoes are tender. Drain clams and reserve liquid. Add cornstarch to clam liquid and stir. Add clams and liquid to vegetable mixture. Bring to a boil over medium heat, stirring constantly. Cook until slightly thickened.
Yield: 10 cups.

Betty M. Martin
Lincoln, Alabama

LOUISIANA CATFISH ETOUFFEE
"Truly Cajun"

5   tablespoons brown roux
    (equal mixture of oil and flour
    that is browned)
2   cups onions, finely chopped
½   cup celery, finely chopped
1   cup green bell pepper, finely
    chopped
1   teaspoon garlic, finely
    chopped
3   cups chicken broth
½   teaspoon red pepper sauce
    (less if you don't want it hot)
⅛   teaspoon cayenne pepper
1   16 ounce can tomatoes,
    drained and chopped
1   cup white cooking wine

1   teaspoon fresh lemon juice
1   tablespoon Worcestershire
    sauce
1   6 ounce can tomato paste
1   small bay leaf
1   teaspoon bottled brown
    bouquet sauce
Salt to taste
2   pounds catfish fillets-skinned
    and cut into 1 inch chunks
1   cup green onions, finely
    chopped
½   cup parsley, finely chopped

Heat brown roux in large Dutch oven over low heat, stirring constantly. Add the onions, celery, green pepper, and garlic. Stir frequently. Cook uncovered until vegetables are soft. Add broth and remaining ingredients; except catfish, green onions and parsley. Simmer for 1 hour. Add catfish, green onions, and parsley. Cook 10 minutes or until fish is flaky. Serve over rice. Yield: 8 servings.
Note: This is well worth the trouble. May substitute fresh, peeled, deveined shrimp for a different shrimp creole. Can be reheated.

Mrs. Mike Riley (Pam)

WEST INDIES SALAD

1   medium onion, chopped
1   pound lump crabmeat
½   cup vegetable oil

⅜   cup cider vinegar
½   cup ice water
Salt and pepper to taste

Spread half of onion over bottom of large bowl. Cover with separated crab lumps and then remaining onion. Pour oil, vinegar, ice water, salt, and pepper over all. Cover and marinate 2 to 10 hours. Toss lightly before serving. Yield: 4 to 6 servings.

Catherine C. Thomson

Never re-freeze fish. Once thawed, fish should be cooked immediately.

SEAFOOD GUMBO

½ cup vegetable oil
½ cup all-purpose flour
4 celery stalks, chopped
2 medium onions, chopped
1 green pepper, chopped
1 garlic clove, minced
½ pound okra, sliced
1 tablespoon vegetable oil
1 quart chicken broth
1 quart water
¼ cup Worcestershire sauce
1 teaspoon hot sauce
¼ cup catsup
1 tomato, chopped
1 teaspoon salt

2 slices bacon, chopped
1 bay leaf
¼ teaspoon dried whole thyme
¼ teaspoon dried whole rosemary
¼ teaspoon red pepper flakes
2 pounds unpeeled medium fresh shrimp
2 cups cooked chicken, chopped
1 pound fresh crabmeat
1 12 ounce container fresh oysters, undrained
Hot cooked rice
Gumbo File

Combine ½ cup oil and flour in a large Dutch oven and cook over medium heat, stirring constantly for 15 to 20 minutes, until mixture becomes a carmel color. Stir in celery, onion, green pepper and garlic. Cook for 45 minutes, stirring occasionally. Fry okra in 1 tablespoon of hot oil until browned. Add to gumbo mixture and stir well over low heat for a few minutes. Add the next 12 ingredients and simmer for 2½ hours, stirring occasionally. Peel and devein shrimp. Add seafood during the last 10 minutes of simmering. Remove bay leaf. Serve over rice. Add gumbo file. Yield: 15 one cup servings.

Amy M. Mathison

CREOLE FLOUNDER

1 15 ounce can tomato sauce
1 medium tomato, chopped
1 clove garlic, minced
½ cup green pepper, chopped

½ cup onion, chopped
1 bay leaf
1½ pounds flounder fillets
Salt or pepper, if desired

Mix tomato sauce, tomato, garlic, peppers, onions, and bay leaf in saucepan. Cook at low heat until tender. Pour over fish evenly prior to baking or broiling. Cook 20 to 25 minutes at 375 degrees or broil for 8 to 12 minutes. Yield: 4 servings.

Jerry Woodard

EASY CATCH-OCEAN PERCH

1   10 ounce package chopped frozen spinach, thawed and drained
1   16 ounce package ocean perch fillets
1   10¾ ounce can cream of shrimp soup

⅓   cup mayonnaise
6   ounces Cheddar cheese, shredded
¼   teaspoon chopped dill weed (for a stronger dill taste increase ½ teaspoon)

Thaw and drain spinach. Pat spinach into lightly greased 9x9 inch glass baking dish. Arrange fillets on top of spinach with skin side up. In another bowl, mix together cream of shrimp soup and mayonnaise. Spread soup mixture over fillets. Bake for 20 minutes at 350 degrees. Remove from oven and cover with shredded Cheddar cheese. Sprinkle dill weed evenly on top of cheese. Return to oven and continue to bake at 350 degrees for 30 to 35 minutes longer. Serve hot.
Yield: 4 to 6 servings.
Note: This dish may be reheated.

Mrs. Julian M. King, Sr. (Donna)

LOTTIE BELL PARKER'S DEVILED CRAB

1   large onion, chopped
1   bell pepper, chopped
½   cup celery, chopped
1   clove garlic, minced
1   tablespoon butter
1   pound crabmeat
1   cup mayonnaise
1   tablespoon Worcestershire sauce

1   teaspoon mustard
2   teaspoons ketchup
2   eggs
Salt and pepper to taste
1   dash hot pepper sauce
1   tablespoon lemon juice
½   cup tomato
1   cup bread or cracker crumbs
Cheddar cheese, shredded

Sauté onion, bell pepper, celery, and garlic in butter for 5 minutes. Add crab and mix well. Add remaining ingredients except cheese and stir. Add additional bread crumbs/crackers until proper consistency is reached. Place in shallow buttered pan or crab shells and top with additional bread crumbs. Bake 350 degrees for 10 minutes. Sprinkle with grated cheese and bake until melted.

Marvel Babcook
Sloatsburg, New York

CRAB DEMOS

4	teaspoons prepared mustard	1	cup mayonnaise
3	teaspoons curry powder	½	cup cooked wild rice
½	teaspoon salt	6	ounce lump crabmeat
2	teaspoons lemon juice		Parmesan cheese, grated

Mix mustard, curry powder, salt, and lemon juice with the mayonnaise. Divide the wild rice into 2 shells. Cover with crabmeat. Spread the above mixture over the crabmeat. Sprinkle with grated Parmesan cheese and place in 400 degree oven for about 20 minutes. Serve hot.

Hattie Wallace Coker

CRABMEAT AU GRATIN

2	tablespoons butter	¼	cup mozzarella cheese, shredded
2	tablespoons all-purpose flour		
1⅓	cups milk	¼	cup Parmesan cheese, grated
½	teaspoon salt	¼	cup fresh breadcrumbs
⅛	teaspoon white pepper	¼	teaspoon paprika
2	6 ounce packages frozen crabmeat, thawed and drained		Hot cooked rice

Melt butter in a saucepan over low heat; add flour, stirring until thoroughly mixed and smooth. Cook 1 minute, stirring constantly. Slowly add milk, cook over medium heat, stirring constantly, until thickened and bubbly. Stir in salt, pepper and crabmeat. Spoon mixture into a lightly greased 1½ quart casserole. Bake at 350 degrees for 15 minutes. Combine cheeses, breadcrumbs, and paprika. Sprinkle over crabmeat mixture and bake an additional 3 minutes or until cheese melts. Serve over rice.
Yield: 4 servings.

Amy M. Mathison

Add celery leaves to boiling water to prevent seafood odors.

NEVER FAIL CRAB GUMBO

S
E
A
F
O
O
D

2 tablespoons lard, shortening or bacon drippings
2 tablespoons all-purpose flour
2 medium onions, finely chopped
2 stalks celery, finely chopped (optional)
1 green pepper, finely chopped
2 16 ounce cans of tomatoes
1 pound okra, sliced round
1 pound raw shrimp, cleaned and de-veined
8-12 crabs, cleaned or 1 pound crabmeat
1 tablespoon salt
Black and red pepper to taste
Hot pepper to taste

Make a golden roux in heavy skillet of shortening and flour. Melt the shortening or bacon drippings in thick pot or preferably an iron skillet. Add the flour, stirring constantly until dark brown. Be careful not to burn. If there is the slightest indication of over browning, dispose of the roux and start over. Stir onions, celery, green pepper into the roux and simmer a few minutes, stirring constantly. Add undrained tomatoes and okra. Simmer until okra is tender. Place in large soup pot, add shrimp, crabs, and three quarts of water. Add seasonings and cook slowly over low heat for several hours. The longer the better. Serve in soup bowls with rice.
Note: May add ½ pint oysters-makes for a rich gumbo.

Linda B. Miller
Kenner, Louisiana

FRESH CRABMEAT AND MUSHROOMS

1 medium onion, chopped
½ pound fresh mushrooms, thinly sliced
4 tablespoons butter
¼ cup all-purpose flour
1½ cups half and half
1 pound fresh crabmeat
Juice of ½ lemon
2 tablespoons white wine (optional)
½ teaspoon paprika
Salt and pepper to taste
1 cup bread crumbs, buttered

Preheat oven to 350 degrees. Sauté onions and mushrooms in butter until soft. Sprinkle with flour and cook for 3 minutes. Gradually add milk and cook until thickened. Fold in crabmeat. Add lemon juice, wine, and adjust seasoning with paprika, salt, and pepper to taste. Fill 6 shells or ramekins with crabmeat mixture. Sprinkle liberally with buttered bread crumbs. Bake 20 to 25 minutes until brown and bubbly. Serve immediately.

Becky Heacock (Mrs. James W.)

135

LYNN'S SCALLOPED OYSTERS

1 cup celery, chopped
1 cup onion, chopped
1 cup butter or margarine
Cracker crumbs (saltine)
1 pint fresh oysters (use more if desired)

Salt and pepper to taste
Chicken broth (the richer the better)
1 egg

Cook onions and celery in ½ cup butter until tender. In the bottom of baking dish put a layer of cracker crumbs, celery and onions, then a layer of oysters. Sprinkle salt and pepper and dot with butter (if chicken broth is well seasoned the salt and pepper may not be needed). Repeat the layers until the dish is ⅔ full, cover top with cracker crumbs. Pour enough hot, rich chicken broth over this to moisten the crackers well. The oysters should be fixed and let hot broth stand on them 5 minutes before baking. Bake at 350 degrees for 20 minutes, or until well set and light brown. Beat 1 egg thoroughly and pour over top and brown well. Serve piping hot.
Note: Do not crumble crackers too fine.

Lynn Barnett
Similar recipe submitted by: *Mrs. Mike Walker (Charlene)*

SHRIMP AND GREEN NOODLES

1 8 ounce package spinach noodles, cooked and drained
1 10¾ ounce can cream of mushroom soup
1 soup can full of mayonnaise

1 soup can full of sour cream
1 to 1½ pounds shrimp, peeled and boiled
4-6 ounces Cheddar or Swiss cheese, shredded

Place noodles in large, 2 quart, buttered casserole dish. Mix soup, mayonnaise, and sour cream into a sauce. Layer shrimp over noodles, sauce over shrimp, and cheese on top. Bake at 375 degrees for 25 minutes.
Yield: 4 to 6 servings.

Sally Bingham
Athens, Georgia

136

SHRIMP MELBA

¼ cup plus 2 tablespoons water
¼ cup margarine, melted
2 teaspoons fresh parsley, chopped
1 teaspoon paprika
32 large fresh shrimp, peeled and deveined
1 cup frozen English peas, thawed
1 cup almonds, sliced
½ cup green onions, sliced
½ cup fresh mushrooms, sliced
3 tablespoons margarine, melted
2 cups saffron rice, cooked
Salt to taste

Combine water, margarine, parsley, and paprika in a 13x9x2 inch broiling pan; add shrimp, tossing well to coat. Broil shrimp 4 inches from heat, 3 to 4 minutes; turn and broil and additional 3 to 4 minutes or until done. In a large skillet, sauté peas, almonds, onions, and mushrooms in margarine for 5 minutes or until almonds are toasted. Add rice and salt; cook until thoroughly heated. To serve, spoon shrimp over rice mixture. Garnish with mushrooms, cherry tomatoes, watercress if desired.
Yield: 4 servings.

Fran Barksdale (Mrs. Larry)

SHRIMP NEWBURG

3 cups shrimp, cooked and cleaned
½ cup sherry
3 tablespoons butter, melted
2 tablespoons all-purpose flour
1 cup heavy cream
4 egg yolks, hard-boiled pressed through sieve
1 teaspoon salt
¼ teaspoon dry mustard
1 dash pepper
2 tablespoons lemon juice
4 cups rice, hot cooked

Sprinkle shrimp with sherry and let stand 1 hour. Combine butter and flour in top of double boiler. Add cream and stir until sauce is thick and smooth, but not boiling. Rub egg yolks to a paste and add gradually to sauce. Stir until smooth, then add salt, mustard, pepper, and lemon juice. When ready to serve, stir in shrimp. (Sherry in which shrimp were marinated may be added to taste). Heat thoroughly. Serve over hot cooked rice.
Note: Especially pretty served over browned or wild rice. This recipe was originally made with lobster.

Mrs. Hattie Wallace Coker

SHRIMP JAMBALAYA

1½ pounds unpeeled fresh
  shrimp
¼ cup onion, chopped
¼ cup green pepper, chopped
¼ cup butter or margine, melted
1 tablespoon all-purpose flour
2 teaspoons chili powder
½ teaspoon salt
¼ teaspoon garlic powder
¼ teaspoon pepper

⅛ teaspoon red pepper
¼ cup Worcestershire sauce
1 tablespoon vinegar
2 cups tomatoes, peeled and
  chopped
1 10 ounce package frozen
  sliced okra, thawed
2 cups hot cooked rice

Peel and devein shrimp. Sauté onion and green pepper in butter until tender.
Combine flour and dry seasonings, and stir into onion and green pepper
mixture. Stir in Worcestershire sauce and vinegar and mix thoroughly. Add
tomatoes and okra, stirring constantly until mixture thickens. Add shrimp
and simmer uncovered for 15 minutes. Stir in rice.
Yield: 6 servings.

Mrs. Edward D. Robertson (Jean)
Northport, Alabama

SEAFOOD NEWBURG

½ cup butter
½ cup all purpose flour
1 pint half and half
⅓ cup dry sherry
1 pound fresh crabmeat

1 pound fresh cooked shrimp,
  peeled and deveined
1½ cups Cheddar cheese,
  shredded
Hot cooked rice

Melt butter over medium heat. Stir in flour until smooth. Slowly stir in half
and half and cook until mixture thickens. Add sherry, crabmeat and shrimp.
Pour mixture into a buttered 2 quart casserole dish and top with cheese.
Bake for 15 minutes or until bubbly at 350 degrees. Serve with rice.

Leigh B. Hulsey
Anniston, Alabama

CREAMED SEAFOOD

3   tablespoons butter
4   tablespoons all-purpose flour
2   cups milk
1   teaspoon dry mustard
3   tablespoons onion, grated
1   8 ounce package of sharp pasteurized process cheese spread

2   6½ ounce cans shrimp
1   6½ ounce can crabmeat
1   4 ounce can mushrooms
Sherry to taste (optional)
Grated Parmesan cheese

Make cream sauce with butter and flour. Cook over medium heat until bubbly. Add milk slowly and mix with a whisk. Add dry mustard and onion. Add cheese and melt. Add drained canned goods. Add sherry to taste. Sprinkle with Parmesan cheese.

Frieda Rogers Meacham

HOT CURRIED SEAFOOD SALAD
"Your bridge group would love this for lunch."

1   large green pepper, chopped
1   medium onion, chopped
1   cup celery, chopped
½   pound crabmeat, flaked
1   pound shrimp, cooked and cleaned
1   cup prepared salad dressing or mayonnaise

1   tablespoon Worcestershire sauce
1   teaspoon curry powder
Dash of salt and pepper
½   cup round, buttery cracker crumbs

Combine all ingredients except cracker crumbs and mix well. Place in a 13x9 inch baking dish. Sprinkle with cracker crumbs. Bake at 350 degrees for 30 minutes.
Yield: 6 servings.

Mrs. Freeman J. Deitz (Miriam)

ABBONDANZA CREPES

"As a pie or as individuals crêpes,

you'll want to try these often."

4 eggs	Seasoned cream cheese
⅛ teaspooon salt	Parmesan cheese
2 cups all-purpose flour	Suggested fillings: ham, Swiss
2⅛ cups milk	cheese, turkey, salami, spinach,
¼ cup margarine, melted	lettuce, and/or tomatoes.
Mayonnaise	

To prepare crêpes, mix eggs and salt in a bowl. Add flour alternately with milk, beating until smooth. Beat in melted margarine. Pour 4 tablespoons of batter into heated and buttered 6 inch skillet or crêpe pan. Turn crêpes when slightly brown. Cook 30 seconds on the other side. Stack crêpes while preparing.

To serve as a pie, layer crêpes alternately with fillings, occasionally spreading a crêpe with mayonnaise or seasoned cream cheese. Sprinkle Parmesan cheese on top. Slice and serve pie style.
Note: May be prepared as individual crêpes. Just fill and fold.

Barbara McCollum
Athens, Alabama

SCALLOPED HAM AND CHEESE CASSEROLE

4	Irish potatoes, sliced	¼	teaspoon salt
2	medium onions, sliced		Pepper to taste
1	10¾ ounce cream of	2	cups cooked ham, diced
	mushroom soup	½	cup mild Cheddar cheese,
½	cup milk		shredded

Wash and slice potatoes, slice onions and set both aside. Combine mushroom soup, milk, salt and pepper together and set aside. In 2 quart casserole dish, line bottom layer with ½ of diced ham, then ½ of sliced potatoes, then ½ of sliced onion. Pour ½ of soup/milk mixture over the layer. Layer again with ham, potatoes and onions and pour remainder of soup/milk mixture over top. End up with cheese on top. Bake 350 degrees for 45 minutes or until potatoes are done. This can also be prepared in microwave following same directions and cooking for approximately 15 minutes on high until potatoes are done.
Yield: 6 to 8 servings.
Note: Recipe may be doubled or halved. This is an excellent dish for left-over ham.

Mrs. Gary Highfield (Dona)

SAUSAGE AND EGG BAKE

1 tablespoon butter
1 medium onion, chopped
1 medium red pepper, chopped
1½ cups fresh mushrooms, sliced
½ pound Italian sausage
5 eggs
4 ounces Monterey Jack cheese, shredded
1 10 ounce package frozen chopped broccoli, thawed and drained
1 cup ricotta cheese
1 tablespoon parsley flakes
20 frozen phyllo pastry sheets, thawed
¾ to 1 cup butter, melted

In a large skillet over medium heat, melt butter. Sauté onion, red pepper and mushrooms until tender; remove from skillet. In same skillet, brown sausage; drain. Add to mushroom mixture. Beat eggs slightly; stir in Monterey Jack cheese and mushroom-sausage mixture. In another bowl, combine broccoli, ricotta cheese, and parsley flakes. Heat oven to 350 degrees. Unroll phyllo sheets; cover with plastic wrap. Place 1 phyllo sheet in a 13x9 inch baking dish. Brush with melted butter. Continue layering and brushing with butter 4 additional sheets. Spread half of mushroom sausage mixture evenly over dough. Layer and brush with butter 5 more sheets; spread with all of broccoli mixture. Layer and brush with butter 5 more sheets. Spread with remaining mushroom-sausage mixture. Layer and brush with butter remaining 5 sheets. Brush tops with butter. Score top of phyllo dough in diamond shape. Bake at 350 degrees for 50 to 60 minutes or until puffed and golden brown.
Yield: 9 to 12 servings.

Mrs. Larry Edmiston (Donna)

BREAKFAST SOUFFLE
"Great make-ahead breakfast"

1½ pounds bulk sausage
9 eggs, beaten
3 cups milk
1½ teaspoons dry mustard
1 teaspoon salt
3 slices bread, cut into ¼ inch cubes
1½ cups Cheddar cheese, shredded

Cook sausage over medium heat until done, stirring to crumble. Drain well on paper towels. Combine sausage and other ingredients; mixing well. Pour into well greased 13x9 inch baking dish. Refrigerate overnight. Remove from refrigerator 30 minutes before baking. Bake at 350 degrees for 1 hour.
Yield: 8 to 10 servings.

Nina Nabors

Similar recipe submitted by *Arazell R. Barnes*

BREAKFAST PIZZA

1   pound pork sausage
1   8 ounce package refrigerated
    crescent dinner rolls
4   ounces sharp Cheddar
    cheese, shredded
4   ounces mozzarella cheese,
    shredded

6   eggs, beaten
½   cup milk
¾   teaspoon dried whole
    oregano
⅛   teaspoon pepper

Cook sausage in a medium skillet until browned. Drain and set aside. Separate crescent rolls into triangles. Place triangles with points toward the center in a greased 12 inch pizza pan. Press bottom and side to form a crust. Seal perforations. Bake at 375 degrees for 5 minutes on lower oven rack. (Crust will be puffy when removed from oven.) Reduce temperature to 350 degrees. Spoon sausage over dough, cover with cheeses. Combine eggs, milk, oregano, and pepper. Pour this mixture over sausage. Bake at 350 degrees on lower rack for 30 to 35 minutes.
Yield: 6 to 8 servings.

Mrs. H.J. Hagan
Alexander City, Alabama

CHEESE SOUFFLE

5   sandwich bread slices or
    4 large white bread slices
¼   cup butter or margarine
¾   pound sharp cheese,
    shredded

4   whole large eggs
1   teaspoon salt
2½ cups whole milk, not skim
1   teaspoon Worcestershire
    sauce

Cut crust off bread, butter generously and cut into cubes. Place in bottom of 8 inch square pyrex dish. Sprinkle cheese over bread cubes. In separate bowl beat eggs and add salt. Add milk and Worcestershire sauce and stir to blend. Pour over bread and cheese, covering them completely. Cover and refrigerate overnight. Remove one hour before baking. Fluff with a fork and bake uncovered 45 minutes at 325 degrees in middle of oven. Serve immediately.
Yield: 8 servings.
Note: Good to serve for breakfast because it can be made ahead of time.

Mrs. Fred Hahn (Martha)

HAM AND BROCCOLI QUICHE

1   10 ounce package chopped broccoli, thawed and well drained
2   cups Swiss cheese, shredded
2 to 3 cups cooked ham, chopped
2   deep dish pie crusts, thawed
6   eggs
2   pints whipping cream
½   teaspoon salt

Mix broccoli, cheese, and ham. Put ½ mixture in each pie crust. Mix 3 eggs with 1 pint whipping cream, using a wire whisk. Add ¼ teaspoon salt to this mixture and pour over quiche. Repeat above with the three other eggs and whipping cream. Bake for 1 hour at 375 degrees.

Judy Elliott (Mrs. Joel)

Similar recipe submitted by *Beth Lumpkin (Mrs. Bobby)*

QUICK SPINACH QUICHE

3   eggs, beaten
1   cup half and half
¼   cup Parmesan cheese, grated
½   teaspoon salt
½   teaspoon pepper
¼   teaspoon nutmeg
½   cup sausage, cooked
1   10 ounce package frozen spinach, cooked or
1   bunch spinach, cooked and drained
1   cup Swiss cheese, shredded
1   9 inch pie shell

Beat eggs; add and mix together milk, Parmesan cheese and spices. Layer sausage, spinach, and Swiss cheese on bottom of pie crust. Pour egg mixture over layered ingredients. Bake at 350 degrees for 40 to 50 minutes or until knife inserted near center comes out clean.
Yield: 6 servings.

Rickey Hatcher

EGGS A LA GREGORY

1   loaf white bread, long loaf
10 ounces Cheddar cheese, shredded
8 to 9 eggs
1   12 ounce can evaporated milk
½   cup butter, melted
Pinch of salt

Grease or spray with non-stick coating spray a 13x9 inch glass dish. Layer white bread with crust trimmed off. Top with ½ of cheese. Put another layer of bread and remaining cheese. Blend eggs and evaporated milk. Pour on bread and cheese layers. Cover and refrigerate overnight. Before cooking, top with melted butter. Bake 30 minutes at 375 degrees.
Yield: 10 to 12 servings.
Note: May add bits of ham or cooked sausage.

Betty Barber

OLD FASHIONED MACARONI AND CHEESE

1	8 ounce package elbow macaroni	½	teaspoon salt
3	tablespoons butter	⅛	teaspoon white pepper
3	tablespoons flour	⅛	teaspoon paprika
2½	cups milk, warmed	2	cups longhorn Cheddar cheese, shredded

Cook macaroni as directed and drain. Meanwhile over low heat, blend butter with flour in saucepan and using whisk, add warmed milk gradually. Cook over medium heat, stirring constantly until creamy. Add salt, pepper and paprika. Add ⅔ cheese and stir until cheese is melted. Turn macaroni into a well greased 2 quart casserole. Pour sauce over macaroni and stir. Sprinkle remaining cheese over top. Bake 375 degrees uncovered for 30 minutes. Yield: 8 to 10 servings.

Mrs. Charles Killough (Dot)

MACARONI CHEESE SUPREME

1	8 ounce package elbow macaroni	1	pound sharp cheese, shredded (reserve ½ cup)
1	10¾ ounce cream of mushroom soup	1	cup mayonnaise
½	cup milk	½	cup bell pepper, chopped
1	medium onion, chopped	1	4 ounce jar pimento, chopped
1	4 ounce can mushrooms, sliced		Bread crumbs (optional)

Cook macaroni according to package directions. Mix all other ingredients while macaroni is cooking. When macaroni is tender, drain and·mix with other ingredients. Pour into large casserole dish, cover and cook at 350 degrees for 45 minutes. Remove from oven, sprinkle with remaining cheese and bread crumbs. (If casserole seems too dry add a little milk.) Return to oven, uncovered for about 10 minutes.

Mrs. Doris Spainhour

Similar recipe by *Mrs. Nina Nabors*

Salads
and
Dressings

EXOTIC CHICKEN SALAD

8 cups cooked chicken, coarsely chopped
1 pound red seedless grapes, chopped
2 12 ounce cans water chestnuts, drained and chopped
2 cups celery, finely chopped

3 cups pecans, chopped
3 cups mayonnaise
2 tablespoons lemon juice
1 tablespoon curry powder
2 tablespoons soy sauce
1 20 ounce can crushed pineapple

Blend mayonnaise, lemon juice, curry powder, and soy sauce. Mix with all other ingredients.

Mrs. Britt Parker (Jody)

LAYERED CHICKEN SALAD

"Add bread and this is a meal."

Salad:

3 cups chicken, cooked, chopped, and divided
2 cups lettuce, torn
1 cup cooked long-grain rice
1 10 ounce package frozen green peas, thawed
¼ cup fresh parsley, chopped

2 large tomatoes, seeded and chopped
1 cup cucumber, thinly sliced
1 small sweet red pepper, chopped
1 small green pepper, chopped
Red pepper rings

Layer 1½ cups chicken and lettuce in a 3 quart bowl. Combine rice, peas, and parsley; spoon evenly over lettuce. Layer tomatoes, cucumber, chopped red pepper, green pepper, and remaining 1½ cups of chicken.

Dressing:

1 cup mayonnaise
½ cup sour cream
½ cup raisins
½ cup onion, finely chopped
¼ cup sweet pickle relish

2 tablespoons milk
½ teaspoon celery seeds
½ teaspoon dillseeds
½ teaspoon dry mustard
½ teaspoon garlic salt

Combine all ingredients; stir well. Spoon evenly over top of salad, sealing to edge of bowl. Top with red pepper rings; cover and chill 8 hours. Toss before serving.
Yield: 8 servings.

Mrs. Larry Edmiston (Donna)

CHICKEN SALAD

2 envelopes unflavored gelatin
1 cup cold water
1 10¾ ounce can condensed chicken broth
1 cup mayonnaise
2 tablespoons lemon juice
1 teaspoon salt
1 teaspoon curry powder
⅛ teaspoon pepper

2½ cups chicken (or turkey), cooked and diced
½ cup celery, thinly sliced
¼ cup onion, finely chopped
¼ cup pitted ripe olives, chopped
¼ cup pimento, finely diced

Sprinkle gelatin on cold water; stir over low heat until gelatin dissolves (about 5 minutes). Remove from heat. Combine remaining ingredients; mix well. Stir in dissolved gelatin; mix thoroughly. Turn into 6 cup (or individual) mold. Chill until firm. Unmold on serving plate. Garnish with chicory and half-slices of canned cranberry sauce.
Yield: 6 to 8 servings.

Mrs. Nauburn Jones, Sr. (Margaret)

SAMPAN SALAD

1 17 ounce can cling peach slices, chilled and drained
2 cups cooked turkey or chicken, diced

1 3 ounce can chow mein noodles
½ cup celery, coarsely diced

Sampan Dressing
¾ cup mayonnaise
¼ cup parsley, minced
1 tablespoon lemon juice

¼ teaspoon salt
½ teaspoon soy sauce

Place peach slices, meat, noodles, and celery in a large bowl. Gently toss peach mixture with Sampan dressing. You might want to leave noodles out until ready to use, if you want crunchy noodles.
Note: May substitute rice for chow mein noodles.

Vivian Davis
Florence, Alabama

SHRIMP SALAD

1 16 ounce package of shrimp
   (cocktail size), cooked
   according to directions or
1 pound fresh shrimp, deveined,
   boiled, and chopped
1 to 1½ cups bell pepper,
   chopped

¼ to ½ cup olives, chopped
¼ to ½ cup pickle relish
Dash of lemon juice
Salt and pepper to taste
Mayonnaise (approximately
   3 tablespoons)

Mix all ingredients together and chill slightly before serving.
Yield: 4 servings.
Note: Can be served in a whole peeled tomato on a lettuce cup.

Mrs. W. J. Munroe (Rachel)

SHRIMP SALAD SUPREME

1 6 ounce package long grain
   and wild rice
1 cup chili sauce
2 tablespoons horseradish
1 tablespoon lemon juice
1 pound shrimp, cooked, peeled
   and cut in half

2 small avocados, peeled and
   diced
2 tablespoons parsley flakes
Spinach or lettuce

Cook rice according to package directions. Transfer to large bowl. Mix chili
sauce, horseradish and lemon juice in small bowl. Add shrimp and chili sauce
mixture to rice. Toss to mix well. Just before serving, fold in avocado and
parsley. Spoon onto bed of spinach or lettuce.
Yield: 6 servings.

Mrs. Dewayne Clark (Marion)

VERMICELLI SALAD

S
A
L
A
D
S

24 ounce package vermicelli
4 tablespoons salad oil
3 tablespoons lemon juice
1 tablespoon Ac'cent Flavor
   Enhancer
1 cup celery, chopped
1 cup pimento, chopped

1 4 ounce can ripe pitted
   medium olives, sliced
1 pint mayonnaise
Salt and pepper to taste
1 chopped green pepper
½ cup minced onion

Cook vermicelli until tender, but do not overcook. Drain. Put vermicelli in a large bowl. Add salad oil, lemon juice, and Accent and mix well with vermicelli. Cover tightly and refrigerate overnight. The next day, with two knives, chop vermicelli into smaller pieces then add remaining ingredients and toss together. Cover and return to refrigerator until ready to serve. This keeps for days (if you can keep it around that long) and makes lots!
Note: This is good served on a bed of lettuce with spinach soufflé and fresh french bread.

Holly H. Gilbert
Birmingham, Alabama

COMPANY POTATO SALAD
"Wonderful variation of old-fashioned potato salad."

4 pounds red potatoes, boiled
   in skins
½ cup celery, sliced
3 tablespoons onion, chopped
1 small green bell pepper, diced
1 apple, diced
3 eggs, boiled and diced
1 cup sweet pickle relish

1 2 ounce jar pimento
1 cup mayonnaise
¼ cup thousand island dressing
3 to 4 slices bacon, fried crisp
and diced
4 to 5 tablespoons hoop cheese,
shredded
Salt to taste

Boil potatoes until tender, but firm. Cool. Peel skins from potatoes and dice into 4 quart bowl. Add vegetables, apple, eggs, pickle relish, and pimentos. Mix mayonnaise, dressing, bacon, and cheese. Gently stir into potatoes. Salt to taste. Garnish with paprika. Refrigerate for 4 to 6 hours before serving.
Yield: 12 to 15 servings.

Mrs. Carl R. Reaves (Joyce)

CABBAGE AND POTATO SALAD

10 potatoes, boiled in jackets, peeled and sliced	3 green-peppers, in rings
1 head cabbage, shredded	6 boiled eggs, sliced
1 quart mayonnaise	Celery seed
3 onions, in rings	Paprika
	Salt and pepper to taste

Begin with layer of cabbage in a bowl. Add a layer of sliced potatoes, salt, pepper, and sprinkle with celery seed. Add onion and pepper rings. Add sliced eggs and spread mayonnaise over all. Start over and layer again. Refrigerate for 24 hours before serving.
Yield: 15 to 20 servings.

Mrs. Hollis Mann (Joy)

PENNSYLVANIA DUTCH POTATO SALAD

Sauce:

½ cup sugar	2 teaspoons yellow mustard
½ cup vinegar	1 generous teaspoon cornstarch
½ cup water	½ to ¾ tablespoon mayonnaise
1 egg	

Combine first five ingredients in medium saucepan. Stir well. Add cornstarch and bring to a full boil, stirring constantly. Remove from heat. Allow to cool. When cool add ½ to ¾ tablespoon mayonnaise until creamy.

Potato Mix:

4 to 5 medium boiled potatoes, cooked and cubed	½ cup onion, chopped
1 to ½ teaspoons celery seed	1 to 2 stalks of celery, chopped

Mix all ingredients. Gently toss potato mixture with sauce. Sprinkle with celery seed before serving.

Vicki Wirt Hultzapple
Chambersburg, Pennsylvania

HOT GERMAN POTATO SALAD

10 medium potatoes
6 slices bacon
¾ cup onion, chopped
2 teaspoons all-purpose flour
2 teaspoons sugar
2 teaspoons salt
1 teaspoon celery seed

1 dash pepper
¾ cup water
⅓ cup vinegar
1 package smoked sausage or bratwurst
2 teaspoons shortening

Peel potatoes and dice. Boil in salted water (½ teaspoon salt per 1 cup water) until tender. Drain. Fry bacon until crisp in large skillet. Remove bacon. In the same pan, cook and stir onion in bacon drippings until tender. Blend in flour, sugar, salt, celery seed, and pepper. Cook over low heat, stirring until mixture is bubbly. Remove from heat. Stir in water and vinegar. Heat to boiling, stirring constantly. Boil and stir for one minute. Crumble bacon and carefully stir bacon and mixture into potatoes. Heat 2 teaspoons shortening in skillet, then brown bratwurst or smoked sausage. Serve on top of potato salad.

Hilda Fannin
Similar recipe submitted by *Jane B. Davis*
Tuscaloosa, Alabama

CORNBREAD SALAD
"Such a tasty dish."

1 8 ounce box quick cornbread mix
1 bell pepper, chopped
1 medium onion, chopped
1 16 ounce can pinto beans

1 cup sweet pickles, chopped
1 12 ounce package bacon, fried and crumbled
2 medium tomatoes, chopped

Cook cornbread according to package directions. Crumble in bottom of 9x13 dish. Layer other ingredients as listed.

Topping:
1 cup mayonnaise
½ cup sweet pickle juice

1 tablespoon sugar

Mix ingredients together and pour over top of cornbread mixture.

Mrs. William Casaday

HARVEST RICE

2 cups cooked rice
2 tablespoons onion, finely chopped
1 tablespoon vinegar
2 tablespoons salad oil
¾ teaspoon curry powder

2 teaspoons salt
1 10 ounce package frozen green peas, cooked, drained, chilled
1 cup celery, chopped
¾ cup mayonnaise

In large bowl, mix hot rice, onion, vinegar, salad oil, curry powder, and salt. Chill at least 3 hours or overnight. Just before serving, toss with peas, celery and mayonnaise.
Note: Good stuffed in a tomato or on a lettuce leaf.

Mrs. Fred Hahn (Martha)

COLD RICE SALAD

4 cups chicken stock
2 cups long grain rice
3 6 jounce jars marinated artichoke hearts
½ cup green onions, chopped
1 2¼ ounce can black olives, chopped

1 cup celery, diced
½ cup parsley, chopped
1 teaspoon curry powder
2 cups mayonnaise
Salt to taste
Pepper to taste

Bring chicken stock to boil. Add rice and cook 20 minutes or until done. Cool. Drain artichokes, reserving marinade, and chop. Add artichokes, green onions, olives, celery, and parsley to rice. Combine marinade with remaining ingredients. Toss with rice mixture and refrigerate.
Yield: 12 servings.

Valerie B. McWilliams

SPECIAL SPINACH SALAD

2 10 ounce packages frozen chopped spinach, cooked and drained
½ cup celery, finely chopped
½ cup onion, finely chopped
1 cup sharp pasteurized processed cheese

2 eggs, hard-boiled and chopped or sliced
½ teaspoon hot pepper sauce
1½ teaspoons vinegar
½ teaspoon salt
1¼ cups mayonnaise

Mix all ingredients together; chill. Serve with horseradish if desired.

Ruby Richardson

MARINATED ASPARAGUS

1   15 ounce can green
    asparagus, drained
½   cup cider vinegar
½   cup sugar
½   teaspoon salt

1   teaspoon pepper
½   lemon, juiced
3   teaspoons olive oil
3   teaspoons paprika

Mix ingredients and pour over drained asparagus. Refrigerate overnight.
Serve chilled.
Yield: 4 servings.

Gayle McMillan

VEGETABLE SALAD

1   14 ounce can artichoke
     hearts, drained and quartered
1½ cups carrots, sliced
2   cups cauliflower florets
½   cup purple onion, chopped
½   cup celery, chopped

½   cup Italian salad dressing
½   cup mayonnaise
2   tablespoons chili sauce
1   tablespoon lemon juice
1   teaspoon dried whole
    dillweed

Combine first 6 ingredients. Toss well; cover and chill 2 or more hours. Drain
vegetables. Combine remaining ingredients; pour over vegetables and toss
gently. Serve on lettuce leaves.
Variations: May add broccoli; may top with asparagus.

Mrs. Jeanne R. McKinney

PARMESAN VEGETABLE SALAD

½   head of lettuce, coarsely
    shredded
1   cup celery, chopped
1   cup purple onion, chopped
1   17 ounce can small English
    peas, drained

1   cup green pepper, chopped
1½ cups mayonnaise
1½ teaspoons sugar
Grated Parmesan cheese
4 to 5 slices bacon, cooked and
     crumbled

Layer vegetables in order listed in a 2-quart bowl; spread mayonnaise evenly
over top. Sprinkle salad with remaining ingredients in the order listed. Cover
tightly and chill 8 hours. Can be chilled shorter length of time but flavor
is not as good.
Yield: 4 to 6 servings.

Wanda Embry

BROCCOLI AND RAISIN SALAD

"This uncommon mixture of ingredients will delight both men and women."

1 large bunch broccoli without stems, cut into florets	12 slices bacon, fried and crumbled
1 cup raisins	1 medium red onion, chopped

Mix ingredients and keep refrigerated until ready to serve.

Dressing:

1 cup mayonnaise	¼ cup sugar
2 tablespoons white vinegar	

Mix ingredients together, stir well. Pour over broccoli mixture. Toss together to make salad when ready to serve.

Mrs. Jack Edmiston (Candy)

Variation: Add washed and separated head of cauliflower to salad mixture.

Vickie Wirt Hultzapple
Chambersburg, Pennsylvania

Variation: Add 8 ounces shredded Swiss cheese to salad mixture.

Mrs. Paul Bingham, Jr. (Sally)
Athens, Georgia

Variation: Substitute 1 8 ounce bottle coleslaw dressing for dressing

1 cup nuts	1 cup water chestnuts, chopped

Jody Parker

ITALIAN SALAD

"A meal within itself."

1 head broccoli	1 cup Cheddar cheese, shredded
1 head cauliflower	
2 small zucchini	1 6 ounce can small ripe pitted olives
1 large onion	
2 5 ounce sticks pepperoni	1 8 ounce bottle Italian dressing

Cut up broccoli, cauliflower, zucchini, onion, and pepperoni and put in large bowl. Add cheese, olives, and dressing. Stir well so that all of the ingredients are coated with the dressing. Refrigerate several hours before serving. Yield: 10 to 12 servings.

Mrs. Harvey Hendrix (Laura)

NEAPOLITAN SALAD

3 8 ounce packages cream cheese
2 tablespoons milk
1 cup mayonnaise
1 cup celery, minced
1 cup bell pepper, minced
1 tablespoon onion, minced
1 2 ounce jar pimento, chopped
½ teaspoon paprika

1 tablespoon Worcestershire sauce
Cayenne pepper to taste
Salt to taste
Pepper to taste
1 envelope gelatin, unflavored
¾ cup cold water
1 10¾ ounce can tomato soup

Moisten cream cheese with milk. Add mayonnaise and mix well. Add celery, bell pepper, onion, pimento, and seasonings. Dissolve gelatin in ¾ cup cold water. Heat tomato soup to boiling point, add gelatin. Stir well. Cool . Add cream cheese mixture. Pour into 2 six cup molds. Chill before serving.

Mrs. James N. Montgomery (Ann)

48 HOUR SLAW
"A great dish to prepare ahead to serve a crowd!"

1 medium head of cabbage, shredded

2 medium onions, thinly sliced
¾ cup sugar

Alternate layers of cabbage and onions in a large bowl. Cover with sugar and jiggle, do not stir.

Dressing:
1 teaspoon celery seed
1 teaspoon prepared mustard
1 teaspoon sugar

½ teaspoon salt
1 cup vinegar
1 cup salad oil

Mix first 5 ingredients in a pan and bring to a boil. Add the oil and boil again. Pour boiling hot over cabbage mixture. Refrigerate for at least 24 hours, up to 48 hours. Do not stir until ready to serve. Drain before serving. Yield: 6 servings.

Alicia W. Rogers (Mrs. Phillip)

FREEZER SLAW

1	large cabbage, shredded	2	cups sugar
½	medium bell pepper, chopped (optional)	1	teaspoon dry mustard
		½	cup water
5	large carrots, chopped	1	cup cider vinegar
1	teaspoon salt	1	teaspoon celery seed

Cut cabbage in half and set in cold water with carrots to crisp for 1 hour. Shred cabbage, green peppers, and carrots. Sprinkle with salt and let stand for 30 minutes. Drain off accumulated water. Combine sugar, mustard, water, vinegar, and celery seed in medium saucepan and bring to boil for 3 minutes stirring constantly (will boil over easily). Cool 5 minutes. Pour over cabbage mixture and mix well. May eat now or put into freezer containers and freeze. Thaw in refrigerator.
Yield: 10 servings.

Mrs. Ginny Sims

GREAT SLAW

"Easily made for any size crowd"

1	medium head cabbage, shredded	¼	cup red wine vinegar
		¼	cup sugar
1	cup mayonnaise	1	tablespoon celery seeds

Mix all ingredients together, stir well. Place in tight container, and refrigerate until ready to use. Will keep for several days.
Yield: 6 servings.

Mrs. Bill Perry (Linda)

ENGLISH PEA SALAD

1	cup Cheddar cheese, shredded	1	cup lettuce, chopped
1	8 ounce can sliced water chestnuts	1	cup mayonnaise based salad dressing
1	cup green onions, chopped	1	10 ounce box frozen English peas, thawed and placed on a
1	cup celery, sliced		paper towel to absorb water

Mix together all ingredients. You may serve this on lettuce leaves in a bowl.

Judy Griffin

156

FRUIT SALAD

1	large can pineapple chunks	1	small tub cool whip
1	large can fruit cocktail	1	can cherry pie filling
1	can condensed milk		

Drain and mix pineapple chunks and fruit cocktail. Stir in condensed milk and cool whip. Fold in cherry pie filling. Refrigerate for 2 hours or overnight.

Pat King
Pinchard, Alabama

FRUIT COMBO

1	15¼ ounce can pineapple chunks, packed in juice	1	cup strawberries, cut in halves
3	cups cantaloupe or honeydew melon balls	¼	cup orange marmalade
		2	tablespoons orange liqueur

Drain pineapple chunks, reserve juice. In a mixing bowl combine pineapple, melon balls and strawberries. Combine the reserved juice, marmalade, and liqueur. Pour over the fruit. Stir gently. Chill 1 to 2 hours, stirring occasionally.
Yield: 6 servings.

Mrs. Matt Mihelic (Ree)

MARINATED FRUIT SALAD

10 cups fresh fruit in season,
   sliced and cubed
½ cup sugar
1 cup water
½ teaspoon lemon juice

2 cinnamon sticks
½ teaspoon whole cloves
½ teaspoon whole allspice
½ cup Kirsch liqueur

In a small saucepan; combine sugar, water, lemon juice and cinnamon sticks. Then tie cloves and all spice in cheese cloth and add to mixture. Bring to a boil over medium heat. Lower heat, cover and simmer 5 minutes remove heat and cool. Remove cinnamon and spices, stir in Kirsch. Pour mixture over fruit and cover and refrigerate several hours or over night.
Yield: 12 servings.

Linda D. Taconis
Charlotte, North Carolina

CONGEALED CORNED BEEF SALAD

1 can jelled beef consommé
Juice of ½ lemon
1 3 ounce box lemon flavored
   gelatin
1 12 ounce can corned beef,
   crumbled
1 cup mayonnaise

1 cup celery, diced
1 small onion, chopped
2 eggs, hard boiled
1 tablespoon bell pepper,
   chopped
1 teaspoon Worcestershire
   sauce

Heat consommé and lemon juice to boil. Add gelatin. Stir well. Cool. Add other ingredients. Mix well. Pour into molds. Cover with plastic wrap and congeal.

Mrs. James N. Montgomery (Ann)

TANGY CANTELOUPE SALAD

1 medium sized canteloupe, cut
   in bite sized pieces
1 16 ounce can pineapple
   chunks, drained
1 12 ounce can fruit cocktail,
   juice included

4 ripe bananas, sliced
¾ cup orange flavored breakfast
   drink mix, dry

Combine all fruits. Sprinkle fruit drink mix over them, stir lightly and chill.

Mrs. Frank Spears (Sarah)
Dothan, Alabama

HOLIDAY AMBROSIA

"This family favorite is requested every Christmas."

12 oranges
4 pink grapefruits
½ cup nuts, chopped

1 3½ ounces can flaked coconut
½ to 1 cup confectioners sugar

Peel oranges and grapefruit. Remove seeds and membranes. Place in large bowl and add nuts and coconut. Sweeten with confectioners sugar to taste. Mix well. Chill before serving.
Note: May be garnished with maraschino cherries. Keeps well for several days in refrigerator.

Mrs. Carl Reaves (Joyce)

AB'S FROZEN FRUIT SALAD

1 cup mayonnaise
1 8 ounce package cream cheese, softened
2 tablespoons confectioners sugar
1 cup pineapple tidbits, drained

1 cup fruit cocktail, drained
½ cup maraschino cherries, chopped
1 cup miniature marshmallows
1 cup frozen whipped non-dairy topping

Mix mayonnaise and cream cheese. Add confectioners sugar, fruits, and marshmallows; mix well. Fold in whipped topping. Spoon into lightly greased 9x13 inch dish, cover and freeze. Cut in squares and serve on lettuce leaves. Top with a half maraschino cherry.
Yield: 10 to 12 servings.

Arazell R. Barnes
Oklahoma City, Oklahoma

Save time chopping raisins, marshmallows, and dates by using scissors.

MANDARIN ORANGE SALAD

Salad:
¼ cup sugar
¼ cup almonds, chopped and slivered
1 cup celery, diced
2 green onions and tops, sliced
½ to 1 head Romaine lettuce, shredded
1 11 ounce can mandarin oranges, drained

In small saucepan, melt sugar over medium heat, stirring constantly. Add almonds and stir until coated, about 5 minutes. Turn out onto a plate. Cool, break into small pieces and reserve. Combine celery, onions, and lettuce in a large bowl. Add oranges and reserved almonds; toss.

Dressing:
¼ cup vegetable oil
½ teaspoon salt
½ teaspoon hot sauce
2 tablespoons vinegar
2 tablespoons sugar

Combine ingredients and toss with salad.
Yield: 6 servings.
Note: Also looks pretty arranged on separate salad plates instead of tossing.

Mrs. Tom West (Margaret)
Similar recipe submitted by *Mrs. Marion Molliston*

CATRIONA'S CELESTIAL SALAD

Salad:
1 11 ounce can mandarin oranges, drained
1 cup green seedless grapes
¼ cup green onions, chopped
½ cup toasted almonds, sliced
1 head lettuce, cut up or fresh spinach

Combine salad ingredients.

Dressing:
⅔ cup salad oil
⅓ cup orange juice
¼ cup sugar
1 dash salt
3 tablespoons vinegar
1 teaspoon celery seed
2 tablespoons parsley, chopped
1 dash dry mustard

Combine ingredients and pour over salad. Refrigerate overnight.

Connie B. Barnes

CITRUS BOWL SALAD

2 11 ounce can mandarin
   oranges, drained
2 8¼ ounce cans crushed
   pineapple, drained
1 16 ounce carton cottage
   cheese

1 9 ounce carton frozen
   whipped non-dairy topping
½ cup pecans, chopped
1 6 ounce package sugar-free
   orange gelatin

Combine first five ingredients in a bowl and mix well. Sprinkle dry gelatin over this and mix well. Let stand overnight in refrigerator.
Note: You could reserve some mandarin oranges to place on top.

"Tee" J. Albright
Plant City, Florida

RED RASPBERRY SALAD

16 large marshmallows
1   cup milk
1   8 ounce package cream
    cheese
1   6 ounce package lemon
    gelatin

2   cups hot water
1   20 ounce can crushed
    pineapple
½   cup pecans, chopped
1   3 ounce envelope whipped
    topping mix

Dissolve marshmallows in one cup hot milk. Cream together cream cheese, lemon gelatin; add hot water. Stir until dissolved and add to marshmallow mixture. When cooled, add pineapple including juice, pecans, and whipped topping mix. Place in 9x13 inch baking dish. Refrigerate until firm. Then add topping.

Topping:
2½ cups hot water
2   6 ounce packages raspberry
    gelatin

2   10 ounce packages frozen red
    raspberries

Mix hot water and gelatin until gelatin dissolves. Then add raspberries. Put on first layer and refrigerate.

Jane B. Davis
Tuscaloosa, Alabama

CREAMY FROZEN FRUIT SALAD

1   20 ounce can fruit cocktail
1   cup liquid drained from
    cocktail
1   3 ounce package strawberry
    gelatin
1   8 ounce package cream
    cheese, softened
⅓   cup mayonnaise

1   cup pecan halves
20 maraschino cherries,
    quartered
2   cups small marshmallows
1   pint whipping cream or
    1 12 ounce container frozen
    whipped non-dairy topping

Drain cocktail, measure syrup and add water to make 1 cup. Bring liquid to boil and add to gelatin. Chill until syrupy. Beat softened cream cheese and mayonnaise until smooth. Fold in remaining ingredients. Freeze and use as desired.
Note: Absolutely must be served frozen for the best product.

Lera Jenkins

STRAWBERRY PRETZEL SALAD

"It's a salad, but good enough to be a dessert."

Crust:
1½ cups crushed pretzels
3   tablespoons sugar

½   cup margarine

Mix all ingredients and press into a 13x9x2 glass dish. Bake 10 or 15 minutes at 350 degrees. Cool.

Middle Layer:
1   8 ounce package cream
    cheese

1   12 ounce carton frozen
    whipped non-dairy topping
⅔   cup sugar

Whip together until smooth and spread on pretzel layer.

Topping:
2   3 ounce packages of
    strawberry gelatin
2   cups hot water

2   10 ounce cartons sliced,
    frozen strawberries

Mix together and chill until slightly set. Pour over second layer and chill until firmly set.

JoAnn Mullins

APRICOT SALAD

1   6 ounce package apricot
    gelatin
⅔   cup boiling water
1   8 ounce package cream
    cheese, softened
1   15¼ ounce can crushed
    pineapple, undrained

2   7¾ ounce jars apricot baby
    food
1   8 ounce carton frozen
    whipped non-dairy topping,
    thawed
Lettuce

Dissolve gelatin in boiling water, cool and set aside. Beat cream cheese until smooth. Gradually add gelatin, beating well. Stir in pineapple and baby food. Fold in whipped topping. Pour into 12x8x2 inch dish; cover and chill until firm. To serve, cut into squares and place on lettuce.

Kathryn Rogers
Stone Mountain, Georgia

FROSTED CRANBERRY SALAD

1   15½ ounce can crushed
    pineapple
2   3 ounce packages lemon
    gelatin
1   7 ounce bottle ginger ale
1   1 pound can jellied cranberry
    sauce

1   2 ounce package whipped
    topping mix
1   8 ounce package cream
    cheese, softened
½   cup pecans, chopped

Drain pineapple, reserving syrup. Add water to make 1 cup. Heat to boil. Dissolve gelatin in hot liquid, and let cool. Stir in ginger ale. Chill until partly set. Add pineapple and cranberry sauce to gelatin mixture. Blend well. Pour into a 9x9x2 inch pan. Chill until firm. Prepare topping according to package directions. Blend in cream cheese. Spread over gelatin. Toast nuts in 1 tablespoon butter at 350 degrees for 10 minutes. Sprinkle nuts over top of salad. Chill.
Yield: 8 to 10 servings.

Mrs. J. Milton Coxwell, Jr. (Kathi)
Monroeville, Alabama

CRANBERRY RELISH MOLD

2 3 ounce packages cherry
   gelatin
1 teaspoon unflavored gelatin
2 cups boiling water
1 16 ounce can whole berry
   cranberry sauce

1 7 ounce can crushed
   pineapple, drained
¼ cup chopped celery
Fresh cranberries for garnish,
   (optional)
Mayonnaise

Dissolve cherry and unflavored gelatins completely in boiling water. Let cool slightly, then stir in cranberry sauce, drained pineapple and celery. Pour into a glass serving bowl or 6 cup mold that first has been rinsed under cold water. Chill gelatin until firm. At serving time, dip mold briefly in a pan of hot water to loosen and unmold onto chilled plates. Garnish with fresh cranberries, if desired. Top each portion with a small dollop of mayonnaise. Yield: 8 to 10 servings.

Mrs. Rex Killough (Sharon)

CHERRY SALAD

1 6 ounce box cherry flavored
   gelatin
1 cup hot water
1 cup cold water
1 8¼ ounce can crushed
   pineapple, drained

1 21 ounce can cherry pie filling
1 8 ounce package cream
   cheese, softened
1 cup sour cream
½ cup sugar
½ cup pecans, chopped

Mix the flavored gelatin dessert with the hot water in a 9x12 inch glass dish. Dissolve well. Stir in cold water. Add the drained pineapple and cherry pie filling. Congeal for one hour. In a mixing bowl, combine softened cream cheese, sour cream and sugar. Mix well. Spoon and spread on top of congealed mixture. Sprinkle with chopped pecans. Refrigerate until ready to serve.
Yield: 8 servings.
Note: May substitute whipped non-dairy topping for cream cheese mixture. Also can substitute cherry gelatin and pie filling with other flavorings as blueberry or blackberry.

Mrs. Bill (Nancy) Hopewell

ORANGE CHEDDAR SALAD

1   20 ounce can crushed pineapple, undrained
1   6 ounce package orange gelatin
1   cup mayonnaise
1   cup sharp cheese or New York sharp cheese, shredded
1   12 ounce can evaporated milk

Heat pineapple in a saucepan over medium heat to boiling. Stir in gelatin until dissolved. Remove from heat and cool until mixture is warm. Stir in mayonnaise and cheese until mixed. Stir in evaporated milk until blended. Pour mixture into shallow 2 quart casserole. Chill until firm.

Mary Frances Peeples

GREEN GOLD SALAD

1   3 ounce package lime gelatin
1   cup boiling water
1   cup crushed pineapple
2   cups miniature marshmallows
1   cup sharp Cheddar cheese, shredded
1   cup chopped nuts
½   pint whipping cream

Add gelatin to water, slightly congeal, whip until fluffy. Add other ingredients except cream. Whip cream and fold into mixture. Mold as desired. Chill before serving.

Mary Virginia Avery

CONGEALED ASPARAGUS SALAD

1   cup water
½   cup vinegar
¾   cup sugar
½   teaspoon salt
½   cup pecans, chopped
¼   cup spring onions, chopped
2   envelopes unflavored gelatin
1   10½ ounce can chopped asparagus spears
Juice of ½ lemon
½   cup water chestnuts, chopped
1   4 ounce jar chopped pimento

Bring to a boil the first six ingredients. Add enough water to the juice from the asparagus to make ½ cup and dissolve the gelatin in this liquid. Mix this with the hot ingredients and pour over the asparagus. Let cool. Add the remaining ingredients. Stir well. Refrigerate 3 hours.
Yield: 10 small molds or 9x9 glass baking dish.

Mrs. J.B. Boykin (Evelyn)

LIME SALAD

1 6 ounce package of lime gelatin	1 8¼ ounce can crushed pineapple, drained
2¾ cups hot water	¾ cup nuts, chopped
1 8 ounce package of cream cheese, softened	¾ cup apple, chopped
	¾ cup celery, chopped

Dissolve gelatin in hot water, add cream cheese. Stir until well blended. When gelatin is partially congealed, add remaining ingredients. Chill until firm. (2 hours)

Mrs. James C. Rogers (Marian)

JERRY'S COLE SLAW AND SAUCE

5 heaping tablespoons mayonnaise	2 tablespoons hot pepper sauce
2 tablespoons mustard	1 tablespoon garlic salt
2 tablespoons olive oil	Juice of one lemon
2 tablespoons catsup	Black pepper as desired
2 tablespoons Lea and Perrins steak sauce	

Blend all sauce ingredients together.

½ head of cabbage, chopped	½ cup white onion, chopped
½ cup red onion, chopped	½ cup bell pepper, chopped

Combine cabbage, onions, and bell pepper. Add cole slaw sauce if desired. Mix well and serve.

Mrs. Jerry Woodard

AUNT JIMMIE'S SLAW DRESSING

¾ cup sugar	1 teaspoon Worcestershire sauce
½ cup water	
1 12 ounce bottle chili sauce	½ large onion, chopped
¾ cup oil	Juice of ½ lemon
¾ cup mayonnaise	Onion powder, generous sprinkle
1 tablespoon tarragon vinegar	Paprika, generous sprinkle

Bring sugar and water to boil. Cool. Add all other ingredients and put in blender. Store in refrigerator.

Mrs. Pearino Gaither (Mary)

ALMOST JOHN'S SLAW DRESSING

1 cup sugar	1 tablespoon prepared mustard
2 cups mayonnaise	1 teaspoon Lea & Perrins
½ cup ketchup	Sauce
½ cup white vinegar	½ teaspoon salt

Mix until sugar dissolves. Store covered in the refrigerator.
Yield: 1 quart.

Andrea Montgomery
Similar recipe submitted by *Hyland Camp (Mrs. Jeffrey)*

DAVID'S FAVORITE 1000 ISLAND DRESSING
"A rich, creamy dressing."

1 cup salad dressing	1 teaspoon onion, cut fine
1 or 2 boiled eggs, chopped	2 tablespoons tomato catsup
½ cup sweet pickles, chopped	Salt to taste

Mix all ingredients. Cover and chill. Serve over tossed green salad.
Yield: 6 servings.
Note: Chili sauce may be substituted for catsup.

Mrs. Janie Cravens

SUNNY HONEY DRESSING FOR FRUIT

4 ounces honey	1 teaspoon paprika
2 tablespoons vinegar	1 teaspoon celery seed
1 teaspoon salt	1 cup vegetable oil
1 teaspoon dry mustard	

Mix all ingredients except oil in mixing bowl. Mix with electric mixer at medium speed. Very slowly, add the oil. The mixture will thicken to a consistency like mayonnaise. Store indefinitely in covered jar in refrigerator. Serve on fresh fruit or well-drained canned fruit.

Mrs. W. A. Davis (Mona)
Variation: Substitute ½ cup sugar for honey.

Catherine C. Thomson

FRIPP ISLAND DRESSING

1   cup mayonnaise
4   teaspoons prepared mustard
3 or 4 teaspoons sugar

1¼ teaspoons salt
1   small onion, minced

Mix ingredients well. Pour into covered jar. Keep in refrigerator.
Note: Keeps well for long period of time.

Mrs. Bailey Dixon (Gail)
Clinton, South Carolina

HOT BACON DRESSING FOR SPINACH SALAD

12 slices bacon
6   tablespoons cider vinegar
1   tablespoon Worcestershire
    sauce
Salt and pepper to taste

Bacon, cooked and crumbled
Bean sprouts, chilled
2   eggs, hard-boiled and
    chopped

Cook bacon until crisp. Drain and cool. Add vinegar, Worcestershire, salt, and pepper to bacon drippings. Bring to a boil and boil 1 minute. Remove and serve, while hot, over fresh, chilled spinach leaves. Garnish with crumbled bacon, chilled bean sprouts, and 2 chopped hard boiled eggs. Yield: 4 to 6 servings.

Mrs. Mike Walker (Charlene)

NEW PERRY HOTEL SALAD DRESSING

2   cups sugar
2   tablespoons onion, grated
3   tablespoons salt
2   tablespoons Worcestershire
    sauce

1   cup catsup
2   cups vegetable oil
2   cups celery, minced
1½ cups vinegar

Mix all ingredients together. Cover and refrigerate. Keeps indefinitely.

Valerie B. McWilliams

Sauces
and
Soups

MAYONNAISE BBQ SAUCE
"So easy and so tasty."

6	tablespoons mayonnaise	3	tablespoons lemon juice
1	tablespoon black pepper	3	tablespoons vinegar
1	tablespoon salt	2	tablespoons sugar

Mix all ingredients. Use for basting chicken on an open grill. When using on chicken in oven, place chicken on a broiler pan, turn and baste frequently for about 45 minutes to 1 hour in a 375 degree oven.
Yield: ½ cup of sauce.

Mrs. Frankie Newman

BROWN SAUCE

½	cup vinegar	1	tablespoon salt
¼	cup butter	¼	teaspoon pepper
1	tablespoon catsup	½	teaspoon dry mustard
1	teaspoon brown sugar		
2	tablespoons Worcestershire sauce		

Mix all ingredients in saucepan, stir until butter melts. Simmer 15 or 20 minutes, uncovered, until sauce thickens. (Very good for any barbecue when you do not want a catsup based sauce.) Makes approximately 1 cup of sauce.
Note: Makes a good basic brown sauce.

Mrs. John W. Bryant (Mary Carson)

Freeze leftover gravy in ice cube trays. Label and store in a plastic freezer bag.

ITALIAN MEAT SAUCE (for Spaghetti)

1	cup onion, chopped	2	teaspoons salt
1½	pounds lean ground chuck	½	teaspoon monosodium
2	cloves of garlic, chopped		glutamate
2	1 pound 12 ounce cans	3	teaspoons dried oregano,
	tomatoes		crushed
1	6 ounce can tomato paste	¼	teaspoon dried thyme,
6	ounces water		crushed
2	stalks celery, finely chopped	1	bay leaf

Put all ingredients in crock pot. Stir thoroughly. Cover and cook on medium heat for 6 to 8 hours or low 10 to 16 hours.

Mary Catherine Harris

SAUCE FOR LAMB ROAST

"Lamb roast is not complete without this sauce."

2	16 ounce cans of peeled, whole tomatoes	2	stalks celery, chopped
		1	lemon, thinly sliced
1	cup vinegar		Dash of Worcestershire sauce
2	cups sugar		
1	medium onion, finely chopped		

Combine all ingredients in 2 quart saucepan and bring to a boil. Lower heat and simmer for 1 hour or until tomatoes fall to pieces. Stir occasionally. Serve hot over lamb.

Mrs. Mike Walker (Charlene)

WHITE SAUCE FOR GRILLED POULTRY

1	cup mayonnaise	Salt to taste
1	tablespoon white vinegar	Pepper to taste
1	tablespoon concentrated lemon juice	

Combine ingredients. Mixture will be soupy. Baste poultry occasionally while grilling. May also be used as a dipping sauce.
Yield: approximately 1 cup.
Note: May be doubled. Will keep in the refrigerator for several weeks.

Mr. Tommy Burch
Baton Rouge, Louisiana

DANDY! MINT SAUCE

1 cup marshmallow creme
½ cup mint jelly, with leaves

Combine ingredients, mix well and store in refrigerator. Serve over ice cream, chocolate wafers, or brownies.

Betty Lou Camp

CHOCOLATE SAUCE

½	cup margarine	4	squares semi-sweet chocolate
2	cups sugar	18	large marshmallows
¼	teaspoon cream of tartar	¼	teaspoon salt
1	5 ounce can evaporated milk	Nuts as desired	

Melt margarine and sugar in double boiler. Stir in remaining ingredients. Heat until chocolate and marshmallows are melted. May be served hot or cold.
Yield: approximately 4 cups.
Note: Keeps well in refrigerator.

Susan Reeves
Beaumont, Texas

ALMOND SAUCE

"Terrific topping for angel food cake."

½	cup butter	¼	cup water
1	cup sugar	2	teaspoons almond extract

Mix all ingredients in a small saucepan. Heat until sugar is smooth. Pour over angel food cake.
Yield: About 2 cups.

Susan Reeves
Beaumont, Texas

BEEF STEW WITH ALE

4	pounds top or bottom round of beef, cut into 1½ inch cubes	1	13¾ ounce can beef broth
½	cup all-purpose flour	1	cup ale or beer
⅓	cup olive oil	2	bay leaves
3	medium yellow onions, coarsely chopped	1	teaspoon dried thyme leaves
3	large garlic cloves, peeled and chopped	½	teaspoon salt
1	6 ounce can tomato paste	1	10 ounce package frozen green peas
		1	12 ounce bag frozen baby carrots

Toss beef in flour until evenly coated. In a large heavy Dutch oven, over medium high heat, heat 2 tablespoons oil until very hot. Add a few pieces of meat and cook until well browned on all sides. Remove browned pieces with a slotted spoon, and set aside. Continue with remaining beef, adding more oil to the Dutch oven if necessary. Add the onions and garlic to the Dutch oven and cook, stirring frequently, until soft but not browned. Stir in tomato paste and cook, stirring, one minute. Add beef broth, ale or beer, bay leaves, thyme leaves, and salt. Return the beef to the pan. Heat to boiling, over high heat. Reduce heat to low, partially cover and simmer stew slowly for about 1½ hours or until meat is tender when pierced by a fork (See note). Add peas and carrots and cook 10 minutes or until vegetables are tender-crisp.

Note: Stew can be made ahead up to this point; cool and refrigerate up to 2 days. Before serving, heat to boiling, add frozen vegetables and proceed as above.

Yield: 8 servings.

Mrs. Larry Edmiston (Donna)

Add one or two tablespoons of vinegar to beef stews to tenderize the meat.

5 HOUR STEW

2	pounds stew meat	2	tablespoons sugar
2	cups celery, sliced	1	teaspoon salt
2	cups carrots, sliced	1	teaspoon pepper
4 to 5 onions, sliced		1	slice bread, crumbled
6	potatoes, sliced	1	24 ounce can cocktail
2	tablespoons all-purpose flour		vegetable juice

Put in a large Dutch oven in order listed. Cook covered at 250 degrees for 5 hours. Do not bother.
Yield: 16 servings.
Note: Great to put in the oven on Sunday morning.

Mrs. Andrea Montgomery

FRENCH STEW

"Easy enough, yet with a gourmet touch."

3	pounds stew meat	1	cup white wine (optional)
3	large carrots, sliced	¼	cup tapioca
1	8½ ounce can onion, drained	1	tablespoon dark brown sugar
1	16 ounce can tomatoes	1	bay leaf
1	16 ounce can small peas, drained	½	cup fine dry bread crumbs
1	10¾ ounce can beef consommé	1	tablespoon salt
		¼	teaspoon pepper
1	16 ounce can whole green beans, drained		

Combine all ingredients and bake in covered large pot 6 to 8 hours at 250 degrees or in large crock pot for 8 to 10 hours on low. Serve over wild rice.
Yield: 12 servings.

Sue Wright Nicholls
Also submitted by *Susan Nicholls Reeves*, Beaumont, Texas

MEAT BALL CHOWDER
"Hot and hearty."

2	pounds lean ground beef	3	onions, cut in eighths
2	teaspoons salt	6	carrots, sliced
⅛	teaspoon pepper	3	cups celery, sliced
2	eggs, slightly beaten	4	potatoes, diced
⅓	cup fine cracker crumbs	¼	cup long grain rice
2	teaspoons milk	1	tablespoon sugar
3	tablespoons all-purpose flour	2	teaspoons salt
1	tablespoon salad oil	2	bay leaves
6	cups tomato juice	¾	teaspoon marjoram
6	cups water	1	12 ounce can Mexicorn
6	beef bouillon cubes		

Combine meat, salt, pepper, eggs, cracker crumbs, and milk. Mix thoroughly. Form into balls about the size of a walnut. Dip in flour. Heat oil in 8 to 10 quart soup pot. Lightly brown meat balls on all sides. Add remaining ingredients (except add corn last 10 minutes of cooking). Bring to a boil. Cover. Reduce heat and cook at a slow boil for 1½ to 2 hours. Serve in big soup plates.
Yield: 6 to 7 quarts.

Mrs. Charles Killough (Dot)

VERY SPECIAL CHILI

1½ to 2 pounds ground beef		1½	tablespoons chili powder
1	6 ounce can of sliced mushrooms	½	teaspoon crushed red pepper
1	medium onion, chopped	1	teaspoon sage
4	8 ounce cans tomato sauce	1	teaspoon oregano, ground
1	10¾ ounce can mushroom soup	1½	teaspoons black pepper
1	package dried onion soup	1	teaspoon allspice
2	15 ounce cans kidney beans, drained	1	teaspoon onion powder
		¼	cup soy sauce
		¼	cup teriyaki sauce

Brown beef with onions and mushrooms, drain. Add rest of ingredients and simmer 45 minutes.

Janis McCardle

S
O
U
P
S

RICKEY'S CHILI

2 pounds ground beef	1 tablespoon Worcestershire
1 medium onion, chopped	sauce
2 cloves fresh garlic, chopped	2 or 3 drops hot pepper sauce
1 28 ounce can whole	Salt to taste
tomatoes, chopped, reserve	Pepper to taste
juice	Chili powder to taste
2 16 ounce cans hot chili beans	Cayenne pepper to taste

In a large skillet, brown beef, onion, and garlic. Drain and place in large Dutch oven. Add remaining ingredients including reserved tomato juice. Simmer at least 1 hour. Flavor is enhanced with longer cooking time. Top with shredded Cheddar cheese or serve with cheese toast.
Note: Cayenne pepper makes chili "hot" to taste, especially when reheated as a leftover.
Yield: 6 servings.

Rickey Hatcher

CHASSEN CHILI

1 16 ounce package dried pinto	½ cup parsley, chopped
beans	½ cup butter
2 16 ounce cans tomatoes	2½ pounds ground chuck
1 ground green pepper,	1 pound hot pork sausage
chopped	¼ cup chili powder
¼ cup salad oil	2 tablespoons salt
1½ pounds onions, chopped	1½ teaspoons pepper
2 cloves of garlic, minced	1½ teaspoons ground cumin seed

Wash beans and place in bowl. Fill bowl with water 2 inches above beans. Soak overnight. Simmer uncovered in same water until tender. Add tomatoes and simmer 5 minutes. Sauté green pepper slowly in oil for 5 minutes. Add onions and cook until tender. Add garlic and parsley. In large skillet, melt butter and sauté beef and pork for 15 minutes. Add meat to onion mixture and stir in chili powder. Cook 10 minutes, then add to beans. Season with salt, pepper, and cumin. Cover and simmer for 1 hour. Remove cover and cook 30 minutes longer.
Yield: 10 servings.

Leigh Hardwick Hardy

ELAINE'S BEER-CHEESE SOUP
"A Great First Course"

¼ cup margarine
5 tablespoons self-rising flour
3 cups milk
¾ teaspoon salt
1 16 ounce jar pasteurized
   processed cheese spread

¼ to ½ cup light beer
5 dashes hot pepper sauce
Parsley or bacon bits (optional)

Melt margarine in double boiler (over boiling water). Remove from heat and stir in flour. Add 4 tablespoons milk and stir until smooth. Gradually add remaining milk, stirring until smooth. Add salt. Return to heat over boiling water in double boiler. Stir until thickened. Add cheese spread gradually, stirring until melted. Add beer and pepper sauce. Serve hot in small portions. Sprinkle parsley or bacon bits over soup when in individual bowls, if desired. Serve with toasted bread rounds or croutons.
Yield: 4 servings.

Mrs. Jackie F. Stephens (Elaine)

CHICKEN AND BROCCOLI SOUP

1 10 ounce package frozen
   broccoli
⅜ cup onion, chopped
1 tablespoon margarine
3 chicken bouillon cubes
½ teaspoon salt
3 cups water

4 ounces egg noodles
½ teaspoon garlic powder
3 cups milk
½ pound pasteurized processed
   cheese block

In a medium boiler, cook broccoli and drain. Sauté onions and margarine. In another boiler, cook and bring to a boil bouillon cubes, salt, and water. Add noodles and sauteéd onions and cook 3 minutes. Add broccoli and garlic powder, and cook 3 more minutes. Add milk and cheese. Stir until cheese is melted. Soup is ready!

Cathy Hurst

15 BEAN SOUP

2 cups mixed dried beans
2 tablespoons salt
2 quarts water
2 cups diced ham or ham bone
1 large onion, chopped

1 clove garlic, minced
1 teaspoon chili powder
1 28 ounce can tomatoes, chopped
2 tablespoons lemon juice

Rinse beans and place in large kettle, cover with water. Add salt and soak overnight. Drain. Add 2 quarts water, ham or ham bone, and simmer about an hour on medium heat. Add onion, garlic, chili powder, tomatoes, and lemon juice. Simmer about 45 minutes. Add salt and pepper to correct the seasoning if desired.
Yield: 2 quarts.

Nell J. Fears
Madison, Georgia

MUSHROOM SOUP
"This soup is unusually good!"

$\frac{1}{4}$ cup butter
1 to 2 cloves garlic, minced
12 ounces fresh mushrooms, sliced
$3\frac{3}{4}$ tablespoons flour

2 cups chicken broth
2 cups half and half
$\frac{1}{2}$ cup parsley, chopped
Nutmeg to taste
Salt and pepper to taste

Heat butter in saucepan. Sauté garlic and mushrooms in butter for 5 minutes, stirring constantly. Stir in flour, blending well. Slowly add broth and half and half. Bring to a boil, stirring constantly. Turn heat down and simmer for 5 minutes. Add parsley, nutmeg, salt, and pepper.
Yield: 8 servings.
Note: May use parsley sprinkled on top of soup as garnish.

Sue Nicholls
Recipe of the late *Mary Jane Wright Selden*

If soup is too salty, add a potato to absorb extra salt.

DOUBLE CHEESE FRENCH ONION SOUP

4	large onions, thinly sliced and separated into rings	2	cups water
½	cup butter, melted	¼	cup dry white wine
1	tablespoon all-purpose flour		Fresh ground pepper to taste
1	10¾ ounce can chicken broth	8	slices French bread, toasted
1	10¾ ounce can beef broth	8	slices mozzarella cheese
		½	cup Parmesan cheese, grated

Sauté onions in butter in a Dutch oven until tender. Add flour and stir until well blended. Slowly add chicken and beef broths, water, and wine. Bring to a boil; reduce heat and simmer for 15 minutes. Add pepper. Place 8 oven-proof bowls on a baking sheet. Place 1 slice of French bread into each bowl and ladle soup over bread. Top with 1 slice mozzarella cheese and sprinkle with Parmesan cheese. Broil until cheeses melt.
Yield: 8 servings.

Amy M. Mathison

MRS. MINNIGERODE'S LENTIL SOUP

2	tablespoons butter	Bone from leg of lamb
1	large onion, chopped	1½ cups dried lentils
1	celery stalk with leaves, chopped	Salt and pepper to taste
1	carrot, peeled and chopped	1 teaspoon cumin (or to taste)
8	cups beef broth (not salty)	Juice of ½ lemon

Sauté onion, celery, and carrot in butter. Add beef broth and lamb bone. Simmer until meat falls from bone; approximately 2 hours. Remove grease and skin from broth. Add dried lentils, salt, and pepper to broth. Simmer until lentils are soft; approximately 1½ hours. Add lemon juice and cumin.

Muffett Robbs Conover

EASY VEGETABLE SOUP

1	pound ground beef	4	beef bouillon cubes
1	cup onion, chopped	1	tablespoon dried parsley
1	cup carrots, sliced		flakes
1	cup celery, sliced	¼	teaspoon crushed basil leaves
1	cup frozen green beans	1	teaspoon salt
2	16 ounce cans tomatoes	⅛	teaspoon pepper
½	cup water	1	cup enriched pre-cooked rice

Brown beef and onion. Drain well. Place in large Dutch oven. Add remaining ingredients, except rice. Bring to a boil. Reduce heat and simmer, covered, for 45 minutes. Add rice and stir well. Simmer an additional 10 minutes or until rice is tender.
Yield: 6 to 8 servings.

Mrs. Mike Riley (Pam)

CREAM OF TOMATO SOUP

1	16 ounce can whole tomatoes, undrained	1	teaspoon salt
2	cups water	1½	tablespoons all-purpose flour
1	tablespoon margarine	½	cup milk

With knife, remove cores from tomatoes and mash tomatoes with a fork. Place tomatoes (with juice) in large saucepan. Add water, margarine, and salt. Bring to a boil, then simmer for 10 to 15 minutes. Dissolve flour in milk. Using a strainer, pour milk into hot soup. Cook an additional 5 to 10 minutes over low heat, stirring frequently to avoid scorching.
Yield: 4 servings

Mrs. Carl Reaves (Joyce)

A leaf of lettuce dropped into a pot of soup absorbs the grease from the top of the soup.

Vegetables

*Thank you for letting me be born in the South
and for the cornbread and turnip greens in my mouth.*
Copied.

GREEN BEAN CASSEROLE

1 large onion, chopped	1 teaspoon salt
½ cup butter	3 10 ounce packages frozen
¼ cup self-rising flour	french-style green beans,
1½ cup milk	cooked and drained
¾ pound Cheddar cheese,	1 2 ounce can mushrooms
shredded	1 8 ounce can water chestnuts,
Dash of hot sauce	sliced
2 teaspoons soy sauce	Chopped almonds
½ teaspoon pepper	

Sauté onions in butter. Add flour, then milk. Stir in cheese and hot sauce, soy sauce, pepper and salt. Add beans, mushrooms, and water chestnuts. Pour into casserole and sprinkle with chopped almonds. Bake at 350 degrees until thoroughly heated.

Ms. Hattie Wallace Coker

HARVARD BEETS

"Great dish for beet lovers."

1 16 ounce can diced or sliced beets (reserving ⅓ cup liquid)	¼ teaspoon salt
2 tablespoons sugar	¼ cup vinegar
1 tablespoon cornstarch	2 tablespoons butter

Drain beets; reserving ⅓ cup liquid. Combine sugar, cornstarch, and salt in saucepan. Stir in reserve liquid, vinegar, and butter. Cook and stir until mixture thickens and bubbles. Add beets. Heat thoroughly.
Yield: 4 or 5 servings.

Winser Hayes

182

BROCCOLI, CHEESE, AND RICE CASSEROLE

2   10 ounce packages frozen
    chopped broccoli
1   medium onion, chopped
¼   cup celery, chopped (optional)
2   tablespoons margarine
1   10 ¾ ounce can cream of
    chicken soup
1   10 ¾ ounce can cream of
    mushroom soup

1½ cups of American cheese or
    pasteurized process cheese
1   5¼ ounce can evaporated
    milk
3   cups cooked rice
Cracker crumbs mixed with butter

Cook first 4 ingredients in small amount of water until tender. Drain, reserving liquid. Mix soups, cheese, and milk. Heat until cheese is melted and well mixed (can use microwave for this). Mix broccoli mixture, soup mixture, and rice (if too thick, add some water that broccoli was cooked in). Pour in 9 x 13 inch buttered casserole. Top with crumbs cooked in butter. Bake 30 to 45 minutes at 350 degrees or until set.

Ms. Faye P. Cooley
Similar recipe submitted by *Mary A. Lumpkin*

SAVORY BROCCOLI CASSEROLE

1   bunch fresh broccoli or 2
    10 ounce packages frozen
    broccoli, chopped
2   eggs, beaten
½   cup milk
1   10 ¾ ounce cream of celery
    soup (undiluted)

1   cup mayonnaise or salad
    dressing
1   cup sharp Cheddar cheese,
    grated
20 butter flavored crackers

Cut broccoli into 1 inch pieces. Cook in a small amount of boiling salted water just until tender, combine eggs, milk, soup, mayonnaise and cheese; stir in the cooked broccoli. Pour mixture into greased 2 quart casserole. Crush and sprinkle crackers over mixture. Bake at 350 degrees for 30 to 40 minutes.

Mrs. Nina Nabors
Similar recipe submitted by *Mrs. Larry Edmiston (Donna)*

LEMON-BROCCOLI GOLDENROD

¾	pound fresh broccoli	½	teaspoon onion, grated
¼	cup water	⅛	teaspoon dried whole thyme
⅓	cup mayonnaise	1	teaspoon lemon rind, grated
1	tablespoon lemon juice		

Trim off leaves of broccoli and remove tough ends of lower stalks. Wash broccoli and slice into separate spears. Arrange broccoli spears in a circle in a glass pie plate, placing stems toward the outside. Add water. Cover with heavy-duty plastic wrap and microwave on high for 4 to 6 minutes or until spears are tender. Drain well and arrange on serving platter. Combine next four ingredients in a 1-cup glass measure. Microwave on high for 30 to 40 seconds or until thoroughly heated. Pour over broccoli. Sprinkle with lemon rind.
Yield: 2 to 4 servings.

Mrs. Larry Barksdale (Fran)

SEVEN LAYER CASSEROLE

1½	cups cooked rice	1½	cups sharp Cheddar cheese, shredded
1½	cups ham, cooked and cubed	¼	cup milk
½	onion, chopped	2	slices sour dough bread
1½	cups broccoli, cooked, drained, and chopped	2	tablespoons butter or margarine
1	10 ¾ ounce can cream of mushroom soup		

In a buttered 1½ quart casserole, layer rice, ham, onion, and broccoli. In separate bowl, combine soup, cheese and milk. Spread over broccoli. Bake in 375 degrees for 20 minutes. Make coarse bread crumbs in blender with bread slices. Sauté crumbs in butter over medium high heat until light brown. Sprinkle crumbs over casserole. Continue baking 15 minutes longer or until hot and bubbly.
Yield: 4 servings.

Mrs. Larry Edmiston (Donna)

CARROTS L'ORANGE

2   pounds carrots, julienned
2   cups water
1   tablespoon orange rind, grated
1   cup sugar
1½   tablespoons frozen orange juice concentrate

¼   teaspoon salt
2   tablespoons butter
1   tablespoon cornstarch
4   tablespoons Cointreau

Cook carrots in water until just tender. Drain, reserving cooking liquid. Combine ¾ cup reserved carrot liquid with orange rind, sugar, orange juice concentrate, salt, and butter. Heat to boiling and simmer 5 minutes. Dissolve cornstarch in ¼ cup cold carrot liquid and add to orange mixture. Add cooked carrots and Cointreau.
Yield: 8 servings.

Harriet Heacock

CABBAGE CASSEROLE

1   medium to large head of cabbage, coarsely shredded
3   slices bread, buttered
4   eggs, beaten

2   cups milk
2½   cups sharp cheese, shredded
1   teaspoon salt
¼   teaspoon pepper

Cook cabbage briefly in salted water. Drain well. Put bread in bowl. Combine eggs and milk and pour over bread. Soak 5 minutes. Add cabbage, 1½ cup cheese, salt, and pepper. Mix. Pour in greased 2 quart casserole dish and bake at 250 degrees for 1½ hours. Test with knife (like custard). Sprinkle rest of cheese on top. Heat until cheese is melted.
Yield: 8 to 10 servings.

Connie Barnes

To prevent unpleasant odors while cooking cabbage or cauliflower, place a piece of bread on top of lid.

SAUCY BAKED CARROTS

8   medium carrots, scraped and
    cut in ¼ inch slices
½   cup mayonnaise
¼   cup water
2   tablespoons onion, finely
    chopped
2   tablespoons prepared
    horseradish
½   teaspoon salt
Pepper to taste
½ to 1 cup dry bread crumbs
¼   cup margarine or butter,
    melted

Cook carrots in water until tender, about 8 to 10 minutes. Drain. Combine next six ingredients; mix well. Add carrots and toss gently. Pour into lightly greased 1½ quart casserole dish. Combine bread crumbs and butter. Mix well and sprinkle over carrots. Bake at 375 degrees for 20 to 25 minutes. Yield: 6 to 8 servings.

Jeanne R. McKinney

CHEESY CAULIFLOWER

1   large cauliflower
⅔   cup mayonnaise
1   teaspoon prepared
    horseradish
1   teaspoon prepared mustard
4   ounces medium Cheddar
    cheese, shredded
¼   teaspoon salt

Separate florets of cauliflower and cook in salted water 10 minutes or until crisp tender. Drain and set aside. Meanwhile, mix remaining ingredients well. Place cauliflower with stem ends down in casserole dish. Dot mayonnaise mixture on top. Bake in 350 degrees oven for 10 minutes until bubbly. *Note:* Broccoli is also delicious with this topping.

Melba Hagan
Alexander City, Alabama

CORN PUDDING

6   ears of corn, grated
1   cup milk
1½ tablespoons of sugar
1   tablespoon flour
3   eggs, beaten separately
Salt and butter to taste

Mix all ingredients and pour into greased, deep dish casserole. Bake at 350 degrees for 30 minutes (uncovered).

Mrs. Mike Walker (Charlene)

MEXICORN CASSEROLE

1 12 ounce can mexicorn, undrained
1 10 ounce can cream of mushroom soup
1 cup cooked rice
½ cup onion, chopped
½ cup bell pepper, chopped

¼ cup water
1 cup mild Cheddar cheese, shredded
1 package round buttery crackers; from 3 package box, crumbled
½ cup margarine

Stir first six ingredients together and pour into a greased 8½ inch square casserole dish. Top with cheese. Melt margarine and stir into cracker crumbs. Sprinkle buttered crumbs over cheese. Bake at 400 degrees until bubbly and crumbs are golden brown, approximately 20 to 30 minutes. Yield: 6 to 8 servings.

Mrs. Jackie Stephens (Elaine)
Similar recipe submitted by *Mrs. Matt Mihelic (Ree)*

PREACHER'S CASSEROLE

1 10¾ ounce can cream of chicken soup
1 10¾ ounce can cream of celery soup
4 tablespoons sour cream
1 16 ounce can shoe peg corn (can substitute whole kernel corn), drained

1 16 ounce can French cut green beans, drained
1 small onion, chopped
½ cup Cheddar cheese, shredded
1 stack round buttery crackers
¼ cup butter, melted

Mix soups and sour cream. Add corn, beans, onion, and cheese. Mix well. Pour into casserole dish. Crush crackers and put on top. Pour melted butter over top. Cook about 20 minutes at 350 degrees or until crackers are brown.

Mrs. Randall Stewart (Reba)
Similar recipes submitted by *Mrs. Moody Scroggins (Joan)*
Nancy Hopewell
Mrs. Larry Edmiston (Donna)

Soak a head of cauliflower in ice water, florets down, before cooking to draw out any hidden insects.

CREOLE CORN

2 slices bacon, chopped into
small pieces
1 large onion, sliced
1 bell pepper, chopped
2½ cups fresh tomatoes,
chopped

1 small bay leaf
2 cups whole kernel golden
sweet corn
¼ teaspoon salt
⅛ teaspoon pepper

In large skillet, fry bacon. Remove from skillet reserving drippings. Add onion and bell pepper to drippings in skillet. Cook over medium heat, stirring constantly until crisp-tender. Add tomatoes and bay leaf to onion mixture. Simmer 10 minutes, stirring occasionally. Stir in corn and simmer 10 minutes. Discard bay leaf; stir in salt, pepper, and bacon.
Yield: 6 to 8 servings.

Mrs. Mike Riley (Pam)

QUICKLY BAKED EGGPLANT
"Great recipe for eggplant lovers."

1 medium eggplant, pared and
cut in ¼ inch slices
½ cup butter, melted
¾ cup bread crumbs, fine and
dry
¼ teaspoon salt

1 cup spaghetti sauce with
mushrooms
1 cup mozzarella cheese,
shredded
Oregano according to taste

Preheat oven to 450 degrees. Dip eggplant in butter and then mixture of bread crumbs and salt. Place on greased baking sheet. Spoon sauce over each eggplant slice. Sprinkle with cheese and oregano. Bake at 450 degrees for 10 to 12 minutes or until done.
Yield: 4 to 5 servings.

"Tee" J. Albright
Plant City, Florida

Salt added to the water when boiling corn or added to fresh cream corn while cooking toughens it. Salt after removing from heat.

VIDALIA ONION CASSEROLE

¼	cup butter	2	eggs, beaten
3	medium onions, sliced	¾	cup half & half
¼	cup green pepper, chopped	½	teaspoon salt
¼	cup pimento, chopped	⅛	teaspoon black pepper
1	cup Swiss cheese, shredded	2	tablespoons butter
1	cup cracker crumbs		

Melt ¼ cup butter in sauce pan. Add sliced onions and green pepper. Cook until tender. Add pimento. Place ½ mixture in 2 quart baking dish. Top with half of cheese then half of crackers. Repeat layers. Beat eggs with half & half, salt and pepper. Pour over onions. Top with buttered cracker crumbs. Bake 25 minutes at 350 degrees.
Yield: 6 servings.

Mrs. James W. Heacock (Becky)

VIDALIA ONION PIE

4	large onions, thinly sliced	½	teaspoon white pepper
½	cup butter or margarine	¼	teaspoon hot pepper sauce
3	eggs, well beaten	1	unbaked 9 inch pie shell
1	cup sour cream		Parmesan cheese, grated
¼	teaspoon salt		

Sauté onions in butter. Combine eggs and sour cream. Add to onions. Add seasonings. Pour into pie shell. Sprinkle Parmesan cheese on top. Bake for 20 minutes at 450 degrees and then 20 minutes at 325 degrees.

Betty Lou Camp - compliments of *Mrs. Carl D. Chandler*
Montgomery, Alabama

Celery rubbed between the hands will remove onion odor.

CHEESY POTATO SCALLOP

6 cups cooked new potatoes, thinly sliced	2 cups cottage cheese
2 small onions, sliced and separated into rings	1 cup dairy sour cream
1 teaspoon salt	1½ cups Cheddar cheese, shredded
¼ teaspoon pepper	Paprika

Alternate layers of potatoes and onions in a 2 quart buttered casserole, sprinkle potatoes with salt and pepper as you layer. Combine cottage cheese and sour cream and spoon over potatoes. Top with Cheddar cheese, sprinkle with paprika. Bake in a 350 degree oven for 20 minutes.
Yield: 8 servings.

"Tee" J. Albright
Plant City, Florida

PARMESAN POTATOES

¼ cup butter or margarine	¼ teaspoon white pepper per layer
4 medium baking potatoes, scrubbed but unpeeled	
¼ cup Parmesan cheese per layer, grated	

Preheat oven to 375 degrees and melt butter in 10x8 inch baking dish. Cut potatoes in half lengthwise, then in half lengthwise again. Cut slices into ¼ inch strips; reserve ends that are almost entirely covered with peel. Layer the remaining potatoes crisscross style (first row length of dish—second row-width of dish, etc.) sprinkling each row with pepper and cheese as you go. Top with reserved potato ends, skin side up, ending up with pepper and cheese. Spoon up enough butter over top layer to moisten well. Bake uncovered until tender when tested with fork, about 45 minutes.
Yield: 4 to 6 servings.

Mrs. Wanda Embry (Joe)
Similar recipe submitted by *Mrs. Jeanne R. McKinney*

To freeze potatoes, cook in boiling water or bake in their jackets. Cool, then wrap in foil.

MASHED POTATO CASSEROLE

10 to 12 potatoes, peeled, cooked and mashed
1   8 ounce carton sour cream
2   tablespoons milk
2   tablespoons mayonnaise
1   teaspoon parsley
1   teaspoon onion, grated
¾   cup butter, softened
⅛   teaspoon garlic salt
¼   teaspoon celery seed
⅛   teaspoon lemon pepper
½   cup Cheddar cheese, shredded

Mix all ingredients except cheese. Put in a 2 quart buttered casserole dish. Top with cheese. Bake at 325 degrees for 25 minutes or until browned. Yield: 10 servings.

Mrs. Mike Riley (Pam)
Similar recipe submitted by *Rhonda Lewis*

KENTUCKY BOURBON SWEET POTATOES

"The hint of bourbon is an interesting surprise!"

4   cups sweet potatoes, cooked
    or
2   16 ounce cans sweet potatoes, well drained
1   cup sugar
½   cup bourbon
2   eggs
½   cup margarine
1   teaspoon nutmeg
1   teaspoon vanilla

Mash sweet potatoes. Add sugar, bourbon, eggs, margarine, nutmeg, and vanilla. Beat until well blended. Turn into a 2 quart shallow baking dish.

Topping:
¾   cup pecans, chopped
¾   cup brown sugar
½   cup margarine

In a saucepan, stir margarine, nuts, and brown sugar together. When margarine is melted, spoon on top of potatoes. Bake uncovered at 350 degrees for 30 minutes.
Yield: 6 servings.

Hilda Fannin

SWEET POTATO DELIGHT

1 17 ounce can of golden yams
3 eggs
1 cup liquid from yams—add milk to make 1 cup
⅛ teaspoon salt

1 teaspoon vanilla
½ cup margarine
Corn flakes, crushed
Sugar

Mash yams and mix eggs, liquid, salt, vanilla, and margarine. Put in a covered 1½ quart round casserole dish with crushed corn flakes on top, sprinkle with sugar. Bake 20 minutes at 450 degrees.

Dot Wallis Moosmann
Sun City Center, Florida

MARINATED BLACKEYED PEAS

2 16 ounce packages frozen blackeyed peas (cooked, seasoned, drained)
1 cup wine vinegar
½ onion, finely chopped
1½ teaspoon garlic salt

6 dashes hot sauce
1 cup vegetable oil
¼ cup green pepper, finely chopped
¼ teaspoon pepper
1½ teaspoon Italian seasoning

Combine ingredients in a large bowl. Stir. Cover and marinate in refrigerator 3 days. Garnish with onion rings and green pepper rings. Serve with slotted spoon.
Note: Marinating time may be reduced if necessary.

Hilda Fannin

RICE AND LENTIL PILAF

1 cup dried lentils
2 cups chicken broth
2 cups uncooked instant rice

3 tablespoons olive oil
1 medium onion, chopped

Cook lentils until tender (1 hour). Drain and set aside. Bring chicken broth to a boil and add instant rice. Remove from heat and set aside 5 minutes. Meanwhile, sauté onion in olive oil until tender, do not brown. When onion is ready, add rice and lentils and heat thoroughly.

Diane Grosiak Vita
West Patterson, New Jersey

MOCK WILD RICE

¼ cup butter or margarine
1½ cups uncooked rice
¼ cup onion, chopped
½ pound mushrooms (fresh or canned)
1 cup celery, diced
¼ cup celery leaves, chopped
1½ teaspoons salt

1 8 ounce can water chestnuts, sliced
⅓ cup pecans, chopped
⅛ teaspoon each: pepper, sage, thyme, marjoram
3 cups boiling liquid, water or stock

Melt butter in a large skillet (not iron) with a tight fitting lid. Sauté all ingredients except liquid and herbs, stirring constantly until onion is tender and rice looks milky. In saucepan boil liquid. Add boiling liquid and herbs. Stir to mix well and allow to come to a simmer. Transfer to a covered casserole dish and place in pre-heated oven at 350 degrees for 20 minutes. Do not peek. At the end of 20 minutes, check to see if all liquid has been absorbed. If not, cook a little longer. Stir to mix well.
Yield: 6 servings.

Mrs. J. Milton Coxwell, Jr. (Kathi)
Monroeville, Alabama

HERBED SPINACH BAKE

1 10 ounce package frozen chopped spinach
1 cup cooked rice
1 cup sharp processed American cheese, shredded
2 eggs, slightly beaten
2 tablespoons butter or margarine, softened

⅓ cup milk
1 teaspoon salt
2 tablespoons onion, chopped
¼ teaspoon rosemary (optional)
½ teaspoon Worcestershire sauce

Cook and drain spinach. Mix with cooked rice, cheese, eggs, and butter. Stir in remaining ingredients. Pour mixture into lightly greased 10x6x1½ inch baking dish. Bake at 350 degrees for 20 to 25 minutes. May be cut into squares to serve.
Yield: 8 servings.

Mrs. Al Kline (Naomi)

EASY SPINACH CASSEROLE

4	10 ounce boxes frozen chopped spinach	¼	teaspoon nutmeg
1	pint sour cream		Bread crumbs
1	envelope dry onion soup mix		Margarine
			Fresh Mushrooms

Cook and drain spinach according to directions on box. Combine first 4 ingredients. Pour into buttered 2 quart casserole dish. Top with bread crumbs and dot with margarine. Bake at 300 degrees for 30 minutes. Garnish with fresh sliced mushrooms.
Yield: 12 servings.

Beth Ralston
Charlotte, North Carolina

SPINACH STRATA

54 round, buttery crackers	2½ cups milk
2 10 ounce packages frozen chopped spinach, thawed and well drained	5 eggs
	2 tablespoons dry mustard
2½ cups Cheddar cheese, shredded	

In 2 quart glass baking dish, arrange 18 crackers. Combine spinach and 2 cups shredded cheese. Sprinkle ½ mixture over crackers, repeat layers. Top with remaining crackers; sprinkle with remaining ½ cup cheese.

In medium bowl, beat together milk, eggs and mustard. Pour evenly over mixture in baking dish. Refrigerate for one hour. Bake at 350 degrees for one hour or until puffed and golden. Cut into squares to serve.

Mrs. Tracey Barber (Rick)

POSH SQUASH

2	pounds yellow squash	1	cup mayonnaise
2	eggs, beaten	1	cup Parmesan cheese
¼	cup bell pepper, finely chopped		Salt and pepper to taste
¼	cup onion, finely chopped		Buttered bread crumbs

Cook squash, drain. Combine other ingredients in bowl. Add squash. Pour into buttered casserole dish. Top with crumbs. Bake at 350 degrees for 30 minutes.
Note: This can be frozen, but defrost thoroughly before cooking.

Beth Ralston
Charlotte, North Carolina
Similar recipe submitted by *Nancy Hare,* Montgomery, Alabama

SUMMER VEGETABLE CASSEROLE

*"Don't save this for the summer months.
It is great year-round."*

4 to 5	cups squash	½	cup green peppers, chopped
1	medium onion, chopped	½	cup pimento, chopped
1	10¾ ounce can cream of chicken soup	1	8 ounce package herb seasoned stuffing mix
½	cup mayonnaise	½	cup butter or margarine, melted
½	pint sour cream		
1	cup carrots, shredded		

Cook squash and onion until tender. Drain. Combine soup, mayonnaise, and sour cream. Stir in carrots, pepper, and pimento. Fold in squash and onion. Combine stuffing and butter. Spread ½ in bottom of 12x8x2 inch casserole dish. Spoon in vegetable mixture. Sprinkle remaining stuffing over top. Bake at 350 degrees for 25 to 30 minutes or until bubbly.
Note: Freezes well.

Mrs. Erskine Murray (Betty)
Montgomery, Alabama

SQUASH DELIGHT CASSEROLE

1¼ pound squash	½ cup onion, chopped
¼ cup margarine	¼ cup green pepper, chopped
1 egg, slightly beaten	½ cup pecans, chopped
1 teaspoon sugar	½ cup pimento
½ cup cheese, shredded	1 teaspoon salt
½ cup mayonnaise	½ cup bread crumbs

Cook squash until tender. Drain. Add margarine and mash. Mix together all other ingredients, except bread crumbs. Add to squash. Pour mixture into buttered 2 quart casserole dish. Top with bread crumbs and more cheese to taste. Bake at 350 degrees for 30 to 40 minutes.
Note: Pimento and green pepper may be omitted.

Karan Bush
Birmingham, Alabama

STUFFED SQUASH BOATS

5 medium acorn squash	2 tablespoons butter or margarine
½ pound bulk pork sausage (hot if preferred)	¼ cup bread crumbs
1 large onion, chopped	1 cup medium Cheddar cheese, shredded

Boil squash until done. Drain. Cut squash in half, lengthwise. Remove seeds and pulp. Leave shell intact and set aside. Cook sausage until done. Drain and set aside. Melt butter and sauté onion until tender. Mix squash pulp, onions, bread crumbs, and sausage. Spoon into squash boats and bake at 350 degrees for 10 to 15 minutes. Remove from oven, top with cheese and bake until cheese melts.
Yield: 8 to 10 servings.

Ms. Mary Jim Calhoun

For vegetables that grow above the ground, boil without a cover; for vegetables that grow under the ground, boil with a cover.

LUCRETIA'S ITALIAN ZUCCHINI PIE

4 cups zucchini, thinly sliced	¼ teaspoon sweet basil leaves
1 cup onion, coarsely chopped	¼ teaspoon oregano
½ cup margarine	2 eggs, well beaten
½ cup chopped parsley or	2 cups mozzarella cheese,
2 tablespoons parsley flakes	shredded
½ teaspoon salt	2 tablespoons mustard
½ teaspoon black pepper	2 unbaked pie crust
¼ teaspoon garlic powder	

In 10 inch skillet, cook zucchini and onions in margarine until tender, about 10 minutes. Stir in seasonings. In a large bowl, blend eggs and cheese. Stir in vegetables. Spread unbaked pie crusts with mustard and gently pour in vegetables. Bake at 375 degrees for 18 to 20 minutes. Let stand 10 minutes before serving.

Marion N. Yoe

TOMATO PIE

9 inch pie crust, partially baked	½ teaspoon dried basil or
3 medium tomatoes, cored,	tarragon
peeled and thickly sliced	½ cup mayonnaise
Salt and pepper to taste	1 cup Cheddar cheese, shredded

Bake pie crust at 350 degrees until lightly browned. Line cooled pie crust with tomatoes covering bottom completely. Sprinkle tomatoes with salt, pepper, and basil. In a small bowl combine mayonnaise and cheese. Carefully spread mixture evenly over tomato slices sealing edges of pie crust completely. Bake 30 minutes at 350 degrees or until bubbly. Serve at once. Yield: 6 servings.

Mrs. Rick Barber (Tracey)
Variation: Use 1 cup Parmesan cheese in place of Cheddar cheese.
Mrs. Susan S. Booth

MIXED VEGETABLE CASSEROLE

1	16 ounce can mixed vegetables	½ cup sharp Cheddar cheese, shredded
½	cup mayonnaise	½ cup margarine
½	cup onions, chopped	15 butter flavored salted crackers
½	cup celery, chopped	

Mix vegetables, mayonnaise, onions, celery, and cheese together. Pour in baking dish. Melt margarine. Crush crackers and spread over vegetables. Pour margarine over crackers. Bake until brown at 350 degrees, approximately 30 minutes.

Mrs. James C. Rogers (Marian)

Similar recipe submitted by *Mrs. H. J. Hagan,* Alexander City, Alabama

VEGETABLES WITH DILL SAUCE

1	pound green beans, or 1 pound new potatoes, or 1 pound carrots	3 to 6 tablespoons cider vinegar
½	cup sour cream	¼ cup onions, minced
1	cup mayonnaise	1 tablespoon onion salt
2	tablespoons dill weed	6 slices bacon, cooked and crumbled

Blanche vegetable of your choice or a combination of all for 2 minutes in boiling water. Drain. Combine sour cream, mayonnaise, dill weed, vinegar, onions, and onion salt and mix well. Add vegetables and toss well. Chill overnight. Serve cold or at room temperature with bacon on top.
Yield: 6 servings.

Harriet Heacock

Potpourri

CRANAPPLE-RASPBERRY RELISH

1	pound fresh cranberries, finely chopped	1	10 ounce package frozen raspberries, thawed and drained
2	tart green apples, cored and minced	1	teaspoon lemon juice or to taste
1	cup sugar		
½	cup orange marmalade		

In large bowl, combine all ingredients. May be refrigerated, covered up to 1 month.
Yield: 12 servings.
Note: Leftover relish may be combined with whipped cream and frozen in an ice cream freezer. Makes a special light after holiday treat.

Laine Austin Randall
Greensboro, North Carolina

PEACH JAM—NO COOK FREEZER JAM

2	pounds fresh peaches, peeled, pitted and chopped (Yield: 2¼ cups chopped fruit)	5	cups sugar
		¾	cup water
2	tablespoons fresh lemon juice	1	1¾ ounce box fruit pectin
1	teaspoon ascorbic acid crystals	6	½ pint containers, washed in hot water and dried

Measure 2¼ cups chopped peaches, lemon juice, and crystals into a large bowl, set aside. In a separate bowl measure sugar. Stir sugar into bowl containing fruit. Set aside for 10 minutes. Mix ¾ cup water and 1 box fruit pectin in a small saucepan. Bring to a rolling boil over high heat, stirring constantly. Continue to boil for 1 minute. Stir this mixture into fruit and sugar mixture. Stir for 3 minutes. Fill all containers immediately to ½ inch of tops. Wipe off edge of containers and quickly cover with lids. Let stand at room temperature for 24 hours. Store in freezer until opened. After opening, store in refrigerator up to 3 weeks.

Holly H. Gilbert
Birmingham, Alabama

PEPPER JELLY

½ cup fresh hot peppers, (such as jalapeños)
½ cup bell pepper
1 large onion

1½ cups apple cider vinegar
6½ cups sugar
1 6 ounce package liquid fruit pectin

Seed and chop peppers and onion, using rubber gloves. Pour peppers and onion into blender. Add vinegar and liquify. Add this mixture to sugar in a large saucepan. Bring to a full rolling boil that will not stir down. Remove from heat for 5 minutes. Stir in liquid fruit pectin. Skim, pour into scalded jars and seal. Serve chilled. Spoon over a block of cream cheese and serve with crackers as an hors d'oeuvre. Use all green peppers for green jelly or all red peppers for red jelly. A few drops of food coloring may be added, if desired.
Yield: 4 to 5 pints.

Mrs. Jackie Stephens (Elaine)

GREEN TOMATO PICKLES

Fresh green tomatoes
1 teaspoon salt per quart of tomatoes
Apple cider vinegar to fill quart jars

Hot pepper pods (use 1 or more as desired for each quart jar)

Cut tomatoes into wedges. Pack in sterilized quart jars. Pour one teaspoon salt over each jar of tomatoes. Cover and set aside overnight. The next day heat vinegar to a boil. Add one or more hot pepper pods to each quart of tomatoes. Pour boiling vinegar over tomatoes and seal jars.
Note: Wait 10 to 14 days before opening jars. Serve chilled.

Mrs. Wilson P. Reaves (Beulah)
Wedowee, Alabama

Place a lump of charcoal in an open jar to reduce ice box odors.

CRUNCHY RED PICKLE STICKS

*"Time consuming to make, but really
worth the trouble."*

Ingredients
7   pounds *very* large cucumbers
    (may have started turning
    yellow)
2½ cups pickling lime
4   ounces alum

2   quarts white vinegar
1   tablespoon plain salt
2   tablespoons whole pickling
    spices
5   pounds (10 cups) sugar
Red food coloring

Procedure
First Day: (Start no later than 8:00 p.m.)
Use 7 pounds of *very* large cucumbers that have been peeled, seeded, and cut into sticks. Soak cucumber sticks for 24 hours in solution made of 2½ cups of lime dissolved in 2 gallons of water. (Carefully stir these a bit because the lime has a tendency to settle to the bottom of the container.)

Second Day: (By 8:00 p.m.)
Remove cucumbers from lime solution. Rinse well in clear water. Now soak for 12 hours in alum water—made with 4 ounces alum dissolved in 2 gallons of water.

Third Day: (By 8:00 a.m.)
Remove cucumber sticks from alum water. Soak in clear water for six hours.

Make a syrup of:
2   quarts white vinegar
1   quart water
1   tablespoon plain salt
2   teaspoons red food coloring

5   pounds (10 cups) sugar
2   tablespoons whole pickling
    spice (tied in cloth bag)

Bring syrup to a boil and pour over well-drained cucumbers. Let stand for four hours. Bring to a boil and cook until sticks are transparent—about 30 minutes. (If pickles are not as red as you would like, add more food coloring as they cook.) Remove spices. Pack into standard canning jars. Wipe jar mouths with a clean, damp cloth. Adjust lids and bands, and waterbath for 10 minutes.
Yield: About 12 pints.

Mrs. Becky Newman

SWEET AND SOUR MUSTARD

1   3 ounce can dry mustard
1   cup vinegar
2   eggs

1¼ cups sugar
2   tablespoons cornstarch

Combine mustard and vinegar in a covered saucepan and let stand for 2 hours. Stir until all lumps are dissolved. Beat eggs, add sugar mixed with cornstarch and add to mustard/vinegar mixture. Cook over low heat for about 5 minutes or until mixture thickens. Pour into jars and let cool. Store in refrigerator.

Amy M. Mathison

PICKLED PEACHES

1   29 ounce can peach halves,
    packed in syrup
Whole cloves
½   cup vinegar

½   cup sugar
3   inch cinnamon stick, broken
    in half

Drain peaches, reserving 1 cup syrup. Stud each peach half with 3 or 4 cloves. Combine reserved syrup, vinegar, sugar, and cinnamon stick. Add peaches to syrup mixture. Bring to a boil, then simmer uncovered for 3 to 4 minutes. Cool; then cover and place in refrigerator to chill. Remove cloves and cinnamon before serving.
Note: May be packed while hot in sterilized jars and sealed.

Mrs. Carl Reaves (Joyce)

SWEETENED CONDENSED MILK

1   cup instant dry milk solid
⅔   cup sugar
⅓   cup boiling water (hard boil)

3   tablespoons margarine,
    melted

Combine in a blender and blend well.
Yield: 1½ cups (equivalent to 14 ounce can sweetened condensed milk).

Mrs. Dalton Morgan (Imogene)

CHILI SAUCE RELISH

24 ripe tomatoes	8 bell peppers, chopped
½ box of 1½ ounce size pickling	1½ cups sugar
spice	1 tablespoon salt
10 large onions, chopped	2 cups white vinegar

Pour hot water over tomatoes to peel easily. Chop into large Dutch oven. Tie pickling spice in cheesecloth bag. Add spice bag and remaining ingredients to tomatoes. Cook over medium heat, stirring frequently, until sauce thickens (2 to 4 hours.) Put into sterile, hot jars and seal at once. Yield: 6 to 7 pints.

Mrs. John W. Bryant (Mary Carson)

DELICIOUS HOMEMADE VANILLA

2 cups vodka
5 vanilla beans, cut into 1 inch
  pieces

Combine vodka and vanilla beans in a jar with a tight fitting lid. Cover the jar and let it stand 6 to 8 weeks. Original mixture yields 2 cups. After half the vanilla extract is used, add more vodka to cover the beans, and make another batch. The flavor in the beans is gone when the vodka no longer turns to a dark color after a day or two.

Jayne McDaniel
Birmingham, Alabama

SPICY PICKLED EGGS

12 hard boiled eggs, shelled	½ teaspoon mustard seed
3 cups white wine vinegar	4 to 8 whole cloves
2 tablespoons sugar	4 bay leaves
1 teaspoon salt	1 to 2 chili peppers

Place shelled boiled eggs in a glass jar. Bring the remaining ingredients to a boil, then cool slightly. Pour mixture over eggs. Seal jar and put in the refrigerator. These should stand a week or 10 days unopened, before using.

Myra Elmore

Special Selections

To the Children:

Cooking can be a wonderful learning opportunity and a great adventure. With the recipes in this section, you can prepare meals and snacks for friends, family, and yourself. This section also includes activities that will provide hours of fun.

These are a few rules you should remember as you work:

- **Always have an adult nearby.**
- **Read the entire recipe before you begin.**
- **Clean your hands and work area before you begin.**
- **Gather all ingredients and utensils before you begin.**
- **Be careful around any heated appliance or utensil.**
- **Remember to clean your work area when finished.**
- **Have fun!**

MR. D's DOUGHNUTS

1	10 count canned biscuits	3	tablespoons cinnamon
	Cooking oil		1 small paper sack
1	cup sugar		

Cut a hole in the center of the biscuits. Place enough oil into skillet to cover the biscuits. Heat oil to medium high temperature. Place biscuits in oil and brown on both sides. Drain on paper towels. Mix sugar and cinnamon in paper sack. Shake each doughnut in the sack.

Haley Lawson

CINNAMON BISCUITS

¼	cup butter, melted	1	teaspoon cinnamon
1	small can biscuits, 5 count	⅓	cup sugar

Melt butter. Cut biscuits into 4 pieces. Dip in butter and coat with cinnamon-sugar mixture. Place close together in small pan. Bake at 325 degrees until biscuits are done.
Note: You may wish to use more cinnamon-sugar mixture.

Lesli McCardle

KIDS RAINY DAY CUPCAKES AND ICING
"Great to make with the grandchildren."

1   box butter flavored cake mix
2   cups sugar
1   small can evaporated milk

1   stick corn oil margarine
1   cup caramel, butterscotch, or
    chocolate morsels

Prepare and bake cupcakes following butter flavored cake mix directions. Mix sugar, evaporated milk and margarine in medium saucepan. Cook on low heat until mixture begins to boil. Using timer, cook 5 minutes stirring often (mixture will scorch easily.) Remove from heat and add 1 cup caramel, butterscotch or semi-sweet chocolate morsels. Mix well by hand and continue stirring with wire whisk until spreading consistency. Spread on cupcakes (also makes enough icing for a two layer cake.)
Note: If children are helping be careful as icing remains very hot for several minutes.

Harri Diggs
Lincoln, Alabama

MY VERY OWN BANANA PUDDING

1   vanilla wafer
2   slices of banana
2   tablespoons instant vanilla
    pudding mix

¼   cup milk

Put vanilla wafer in a small jar. Add banana slices and then pudding mix. Pour milk over top and place tight fitting lid on jar. Shake the jar until pudding is thick.
Yield: 1 serving.

Zane Hendrix

SAILBOAT SANDWICHES

4   large soft rolls
1   7 ounce can tuna fish,
    drained
¼   cup celery, chopped

¼   cup mayonnaise
Salt to taste
4   celery stalks with leaves

Cut a big pocket in each roll. Mix the tuna, celery, mayonnaise, and salt in a small bowl. Fill the pockets with tuna mixture. Push the celery stalk down into the top of each roll so it stands up like a sail. Serve immediately.
Yield: 4 servings.

Joshua Riley

IRONED SANDWICHES

"When traveling, this makes a quick snack."

2	slices bread	Sheet of aluminum foil
1	slice cheese	Household iron
2	teaspoons butter	

Take 2 slices of bread and put cheese between slices. Butter outside of both slices of bread. Wrap in foil, like a present. Preheat iron to hottest setting. Iron sandwich for 2 minutes on both sides. Unwrap and enjoy.
Yield: 1 sandwich.

April Edmiston

MINIATURE PIZZAS

1 6 ounce can refrigerated biscuits
2 tablespoons butter, melted
1 14 ounce jar pizza sauce (will not use the whole jar)

1 cup American cheese, shredded

Place biscuits on cookie sheet and flatten them. May use palm of hand. Spread melted butter on biscuits. Bake at 350 degrees for 5 minutes, until very lightly browned. Flatten biscuits once more; this time with a fork. Place pizza sauce on top of bisuits, as much as you like. Cover with shredded cheese. Return to oven and bake at 350 degrees for 5 minutes or until cheese is melted.

Abby Spears

GELATIN EGG

2 or 3 eggs
1 envelope unflavored gelatin
¼ cup fruit juice, boiling, not pineapple

¾ cup cold fruit juice

Rinse egg. Poke hole in each end of egg with ice pick. Break yolk inside egg with ice pick. Blow out inside of egg. Rinse inside of egg. Let stand until dry. Place masking tape over smaller hole. Dissolve gelatin in boiling juice. Add cold juice. Fill egg shell with gelatin using glass measuring cup. Place egg in egg carton. Chill. After gelatin is congealed, crack and remove shell.
Yield: 2 to 3 eggs.

Carly Camp

PUPPY CHOW

"Don't wait for a party—treat the whole family this weekend."

½ cup margarine
1 cup chocolate chips
½ cup creamy peanut butter

8 cups Crispix cereal
2 cups confectioners sugar

Melt margarine and chocolate chips in microwave or over low heat. Add peanut butter and heat until melted. Stir well. Place cereal in large bowl. Pour chocolate mixture over and stir carefully until all cereal is well coated. Shake cereal and confectioners' sugar together in a paper bag until cereal is well-coated. After cooled, store in air tight container.

Beth Ralston
Charlotte, North Carolina

HILLARY'S FRUIT SALAD

1 16 ounce can fruit cocktail, drained
1 11 ounce can mandarin oranges, drained

4 cups multi-colored marshmellows
1 4 ounce container frozen non-dairy topping

Mix all ingredients and chill before serving.
Yield: 8 servings.

Hillary Hendrix

FORGOTTEN COOKIES

2 egg whites, room temperature
¼ teaspoon cream of tartar
¾ cup sugar
⅛ teaspoon salt

1 teaspoon vanilla
1 6 ounce package miniature chocolate chips

Preheat oven to 350 degrees. Beat egg whites and cream of tartar. Add sugar gradually and beat until dissolved. Add remaining ingredients. Drop by spoonfuls on cookie sheets. Place all cookies in the preheated oven, turn off oven immediately and forget them until morning; leaving them in oven until morning.

Kim Scroggins

Similar recipe submitted by *Mrs. W.J. Munroe (Rachel)*

BIRD NEST COOKIES
"A terrific springtime treat."

4 cups cornflakes	½ cup brown sugar
1 cup coconut	1 teaspoon vanilla
½ cup light corn syrup	60 jelly beans (approximately)
1 cup peanut butter	

Mix cornflakes and coconut in a bowl and set aside. Combine corn syrup, peanut butter, and brown sugar in a saucepan and bring to a boil. Remove from heat and add vanilla. Combine both mixtures. Cool. Shape into bird nests. Add 2 or 3 jellybeans to each nest.
Yield: 2 dozen.
Note: Substitute different types of candies to fit your holiday needs.

Rachel Parker

PEANUT BUTTER AND JELLY THUMBPRINT COOKIES

½ cup margarine	2 teaspoons vanilla
½ cup peanut butter	2 cups self-rising flour
½ cup brown sugar	½ cup favorite jelly
2 egg yolks	

Mix the first five ingredients in a large mixing bowl. Add flour and stir until moistened. Roll into small balls. Put thumb in the middle of the ball and press, making a thumbprint. Bake on a greased sheet at 375 degrees for 10 to 12 minutes. Fill thumbprint with jelly.

Sara Parker

AGGRESSION COOKIES

1½ cups brown sugar	1½ cups all-purpose flour
1½ cups margarine	1½ teaspoons baking soda
3 cups oatmeal, uncooked	

Mix all ingredients together and then let your frustrations out. Pound, squeeze, and knead the dough until all lumps of butter and aggression disappear. Roll into small balls and place on an ungreased cookie sheet. Flatten with a fork. Bake 10-12 minutes at 350 degrees. Cool before removing from sheet.
Yield: 5 dozen cookies.

Clint Goodpasture
Oak Ridge, Tennessee

POPCORN CAKE
"Great for children's parties."

½ cup popcorn, unpopped
Oil to pop the popcorn
½ cup butter or margarine
1   10 ounce package of
    marshmallows

1   pound package plain candy
    coated chocolate bits
1   8 ounce jar dry roasted
    peanuts

Pop the popcorn, do not add salt. In saucepan melt butter or margarine. Add marshmallows. Mix together candy, peanuts, and popped popcorn. Add melted ingredients and mix with hands thoroughly. Either press into bundt cake pan or make into popcorn balls. If served as cake, remove from cake pan when cool and set. Slice.
Yield: 12 servings.

Mrs. Jack R. Wood (Jackie Smith)
Heflin, Alabama

SPICE FUNDOUGH

½ cup all-purpose flour
½ teaspoon baking powder
2   tablespoons sugar
¼ teaspoon cinnamon

¼ teaspoon nutmeg
Dash of salt
2   tablespoons water
2   teaspoons oil

Mix dry ingredients together. Add water and oil. Mix with your hands. Store in an airtight plastic bag.
Note: This is an individual recipe. Everyone can make their own.

Clay Goodpasture
Oak Ridge, Tennessee

PLAY DOUGH

1   cup flour
½ cup salt
2   teaspoons cream of tartar

1   cup water
1   tablespoon cooking oil

Mix the above ingredients in the order given. Place over medium heat and stir constantly about 3 minutes or until dough forms a ball. Turn out on waxed paper and knead until smooth. Add food coloring if desired. Store in an air tight container.

Mrs. Pearino Gaither (Mary)

CEMENT ICING
"Use this icing to make Christmas gingerbread houses."

2 egg whites
½ teaspoon cream of tartar

2 cups confectioners sugar

Mix together egg whites and cream of tartar. Beat until stiff. Add 1 cup of confectioners sugar. Beat for 10 minutes. Add second cup of confectioners sugar. Beat for 10 minutes. Keep covered with a cloth while decorating and cementing gingerbread houses.

Mrs. Larry Edmiston (Donna)

HALLOWEEN FACES

2 parts white shortening
3 parts cornstarch
1 part all-purpose flour

Glycerin
Food color or eyeshadow color

Blend the shortening, cornstarch and flour together until a paste is formed. Add a few drops of glycerin to form a smooth creamy consistency like "mother's" makeup. Color with food color or bits of eyeshadow. Use fingers to apply the greasepaint. For brown greasepaint, add plain cocoa powder. Greasepaint can be removed with cold cream.
Note: Please remember to keep away from little eyes and do a skin patch test to be sure there will be no allergic reaction.

Julian Mallory King, Jr. and John Edward King

EGGS IN A BASKET

4 slices soft bread
4 teaspoons margarine

4 medium eggs
1 cup Cheddar cheese, shredded

Preheat oven to 400 degrees. Fit bread slices into custard cups. Place in oven until bread is lightly toasted. Remove from oven. Place 1 teaspoon margarine in each bread basket. Break an egg into each basket. Top with cheese. Return to oven. Bake approximately 12 to 15 minutes at 400 degrees.

Microwave directions: Cover each cup with plastic wrap. Microwave on medium for 4 minutes. Allow to stand covered for 1 or 2 minutes or until white is set.
Note: Carefully remove baskets from custard cups.

George and Lee Sims

Realizing the importance of good health, today's trends in cooking are to prepare foods that are low in cholesterol and fat. In keeping with this concept, we are offering a variety of treats that will help you to keep physically fit.

SESAME CHICKEN KABOBS

4 chicken breasts, deboned and skinned	¼ teaspoon ginger
¼ cup soy sauce	⅛ teaspoon garlic powder
¼ cup Russian dressing, low calorie	1 large onion, cut into 16 pieces or more
1 tablespoon sesame seeds	1 zucchini, thickly sliced
2 tablespoons lemon juice	Cherry tomatoes
	Mushrooms (fresh)

Cut chicken into 1 inch pieces. Chicken cuts easier if partially frozen. Place in shallow container. Set aside. Combine next 6 ingredients in a jar; shake vigorously. Pour over chicken and marinate in refrigerator at least 2 hours. Remove chicken from marinade, reserving marinade for basting. Alternate chicken and chunks of vegetables on skewers. Grill 15 to 20 minutes, basting and turning often (8 skewers.)
Yield: 4 servings
Note: 234 calories per serving—a plateful!

Mrs. Mike Riley (Pam)

CHICKEN POCKETS

2 tablespoons low calorie margarine	1 tablespoon spicy mustard
½ cup onion, chopped or thin rings	¼ teaspoon salt
2 cups carrot strips or rounds	Pepper to taste
1 cup broccoli or green beans	1 to 2 drops hot pepper sauce
½ cup chicken broth	1 7 ounce can water chestnuts
¼ cup skimmed evaporated milk	6 4 ounce chicken breasts, skinless

Preheat oven to 375 degrees. In non-stick skillet, melt margarine. Add onions, carrots, broccoli or green beans. Cook until tender. Add broth, milk, mustard, salt, pepper, hot pepper sauce, and water chestnuts. Cook 2 minutes over medium heat (no boiling.) Place chicken breast and divide vegetable mixture on foil or in individual dishes and cover with foil. Cook 15 to 20 minutes. Open on plates.
Note: Chinese pea pods may be added to vegetable mixture if desired.

Leigh Hardwick Hardy

CHOLESTEROL-LIGHT TURKEY TACOS

1 pound fresh ground turkey	1 package of 10 taco shells
1 package taco seasoning	

Brown ground turkey in skillet. Add prepared taco seasoning and simmer. Fill tacos with meat mixture, then toppings.

Suggested topppings:
⅓ head lettuce, chopped or shredded	½ pound low calorie cheese, shredded
2 tomatoes, diced	Black olives
1 onion, chopped	Picante sauce

Note: Can substitute light tortilla or corn chips and serve as a taco salad. Ground turkey may be substituted for ground beef in many recipes.

Frieda Meacham

LIGHT PAN FRIED CATFISH FILLETS

2 catfish fillets, pond raised	Pepper
Lemon dill seasoning with parsley	2 tablespoons virgin olive oil
Garlic salt	Dash of liquid margarine

Rinse fillets and pat dry with a paper towel. Sprinkle both sides with garlic and pepper. Sprinkle generously on the inside of the fillets, with lemon-dill seasoning with parsley, and let set for 15 minutes. Using a large non-stick skillet, heat oil to hot but not smoking. (Olive oil will burn easily.) Place fillets in the skillet with the outside of the fish down. Cook on moderate-high heat for 5 minutes. Turn with spatula, being careful to keep fillets from breaking apart. Cook an additional 5 minutes and turn again. Add liquid margarine, when it melts remove fillets to a warm platter and serve immediately.
Note: This works well with any white fish.

Harri Diggs
Lincoln, Alabama

"LITE" VEGETABLE SOUP

1   32 ounce can tomato juice
2   medium carrots, chopped
2   celery stalks, chopped
2   beef bouillon cubes

½   small cabbage, shredded
1   16 ounce can green beans
½   teaspoon salt

Combine all ingredients. Cook over medium heat until vegetables are tender.

Mrs. Larry Edmiston (Donna)

SOUTH OF THE BORDER SALAD

1   15 ounce can kidney beans, drained and rinsed
1   cup sharp Cheddar cheese, shredded
1   8¾ ounce can whole kernel corn, drained
½   cup green pepper, chopped

4   green onions, thinly sliced
2   medium tomatoes, diced
½   cup reduced-calorie Russian dressing
½   teaspoon chili powder
1   medium head lettuce, shredded

Combine first 6 ingredients in a large salad bowl. Combine dressing and chili powder; pour over bean mixture, tossing gently. Cover and refrigerate 1 hour. Add lettuce just before serving; toss lightly.
Yield: 5 main dish servings.

Pam Riley

PINEAPPLE CHICKEN SALAD

2   cups cooked chicken, cubed
1   15¼ ounce can pineapple chunks, chilled and drained
1   medium green pepper, cut in strips

½   cup water chestnuts, sliced
¾   cup Zesty Low Calorie Salad Dressing

In salad bowl combine chicken, pineapple, green pepper, and water chestnuts. Pour Zesty Low Calorie Salad Dressing over chicken mixture; toss lightly.
Yield: 4 servings.
Note: See salad dressing recipe in this section.

Teresa Lawson

ZESTY LOW CALORIE SALAD DRESSING

1 tablespoon cornstarch
1 teaspoon sugar
1 teaspoon dry mustard
1 cup cold water
¼ cup vinegar
¼ cup catsup
1 teaspoon prepared
  horseradish

1 teaspoon Worcestershire
  sauce
½ teaspoon salt
½ teaspoon paprika
Dash bottled hot pepper sauce
1 clove garlic, halved

In a small saucepan combine the cornstarch, sugar, and the dry mustard; gradually stir in water. Cook, stirring constantly, over medium heat till thick and bubbly. Remove from heat. Cover surface with waxed paper; stir in the vinegar, catsup, horseradish, Worcestershire, salt, paprika, and hot pepper sauce; beat till smooth. Add garlic. Transfer to storage container; cover and chill. Remove garlic before using.
Yield: 1⅓ cups.

Teresa Lawson

LIGHT APPLE-CHERRY SALAD

1 tablespoon lemon juice
1½ cups unsweetened
  applesauce
1 3 ounce package sugar-free
  cherry gelatin

1 8 ounce can unsweetened
  crushed pineapple with juice
¾ cup sugar-free lemon-lime
  carbonated beverage

Combine lemon juice and applesauce in a boiler; bring to a boil. Remove from heat, add gelatin and stir to disslove. Cool, then add pineapple and lemon-lime carbonated beverage. Spoon into six one-half cup molds or a three cup mold. Chill until firm.
Yield: 6 servings.

Amy M. Mathison

LUSCIOUS FRUIT DIP

1   cup light sour cream
2   tablespoons brown sugar
1   teaspoon poppy seeds

1   cluster grapes
1   pint strawberries

Mix light sour cream and brown sugar until smooth. Add poppy seeds and blend. Serve fruit with dip.

Frieda and Emily Meacham

MARINATED CUCUMBER SALAD

1   medium cucumber
1   small onion
½   cup vinegar

½   cup water
Sugar substitute to taste
¼   teaspoon salt

Thinly slice cucumber and onion into glass bowl. Mix vinegar, water, equal, and salt. Pour on cucumber and onion slices. Cover and refrigerate at least 2 hours.
Note: Can be served immediately.

Judy B. Vinyard

GREEN PEA SALAD
"Makes a great side dish."

1   16 ounce can small green peas
2   hard boiled eggs
4   ounces Cheddar cheese

2 to 3 teaspoons reduced calorie mayonnaise
3   teaspoons onion, diced

Drain peas. Chop eggs and cheese. Mix all ingredients and chill for several hours.

Mary Taylor

HERB BAKED CHICKEN

¼ cup Parmesan cheese, grated
½ cup dry bread crumbs
¼ teaspoon pepper
¼ teaspoon dried whole basil
½ teaspoon dried whole
   oregano

6 chicken breast halves,
   skinned
½ cup buttermilk
Vegetable cooking spray

Combine first 5 ingredients. Dip chicken in buttermilk and dredge in bread crumb mixture. Arrange chicken in a baking dish coated with cooking spray, cover and refrigerate 1 hour. Bake uncovered for 1 hour at 350 degrees, turning after 30 minutes.

Laurie P. Wooten

LITE CHERRY CHEESECAKE

"A low-calorie dessert you'll want more than once."

1½ teaspoons unflavored gelatin
1 tablespoon water
1 cup small curd cottage cheese
2 cups frozen whipped non-
   dairy topping

½ cup confectioners sugar,
   sifted
1 tablespoon lemon juice
1 21 ounce can cherry pie filling
1 9 inch graham cracker crust

Soften gelatin in 1 tablespoon water. Set in container of hot water. Blend with the cottage cheese, frozen whipped non-dairy topping, confectioners sugar, and lemon juice. Pour about ⅓ of the cherry pie filling into a 9 inch graham cracker pie crust. Spoon in other ingredients. Top with remaining pie filling. Chill 2 hours.
Yield: 8 servings.
Note: This makes a very colorful pie. Very easy, quick, and tasty.

Mrs. Hugh M. Parker (Mary Frances)

Cut calories by more than 40% by using nonfat milk in place of whole milk.

LOW CALORIE FRUIT DESSERT

1   8 ounce cottage cheese
1   4 ounce non-dairy whipped
    topping
1   8 ounce can crushed
    pineapple, drained

1   8 ounce can mandarin
    oranges, drained
1   cup peaches, cut in bite-size
    pieces

Mix cottage cheese and non-dairy whipped topping. Add fruit.
Yield: 4 to 6 servings.
Note: This can be used for a salad or a dessert.

Mrs. Rick Barber (Tracey)

BANANA MUFFINS

¾   cup buttermilk*
¼   cup vegetable oil
2   egg whites
2   tablespoons honey
1½ cups whole wheat flour or all-
    purpose flour
3   ounces uncooked
    unprocessed bran

⅔   cup instant nonfat dry milk
    powder
1   teaspoon baking soda
¼   teaspoon ground cinnamon
¼   teaspoon nutmeg
3   very ripe bananas, mashed

Preheat oven to 350 degrees. In a small mixing bowl combine buttermilk, oil, egg whites, and honey; set aside. In a large mixing bowl combine flour, bran, milk powder, baking soda, cinnamon, and nutmeg; add buttermilk mixture and stir until moistened. Gently stir in bananas. Spray twelve 2½ inch diameter muffin pan cups with non-stick cooking spray. Fill each with batter. Bake for 25 minutes until muffins are golden brown. Let muffins cool in pan for 5 minutes, transfer to wire rack and let cool.

*If buttermilk is unavailable, combine 1 cup skim milk and 1 tablespoon lemon juice and let stand for 5 minutes; use as a substitute for buttermilk. Increase baking time to 35 minutes.

Amy Locklin

A tablespoon of vinegar blended with one cup of cottage cheese and ¼ cup skim milk is a tasty low-calorie sour cream substitute.

LOW CALORIE-CHOLESTEROL YEAST BREAD

2 packages dry yeast
½ cup warm water (110 degrees)
⅓ cup sugar
½ cup vegetable oil
4 teaspoons salt
2½ cups 2% skim milk, warm

1 carton egg substitutes
   (equivalent to 2 eggs)
9 to 10 cups enriched all-purpose
   flour
Liquid margarine

Dissolve yeast in ½ cup water, add ½ teaspoon sugar and stir; set aside. Mix sugar, salt, and milk. Add yeast mixture and mix well. Add 4 cups of flour and beat well. Add egg substitute and oil, reserving enough oil to grease pans. Beat mixture well and add remaining flour slowly until forms a stiff dough. Turn dough out on a lightly floured board, cover with bowl and let rest 5 minutes. Knead dough until smooth using as small amount of flour as possible. Place dough into a greased bowl and turn once to grease top of dough; cover with light cloth and let rise until double in bulk about 1½ to 2 hours. Press dough down to remove air bubbles, cover and let rise again for 30 minutes. Press down and divide into 3 equal parts for pound loaves or 6 equal parts ½ pound loaves. Place in greased pans and let rise until double in bulk about 1 hour. Bake in a preheated 375 degree oven until brown. Remove bread from oven and brush lightly with liquid margarine. Turn on baking racks to cool.

Harri Diggs
Lincoln, Alabama

3 O'CLOCK COOLER
"This will help you make it to suppertime."

1 12 ounce can diet carbonated
   beverage, chilled

1 cup ice milk or low-calorie ice
   cream

Put ice milk in bottom of a tall glass. Pour part of the beverage slowly over ice milk. Serve with a straw. As the glass begins to empty, add the rest of the beverage.
Yield: one serving.

Maggie Cravens

220

Today's Southern belle is busy with career, children, and other meaningful activities while at the same time striving to be a wonderful hostess. This section provides easy recipes that take little time to prepare, yet taste like you spent hours in the kitchen.

FRENCH MINT TEA

4 tablespoons instant tea
2 quarts hot water
2 cups sugar
4 tablespoons mint flavored apple jelly

1 12 ounce can frozen lemonade concentrate

In a one gallon container, mix tea, water, and sugar. Add jelly and mix with a whisk until jelly dissolves. Mix lemonade as directed on can and add to tea mixture.

Mrs. Britt Parker (Jody)

LISA'S EASY MICROWAVE SHRIMP DIP

1 clove garlic
1 10¾ ounce can cream of shrimp soup
1 7 ounce can tiny shrimp, drained

1 8 ounce package Swiss cheese, shredded
2 tablespoons cooking sherry

Rub microwave dish with garlic clove. Add soup, shrimp, cheese, and sherry. DO NOT STIR! Microwave 2 minutes uncovered on medium power. Stir well and reheat on medium power 2 or 3 minutes more. Serve hot with sturdy dip crackers.

Denise Murray
Montgomery, Alabama

CRESCENT ROLLS WITH CHEESE

1   package of 8 refrigerated   1   round Gouda cheese
    crescent rolls

Preheat oven to 350 degrees. Open rolls into 4 squares. Press the four squares into one large rectangle on a lightly greased baking sheet. Place the Gouda cheese in the center of the rolls. Pull sides of rolls around the cheese and mash seams together so that cheese is completely covered (making a big round mound). Bake at 350 degrees until lightly browned, 20-25 minutes. Cut into wedges. Serve while warm.
Note: Cheddar cheese can also be used.

Susan H. Holdridge
Alexander City, Alabama

EASY SOUR CREAM BREAD
"Try them for dinner tonight."

1   cup sour cream   2   cups self-rising flour
1   cup margarine, softened

Stir sour cream and margarine together. Add flour and mix well. Press dough into ungreased miniature muffin pans. The bread will not rise, so fill your cups. Bake at 425 degrees for 10 to 15 minutes or until golden brown. Yield: about 30 small rolls.
Note: Recipe may be increased or decreased easily as long as you keep proportions 2 to 1.

Patti Reaves Burch
Baton Rouge, Louisiana
Similar recipe submitted by *Jenni Griffin*

FROSTY FRUIT

4   cups fresh fruit of your
    choice, sliced or chopped
1   6 ounce can frozen
    concentrate lemonade,
    undiluted

Place fruit in mixing bowl. Pour lemonade over fruit. Mix well. Keep in refrigerator.
Yield: 6 servings.

Jane Patterson (Mrs. Gerald)

CHERRY FRUIT FLUFF

1   20 ounce can pineapple
    chunks, drained
1   21 ounce can fruit cocktail,
    drained
1   14 ounce can sweetened
    condensed milk

1   9 ounce tub frozen whipped
    non-dairy topping
1   21 ounce can cherry pie filling

Mix pineapple chunks and fruit cocktail. Add condensed milk and mix. Fold in topping and then pie filling. Refrigerate 2 hours or overnight.

Ms. Pat King
Pinckard, Alabama

PINEAPPLE CASSEROLE
"Good served with pork."

1   20 ounce can chunk
    pineapple
1   cup sugar
3   tablespoons all-purpose flour

1   cup sharp cheese, shredded
½   cup margarine, melted
½   cup saltine cracker crumbs

Drain pineapple, reserve 3 tablespoons juice. Combine sugar, flour, and 3 tablespoons juice. Add cheese and pineapple to sugar and flour mixture. Mix well. Butter 1 quart casserole dish. Pour in mixture. Mix crackers and butter, sprinkle on top. Bake 350 degrees for 20 to 30 minutes or until brown.

Mrs. Mary Frances Peeples
Similar recipes submitted by *Elaine Stephens* and *Cathy Glow*

EASY CORN PUDDING

½   cup sugar
3   tablespoons cornstarch
2   eggs
1   17 ounce can cream style
    corn

1   13 ounce can evaporated milk
Butter

Preheat oven to 350 degrees. Lightly grease 1½ quart baking dish. Combine sugar and cornstarch in medium bowl. Add eggs, corn, and milk and mix well. Turn into a baking dish and dot generously with butter. Bake until center is almost firm, about 1 hour.

Mrs. Freeman Deitz

CHICKEN AND BROCCOLI CASSEROLE

4 large chicken breasts, cooked and cubed	1 cup instant rice, cooked
1 10 ounce package chopped broccoli, cooked and drained	1 8 ounce jar pasteurized processed cheese spread
1 10¾ ounce can mushroom soup, fill empty can with milk	

Mix all ingredients and put into buttered casserole. Cook covered for 40 minutes at 350 degrees. Remove from oven and let stand uncovered for about 10 minutes before serving.

Mrs. Hugh M. Parker (Mary Frances)

CHICKEN AND WILD RICE CASSEROLE

3½ cups cooked chicken, deboned and cut up	1 cup mayonnaise
1 box long grain wild rice	½ cup pimento
1 16 ounce can French cut green beans	1 small onion, grated
1 10¾ ounce can cream of celery soup	Shredded cheese

Mix all ingredients except onion and cheese. Pour mixture into a 2 quart casserole dish. Top with cheese and grated onion. Bake at 350 degrees for 30 to 35 minutes.

Karan Bush
Birmingham, Alabama

HAMBURGER PIE

1   8 count can crescent rolls
1   pound ground beef
1   small onion, diced
1   15 ounce jar spaghetti sauce

1   6 ounce can mushrooms, sliced
4   slices mozzarella cheese

Preheat oven to 350 degrees. Place rolls in a 9 inch pie plate to make a crust. In skillet, brown ground beef and sauté onion; drain. Stir in mushrooms and prepared spaghetti sauce. Pour in crust. Place cheese over meat mixture. Bake at 350 degrees for 25 minutes, or until crust is golden brown and cheese melts.
Yield: 6 servings.

Mrs. Ned Dennis (Althea)
Albertville, Alabama

YAKAMASHI/"KOREAN SEOUL FOOD"

1½ pounds ground beef
2   tablespoons soy sauce
1   teaspoon salt
1   teaspoon pepper
1   medium onion

2   cups carrots
1   clove garlic
1   bell pepper
1   cup celery
2   cups cooked rice

Brown in large pan first four ingredients. Add to mixture all vegetables, finely chopped. Simmer 15 minutes. Add cooked rice. Cook over medium heat 5 minutes, stirring constantly.
Yield: 4 servings.
Note: Extremely flexible recipe. Vegetables may be varied.

Jane B. Davis
Tuscaloosa, Alabama

EASIEST ICE CREAM
"Very Southern, very simple."

2½ cups sugar
5   eggs

½   gallon whole milk
1   teaspoon vanilla

Combine sugar and eggs; add milk and vanilla. Freeze in electric ice cream freezer.

Andrea K. Montgomery

EASY CHEESECAKE
"Quite delicious."

5	large eggs	1	teaspoon vanilla
3	8 ounce packages cream cheese, softened	1	teaspoon lemon juice
1	cup sugar	1	pint sour cream
			Graham cracker crumbs

Grease spring-form pan with butter and dust heavily with crumbs. Heat oven to 350 degrees. Separate eggs and beat whites until stiff, set aside. Beat softened cream cheese, sugar, yolks, and flavorings. Add sour cream. Fold in beaten egg whites by hand and pour in pan. Dust top with more crumbs and bake 35 minutes. Then turn down oven and keep warm in 150 degree oven for 10 minutes. Turn off oven and let stand one hour in oven. Remove and let cool.

Note: More delicious before refrigeration, but can be refrigerated for three or four days or frozen if needed. May purée 1 package frozen raspberries and add sugar to taste. Serve the purée under cheesecake or over top.

Nell J. Fears

GERMAN CHOCOLATE UPSIDE DOWN CAKE

1	cup coconut, shredded	½	cup margarine
1	cup pecans, chopped	1	8 ounce package cream cheese, softened
1	18 ½ ounce box German chocolate cake mix, or regular chocolate cake mix	1	16 ounce box confectioners sugar

Combine coconut and nuts and put into bottom of a greased 9x13 inch pan. Prepare cake mix as directed on box. Pour evenly over pecan/coconut mixture. Place margarine and cream cheese in saucepan and heat until warm. Stir in confectioners sugar amd mix well. Spoon over cake mix. Bake at 350 degrees for 35 to 45 minutes. Do not cut until cool.

Yield: 16 to 20 servings.

Note: In spite of the name, this cake cannot be inverted to a platter.

Mrs. Mike Griffin (Wynelle)

CANDY COOKIES

1½ cups graham cracker crumbs
1   16 ounce box confectioners sugar
1   cup margarine

1   16 ounce jar peanut butter
2   large chocolate bars, ½ pound each

Mix graham cracker crumbs, sugar, and margarine together and press into 13x9 inch glass baking dish. In a double boiler, mix together peanut butter and chocolate. Melt and pour on top of graham cracker crust. Cool and cut into squares.

Mrs. Dot Wallis Moosmann
Sun City Center, Florida

HEATH COOKIES

35 saltine crackers
1   cup margarine
1   cup brown sugar

1   12 ounce package milk chocolate chips

Line a jelly roll pan with foil. Spray with non-stick vegetable spray. Spread crackers side by side in pan. Boil the margarine and brown sugar 1 minute. Pour over crackers and bake at 375 degrees for 8 minutes. Spread chocolate chips over hot mixture; when melted, spread like frosting. Break or cut into squares.

Kathryn Rogers
Stone Mountain, Georgia

DELICIOUS CHOCOLATE CHIP COOKIES

1   package yellow cake mix
¼   cup light brown sugar
¾   cup oil
1   egg

1 to 1½ cups semi-sweet chocolate chips
1   cup nuts, chopped
1   cup raisins

Preheat oven to 375 degrees. In a large bowl stir all ingredients together until well mixed. Drop from a heaping teaspoon onto an ungreased cookie sheet. Bake for 10 minutes or until centers of cookies are brown. Cool on cookie sheet for 1 minute, then remove to rack to finish cooling.
Yield: 3 to 3½ dozen.

Mrs. Brenda F. Warren

BRANDIED ICE CREAM
"Impress your company with this easy dessert."

½ gallon vanilla ice cream,
   softened
¼ cup brandy

¼ cup cremé de cocoa
Chocolate curls or shavings

Combine first three ingredients, mixing well. Pour into shallow container and freeze until firm. Spoon into dishes; garnish with chocolate.

Freida Meacham

EASY BLUEBERRY PIE

1 21 ounce can blueberry fruit
   pie filling
1 20 ounce can crushed
   pineapple
1 18½ ounce box yellow cake
   mix

1 cup margarine, melted
1 4 ounce can coconut,
   shredded
1 cup pecans, chopped
Frozen whipped non-dairy
   topping

Spread pie filling evenly in 9x13x2 inch pan. Spoon pineapple (undrained) over filling. Sprinkle dry cake mix over pineapple. Pour melted margarine over cake mix. Sprinkle coconut and pecans over all. Bake at 350 degrees for approximately 1 hour and 15 minutes. Serve with frozen whipped non-dairy topping.

Chrystal Badders

NANNY PUDDING

1 4 ounce box instant vanilla
   pudding mix
2 cups milk

1 package of graham crackers
4 to 5 bananas

Make pudding according to package directions. Allow pudding to set for 5 minutes. Layer bottom of 8x8 inch dish with graham crackers. Pour half of pudding over crackers. Slice bananas over pudding. Top bananas with another layer of crackers, remaining pudding, and more bananas. Crumble 3 crackers over top bananas. Chill and serve.

Jennifer Cravens

Apple Annie's Delights

APPLE ANNIE

One of the most successful fund-raising projects of the Junior Welfare League of Talladega has been Apple Annie Day. On an autumn day of each year since 1975, League members have donned gingham aprons and have filled baskets with big, juicy, red delicious apples to sell to the folks of the area. All proceeds have been used to fund many, many worthwhile charitable causes within the community. Recent contributions to the community from the Apple Annie Day effort include:

- funding for the art program and other curricula in Talladega City Schools
- playground equipment for Veteran's Park
- equipment for Citizens Hospital
- children's books for the Talladega Public Library
- funding for "Samaritan House" and "Red Door Kitchen" to help needy individuals and families
- funding for Cheahospice
- funding for programs to help abused children

The League appreciates the support of the community, especially the business persons and the Talladega City Schools, for valued help in making Apple Annie Day successful.

RED HOT APPLE CIDER PUNCH

8 to 9 ounces hot cinnamon candy pieces
1 to 2 cinnamon sticks
10 cups apple cider
1 coffee filter

Place cinnamon candy pieces in coffee filter. Place cinnamon sticks on top of candy. Place in brewer of an electric drip coffee percolator. Fill coffee pot decanter with apple cider. Cider can be room temperature or cold. Turn on brewer and warmer of coffee pot. Pour cider from decanter into brewer as you would with coffee. When dripping is complete, turn brewer off. Serve immediately. May be reheated.
Note: Candy pieces and cinnamon sticks may be adjusted according to taste.

Mrs. Hardy Smith (Debbie)

APPLE ANNIE NUT BREAD

1½ cups brown sugar
⅔ cup vegetable oil
1 egg
1 cup sour milk
2½ cups all-purpose flour
1 teaspoon baking soda
1 teaspoon salt
1 teaspoon cinnamon
1 teaspoon ground cloves
1 teaspoon allspice
1½ cups apples, diced
1 cup nuts, chopped
1 teaspoon vanilla
½ cup sugar
2 tablespoons margarine, melted

Stir together brown sugar, oil, egg, and sour milk. Sift flour, soda, salt, and spices; add to first mixture and stir until well mixed. Add apples, nuts, and vanilla. Pour into 2 greased and floured 8x5x3 inch loaf pans. Combine sugar and margarine; sprinkle over top of batter. Bake at 350 degrees for 1 hour.

Mrs. Lucile L. Sharpley

APPLE ANNIE SALAD

2	3 ounce packages lemon gelatin	2	cups cold water
1	cup boiling water	1	cup crushed pineapple
		2	cups apples, chopped

Combine gelatin and water and congeal until syrupy. Then add pineapple and apples. Mix all together and chill until firm.

Topping:

2	eggs, well beaten	1	4 ounce carton non-dairy whipped topping
½	cup sugar		
1	tablespoon lemon juice		Chopped nuts (optional)

Combine eggs, sugar, and lemon juice over slow heat, stirring only until mixture thickens. Cool and fold in whipped topping. Spread over congealed salad. Sprinkle with chopped nuts if desired. Refrigerate.

Mrs. A.D. Welbaum (Clara)

SUGAR CRUSTED APPLES

6	large cooking apples	⅓	cup margarine, softened
⅓	cup plain flour	1	egg, slightly beaten
⅔	cup sugar	¾	cup orange juice
½	teaspoon ground cinnamon		Whipped cream

Core and peel apples. Combine flour, sugar, and cinnamon. Cut in margarine with 2 knives or a pastry blender until mixture resembles coarse cornmeal. Brush apples with egg and roll each in mixture. Arrange apples in a greased, shallow baking dish, fill cavities of apples with any remaining flour mixture. Pour orange juice into pan; bake, uncovered, at 350 degrees for 1 hour, or until apples are tender. Serve warm with pan liquid; top with whipped cream.

Frankie Newman

DANISH APPLE SLICES

Cake:

3 cups all-purpose flour
½ teaspoon salt
1 cup butter or margarine
1½ cups milk
1 egg, separated
6 cups apples, peeled and
    sliced (about 8 apples)

1½ cups sugar
2 tablespoons all-purpose flour
1 teaspoon flour
1 teaspoon cinnamon
2 tablespoons butter or
    margarine

Combine flour and salt. Cut in 1 cup butter or margarine. Combine milk and egg yolk and add to dry ingredients. Mix well. Roll out half of the dough and put in 15x10 inch jelly roll pan. Arrange apples on crust. Combine sugar, flour, and cinnamon and sprinkle over apples. Dot with 2 tablespoons butter or margarine. Roll out rest of dough and put on top. Pinch edges of pastry together. Brush top with slightly beaten egg white. Bake at 375 degrees for 45 minutes. Cool slightly. Frost.

Frosting:

1½ cups confectioners sugar
2 tablespoons margarine

2 tablespoons milk

Combine ingredients. Spread on top of pastry.

Mrs. George Sims (Sylvia)

APPLE CRISP

6 cups (6 medium) apples,
    peeled and sliced
1 tablespoon lemon juice
1 tablespoon water
¾ cup firmly-packed brown
    sugar

½ cup all-purpose flour
½ cup rolled oats
1 teaspoon cinnamon
½ cup butter

Preheat oven to 375 degrees. Place apples in 9 inch square pan. Sprinkle with lemon juice and water. In small bowl combine remaining ingredients until crumbly, sprinkle over apples. Bake at 375 degrees for 40 to 50 minutes or until apples are tender.

Mrs. Steve Turner (Peggy)

GRANDMOTHER'S APPLE DUMPLINGS

4   tart apples
Pastry for 2-crust pie
1   cup sugar, mixed with
    1½ teaspoons cinnamon

8   tablespoons butter or
    margarine

Peel, core, and halve apples crosswise. Use ½ apple for each dumpling. Roll out ⅛ of pie crust in square. Top each ½ apple with 2 tablespoons sugar/cinnamon mixture and 1 tablespoon butter. Pull corners of pastry up around apple and pinch together. Put in 13x9 inch dish.

Sauce:
2   cups water
1   cup sugar

1½ teaspoons cinnamon

Mix sauce ingredients, bring to boil, pour over apple dumplings. Bake uncovered at 400 degrees for 5 minutes. Reduce heat to 350 degrees and bake 35 minutes more. Serve warm with or without cream.
Yield: 8 servings.

Faye P. Cooley

APPLE CAKE

2   cups sugar
1½ cups oil
3   eggs
3   cups all-purpose flour, sifted
1½ teaspoons soda
1   teaspoon salt

½   teaspoon cinnamon
½   teaspoon nutmeg
½   teaspoon cloves
3   cups apples, peeled and
    chopped
1   teaspoon vanilla

Cream sugar and oil. Add eggs one at a time. Combine flour, soda, salt, and spices. Add these dry ingredients to batter. Stir in apples and vanilla. Grease and flour tube pan. Bake at 325 degrees for 1 hour and 15 minutes. Let cool before removing from pan.

Linda McCardle
Variation: Add ¾ cup semi-sweet chocolate chips and 1 cup pecans, chopped.

Mrs. John Morris (Gail)

DRIED APPLE CUSTARD PIE

1 cup dried apples	⅓ cup sugar
2 cups water	1 deep dish pie shell, unbaked

Cook fruit with water until soft. Drain and mash thoroughly. Add sugar and allow to cool. Cover bottom of pie shell with fruit.

Custard:

1 cup sugar	1 cup milk
2 tablespoons all-purpose flour	1 teaspoon vanilla
2 tablespoons butter	Pinch of salt
3 egg yolks	

Cream sugar, flour, and butter. Add other ingredients and mix well. Pour over the fruit in the pie shell. Bake at 350 degrees for 50 minutes or until firm.

Meringue:

3 egg whites	1 teaspoon vanilla
4 tablespoons sugar	

Beat 3 egg whites until stiff, gradually beating in the 4 tablespoons sugar and 1 teaspoon vanilla. Put meringue over the custard and return to oven for 15 minutes or until meringue is browned.

Melba Hagan
Alexander City, Alabama

GRANDMOTHER'S CRUMBLECRUST APPLE PIE

1 cup all-purpose flour	1 dozen cooking apples, peeled
½ cup margarine	and sliced
¼ cup brown sugar	1 tablespoon margarine
1 cup white sugar	

Mix flour, ½ cup margarine, and brown sugar to crumb consistency (sprinkling of cinnamon or nutmeg may be added). Cook apples with white sugar and 1 tablespoon margarine until apples are transparent and soft. Put apples in pie pan; cover with crumb mixture. Bake at 375 degrees for 30 to 35 minutes. May be served with sharp cheese slices, frozen whipped non-dairy topping, or vanilla ice cream.

Mrs. Ray Edmiston (Kara)

NUTTY APPLE PIE CAKE

1	cup sugar	1	teaspoon baking soda
⅓	cup soft butter or margarine	¼	cup warm water
1	egg	2	cups apples, pared and diced
1	cup all-purpose flour	½	cup walnuts or pecans,
1	teaspoon ground cinnamon		chopped
1	teaspoon nutmeg		Whipped cream for garnish
½	teaspoon salt		

Cream sugar and butter until smooth. Add egg. Beat until fluffy. Stir flour with cinnamon, nutmeg, and salt. Mix baking soda with warm water. Add flour mixture along with baking soda and water to creamed mixture. Beat until smooth and fluffy. Fold in apples and nuts. Spread into well-buttered 9 inch pie pan. Bake at 350 degrees for 40 to 45 minutes, or until cake tests done. Serve each wedge while warm with a fluff of whipped cream.
Yield: 6 servings

Mrs. Steve Turner (Peggy)

DUTCH APPLE CAKE

"This is a favorite of children and adults"

1½	cups cooking oil	3	cups fresh apples, diced
2	cups sugar	1	cup pecans, chopped
2	eggs	¾	cup semi-sweet chocolate
1	teaspoon soda		chips
3	cups self-rising flour	1	teaspoon vanilla
1	teaspoon salt		

Mix oil with sugar and eggs. Sift together soda, flour, and salt. Blend with oil mixture. (This will be the consistency of biscuit dough.) Fold in apples, nuts and chocolate chips. Add vanilla. Bake in greased tube pan or loaf pan at 350 degrees for 1 hour and 15 minutes.

Mrs. John Morris (Gail)

The Best From
"When Dinnerbells Ring"

CHEESE STRATA

"A wonderful idea for Brunch.
Add some chopped ham, if you wish."

6	slices light bread	1	teaspoon salt
2	cups aged Wisconsin cheese, shredded	1	teaspoon dry mustard
		1	teaspoon baking powder
3	eggs, well beaten		Dash of red pepper
2	cups sweet milk		

Break up bread in 2 quart greased casserole. Sprinkle 1 layer of cheese in bottom of dish. Mix eggs, milk, salt, mustard, baking powder, and pepper. Pour over bread and cheese and refrigerate at least 1 hour or overnight. Bake at 350 degrees for 45 minutes. This is better if made ahead. The bread absorbs liquid and gives it a lighter texture.
Yield: 6 servings.

Mrs. Winston Legge (Sarah)
Similar recipes submitted by: *Mrs. William Lawrence (Sally), Mrs. Bob Chapman (Mildred), Mrs. Raymond Hammett (Louise)*

CHEESE BISCUITS

1¼	cups flour	6	tablespoons heavy cream
	Dash salt	1	egg, slightly beaten
	Dash cayenne pepper	1	cup Swiss cheese, shredded
6	tablespoons butter	2	tablespoons butter
1	cup Cheddar cheese, shredded		

Sift flour, salt, and pepper. Add butter and Cheddar cheese; mix until mixture resembles meal. Stir in cream and form a ball. Chill several hours. Roll out dough and cut into 2-inch circles. Brush rounds with egg; place on greased baking sheet. Bake at 450 degrees for 6 to 8 minutes or until brown. Cream Swiss cheese and butter; spread on one half of rounds. Cover with remaining rounds and return to oven. Bake until biscuits are heated throughout. Good as hors d'oeuvres or served with lunch.
Yield: 20 biscuits.

Mrs. William B. McGehee, Jr. (Mary Lib)

HOT FRUIT CASSEROLE
"For that special dinner party."

1	29 ounce can sliced peaches	1	10 ounce bottle red cherries
1	29 ounce can pear halves, quartered	1	cup applesauce
		¾	cup dark brown sugar
1	15 ounce can pineapple chunks	⅓	cup butter, melted
		½	cup almonds, slivered
1	29 ounce can pitted plums	2	bananas, sliced

Drain all fruits. Put in large bowl. Add applesauce and ½ cup brown sugar to melted butter. Bring to a boil. Pour over fruit. Refrigerate overnight (or 8 hours.) Butter a 2 quart casserole. Chop bananas and add to other fruit. Put all in casserole dish and bake at 350 degrees for 45 minutes. Mix remaining ¼ cup sugar with almonds. Sprinkle over fruit. Bake again until bubbly. This is a delicious side dish for brunch, lunch, or dinner. Add whipped cream for a dessert.
Yield: 10 servings

Mrs. Dewayne Clark (Marion)

POTATO CASSEROLE
"This will become a family favorite!"

1	2 pound package frozen hash brown potatoes	1	cup sour cream
1	cup onion, chopped	½	cup butter, melted
1	10¾ ounce can cream of chicken soup	1	teaspoon salt
		1	teaspoon pepper
10	ounces sharp Cheddar cheese, shredded	1	can French fried onions

Mix all ingredients except French fried onions. Place mixture in a casserole dish. Top with French fried onions. Bake at 300 degrees for 1 hour.

Mrs. Hardy Conner (Becky)

CHICKEN SPECTACULAR

1 large chicken, cooked, deboned, diced
1 16 ounce can French green beans, seasoned, drained
1 6 ounce box Uncle Ben's curried rice
1 8 ounce can water chestnuts, sliced
1 small onion or 3 tablespoons, chopped
1 10½ ounce can cream of celery soup
1 cup mayonnaise
1 small jar pimento
Salt to taste

In covered boiler cook rice in 2½ cups plus 2 tablespoons chicken broth for 20 minutes. Add onions and cook for 5 minutes more. Stir rice occasionally. Add other ingredients to rice and pour into large greased casserole dish. Bake at 350 degrees for 40 minutes to 1 hour until brown. Yield: 8 to 10 servings.

Jo Ann Mullins
Mrs. James W. Heacock, Sr. (Becky)
Similar recipes submitted by *Mrs. Jackie Stephens (Elaine)* and *Mrs. Carl Reaves (Joyce)*

4-LAYER CHOCOLATE PIE

½ cup margarine, melted
1 cup all-purpose flour
½ cup pecans, chopped
1 8 ounce package cream cheese
1 cup confectioners sugar
1 cup frozen non-dairy whipped topping
2 4½ ounce packages chocolate instant pudding
3½ cups milk
1 teaspoon vanilla
1 13½ ounce frozen non-dairy whipped topping

Combine margarine, flour, and pecans. Pour into 9x13x2 inch pan and bake in 350 degree oven for 15 minutes. Cool. Mix cream cheese, sugar, and 1 cup frozen non-dairy whipped topping until smooth. Spread over crust. Mix pudding, milk, and vanilla according to package directions. Spread over cream cheese mixture. Top with remaining frozen non-dairy whipped topping. Chill before serving.

Mrs. Harold Clark (Bobbye)
Mrs. John Barksdale (Dorothy)
Rickey Hatcher
Joyce Hutchinson
Judy Griffin

"COMPANY'S COMING" COCONUT CAKE
"Tastes like an old timey fresh coconut cake."

2   6 ounce packages frozen coconut
1   8 ounce carton sour cream
1½ cups sugar
1   18 ounce box yellow cake mix
1   4 ounce box instant vanilla pudding

½   cup cooking oil
1   cup water
1   teaspoon vanilla
2   eggs
2   egg yolks

Combine first three ingredients and set aside. In mixing bowl, combine remaining ingredients and beat until smooth. Pour into 2 greased 9-inch cake pans. Bake in 350 degree oven for 30 minutes. Cool 10 minutes on rack. Split layers to make four. Spread coconut mixture between layers while warm. Ice cake.

Icing:

2   egg whites
¾   cup sugar
⅓   cup white corn syrup
1   tablespoon water

¼   teaspoon cream tartar
¼   teaspoon salt
¼   teaspoon vanilla
1   3½ ounce can coconut

In double boiler, combine first 6 ingredients and cook for 5 minutes, beating constantly at high speed. Remove from heat; add vanilla. Spread over cake and sprinkle with coconut.

Mrs. Patrick Duke (Carolyn)

HOT PERKED PUNCH

1   quart cranberry juice
1   quart unsweetened pineapple juice
½   quart water
1   cup brown sugar

1   teaspoon whole cloves
1   teaspoon whole allspice
1   lemon, sliced
2   sticks cinnamon

Pour first three ingredients into large coffee pot. Pour remaining ingredients into basket of coffee pot. Perk as if making coffee.
Yield: 15 cups

Mrs. Tommy Fite (Betty)

FUDGY ICED BROWNIES

½	cup margarine	1	16 ounce can chocolate syrup
1	cup sugar	1	cup pecans, chopped
4	eggs		
1	cup all-purpose flour		

Cream margarine until fluffy. Gradually add sugar and beat. Add eggs, one at a time, beating after each addition. Stir in flour and beat until smooth. Add syrup and nuts and mix. Pour in greased 9x13x2 inch pan and bake at 350 degrees for 25 minutes. DO NOT OVERBAKE.

Icing:

½	cup margarine	½	cup chocolate morsels
1½	cups sugar	1	cup pecans, chopped
⅓	cup evaporated milk		

In saucepan, combine margarine, sugar, and milk and cook over low heat to boiling, stirring constantly. Let boil for one minute without stirring. Remove from heat and add morsels. Stir until melted. Add nuts and mix. Pour icing over brownies while both are hot. Cool. Cut into squares.

Mrs. James Barnett (Lynn)

ORANGE DATE CAKE

"Be sure to use butter — it makes a difference."

1	cup butter	4	cups all-purpose flour
2	cups sugar	1	pound dates, chopped
4	eggs	1	cup pecans, chopped
1	teaspoon soda	2	tablespoons orange rind, grated
⅓	cup buttermilk		

Cream butter and sugar. Beat in eggs, one at a time. Dissolve soda in buttermilk. Dredge dates and pecans in small amount of flour. Add remaining ingredients; blend well. Pour into greased tube pan. Bake in 325 degree oven for 1½ hours. Make tiny holes in top of cake and cover with sauce. Cool in pan. When cooled, loosen edges with knife before turning out on to cake plate. Cake is very tender. Garnish with orange sections.

Sauce:

2	cups sugar	2	tablespoons orange rind, grated
1	cup orange juice		

Mix all ingredients until dissolved. Pour over cake.

Mrs. Carl Monroe (Sula)
Orlean Seals

INDEX

Come and Get It!

Post Office Box 331   •   Talladega, Alabama 35160

Please send _____ copies of **Come and Get It** @ $14.95 each $ _____
Plus postage and handling @ $ 2.50 each $ _____
Alabama residents add applicable local sales tax @ $ 1.20 each $ _____
Total enclosed $ _____

Please send _____ copies of
When Dinnerbells Ring @ $14.95 each $ _____
Plus postage and handling @ $ 2.50 each $ _____
Alabama residents add applicable local sales tax @ $ 1.20 each $ _____
Please make checks payable to: **Junior Welfare League of Talladega**
Total enclosed $ _____

Name _____

Address: _____

City: _____ State: _____ Zip: _____

Proceeds from the sale of **Come and Get It** *and* **When Dinnerbells Ring** *will be used for community projects sponsored by the* **Talladega Junior Welfare League**. *Please allow 21 days for delivery.*

Come and Get It!

Post Office Box 331   •   Talladega, Alabama 35160

Please send _____ copies of **Come and Get It** @ $14.95 each $ _____
Plus postage and handling @ $ 2.50 each $ _____
Alabama residents add applicable local sales tax @ $ 1.20 each $ _____
Total enclosed $ _____

Please send _____ copies of
When Dinnerbells Ring @ $14.95 each $ _____
Plus postage and handling @ $ 2.50 each $ _____
Alabama residents add applicable local sales tax @ $ 1.20 each $ _____
Please make checks payable to: **Junior Welfare League of Talladega**
Total enclosed $ _____

Name _____

Address: _____

City: _____ State: _____ Zip: _____

Proceeds from the sale of **Come and Get It** *and* **When Dinnerbells Ring** *will be used for community projects sponsored by the* **Talladega Junior Welfare League**. *Please allow 21 days for delivery.*

Save **$1.00** on your reorder. Just send us the name, address, and phone number of the best stores in your town that sell cookbooks.

Name of Store _____

Owner or Manager's Name _____

Address _____

City _____ State _____ Zip _____

(Deduct $1.00 off your reorder when this is filled in)

— —

Save **$1.00** on your reorder. Just send us the name, address, and phone number of the best stores in your town that sell cookbooks.

Name of Store _____

Owner or Manager's Name _____

Address _____

City _____ State _____ Zip _____

(Deduct $1.00 off your reorder when this is filled in)